CONJOINED TWINS

LIBRARY OF CONGRESS CATALOGUING-IN-PUBLICATION DATA

Quigley, Christine, 1963–
Conjoined twins : an historical, biological and ethical issues
encyclopedia / by Christine Quigley.
p.    cm.
Includes bibliographical references and index.
ISBN 0-7864-1526-6 (illustrated case binding : 50# alkaline paper)

1. Conjoined twins — Enclyclopedias.   I. Title.
QM691.Q54   2003        616'.043 — dc21           2003005733

British Library cataloguing data are available

Front and back covers: photographs of Violet and Daisy Hilton
(Mütter Museum, College of Physicians of Philadelphia)

Manufactured in the United States of America

*McFarland & Company, Inc., Publishers
Box 611, Jefferson, North Carolina 28640
www.mcfarlandpub.com*

# CONJOINED TWINS

## An Historical, Biological and Ethical Issues Encyclopedia

*by* CHRISTINE QUIGLEY

McFarland & Company, Inc., Publishers
*Jefferson, North Carolina, and London*

# ACKNOWLEDGMENTS

*"No one I have ever talked to about this study has failed to offer in return anecdotes, ranging from pertinent to irrelevant, opinions, ranging from sympathetic to hostile, or information, ranging from reliable to thoroughly undependable."*—Leslie A. Fiedler, *Freaks*

I am grateful to those mentioned below for providing reliable information, since this book builds on the work of others. The research to compile it was made possible in part by a grant from the Francis Clark Wood Institute for the History of Medicine. The research fellowship allowed me to pore through books at the Library of the College of Physicians of Philadelphia and to peruse the shelves and files of the Mütter Museum. In addition to Charles Greifenstein, Curator of Archives and Manuscripts and Interim Director of the Library, and Historical Reference Librarian Christopher Stanwood, I would like to extend a special thank you to Gretchen Worden, Director of the Mütter Museum.

The photographs and illustrations have been reproduced with the kind permission of the following individuals and organizations: Arthur Aufderheide, Department of Pathology and Laboratory Medicine, University of Minnesota; Becker Collection, Syracuse University Library, Department of Special Collections; Jan Bondeson, M.D., Ph.D.; Circus World Museum, Baraboo, Wisconsin; Dicksie Cribb Collection; F. Gonzalez-Crussi; Harvard Theatre Collection, Houghton Library; Harvard University Press; Joanne Martell; Milner Library Special Collections, Illinois State University; Mütter Museum, College of Physicians of Philadelphia; North Carolina Division of Archives and History; Oxford University Press; Royal College of Surgeons of England; Southern Historical Collection, Wilson Library, University of North Carolina–Chapel Hill; Rowena Spencer and the W.B. Saunders Co.; Rob Terteruck; and Wiley-Liss.

I am grateful to those who responded so graciously to my inquiries: Arthur Aufderheide, Lenore Barbian, Bob Blackmar, Will Degeraty, Chris Fellner, Bob Goldsack, Sarah Mitchell, James T. Rutka, and John Templeton, Jr. A special thanks goes to Finn Johnsen for his translation of Danish material.

This book is written in remembrance of Capt. Harvey Lee Boswell (*d.* January 22, 2002), whom I met while researching *Modern Mummies*, and Lessie Montez Swanner (*d.* March 24, 2002), whose strength I admired and whose stories I enjoyed.

I thank those whose own work and passions continue to inspire: Jody Arlington, Jasmine Day, George Higham and Sharon Packer, James Taylor, and Loren Rhoads.

In appreciation of the help and encouragement I receive from my friends and family, I thank Dorothy Cotton, Gail Grella, Donna and Del Gritman, Cris Hastings and Maddy Biggs, the Heilweil Family, Kristina Johnsen, Janice Lane and Katina Stockbridge, Cheryl Locke, Sheila McMullan, Valerie and Roger Meyer, Jim Miller and Chris Sweeters, Jim and Sarah Quigley, Judy Skene, Dorothy Sutton, Deb. Weiner, Eva Wolas, and Nora Wright.

To anyone I may have overlooked: my apologies.

# CONTENTS

*"Get binoculars if you're interested,
get blindfolds if you're not."*—Reba Schappell

\*   \*   \*

*"My name is Lori Schappell and I am one person.
I am not Lori-and-Reba Schappell."*—Lori Schappell

# PREFACE

We've all been told it's not polite to stare, yet our curiosity about those who differ physically from us is entirely natural. These differences take many forms, but the one that never fails to arouse our collective interest occurs when two human ova fail to fully separate during pregnancy. The result is united identical twins, like the famous Siamese brothers Chang and Eng Bunker. Hence the adjective "Siamese" to refer to those who are now called "conjoined." Rather than being individuals fused together in the womb, conjoined twins are physically joined from conception, for reasons still not medically understood, and occur very rarely (being born alive in as few as one in every 200,000 births). They may be linked by ligament, bone, or just flesh, with the majority (nearly 75 percent) joined face-to-face at the abdomen. They often share organs, but what stirs our imagination is whether they share thoughts, sensations, spouses, even souls.

Conjoined twins are therefore of interest to doctors, psychologists, theologians, and lawmakers. They and the general public may consult professional literature to learn more about the research and conclusions in these fields, but may be hard-pressed to find a reference book that concisely covers both recent and historical cases. Gould and Pyle's *Anomalies and Curiosities of Medicine* (1956, originally published in 1896) is a classic reference, but can hardly be considered current. Readers with more of a cultural curiosity — perhaps piqued by a television documentary or recent news broadcast about such twins being delivered or separated — have greater difficulty in satisfying it. They may choose one of the more popular pairs of twins and read a biography like Joanne Martell's *Millie-Christine* (2000) or they may turn to the chapter on Siamese twins in a treatise about sideshow exhibitions of human oddities. Contemporary conjoined twins, of whom there are a surprising number, are similarly challenged when they want to read about how their historical counterparts lived. They may read Leslie Fiedler's ground-breaking *Freaks* (1978), Jan Bondeson's *The Two-Headed Boy* (2000), or Darin Strauss's *Chang and Eng* (2000), depending on whether they want a sociological, medical, or fictionalized perspective on their past, but they will most likely have to delve into newspaper archives for information about their contemporaries.

This book presents the stories of these sometimes famous pairs, of past and present, along with the biological basics, ethical issues about self-support and surgery, and numerous photographs and illustrations. This information, aimed at the lay reader, is organized alphabetically, cross-referenced, and supplemented by a thorough bibliography that will allow consultation of more specific sources.

*Conjoined Twins: An Historical, Biological and Ethical Issues Encyclopedia* attempts to be both comprehensive and accessible. As much information was gathered about as many sets of twins as possible. Some were eliminated because of a lack of biographical data, but most are represented by at least their vital statistics and the basic details of their delivery and, if applicable, their separation. The entries overwhelmingly include sets of conjoined twins, but also include the more well-known instances of parasitic twins and incorporate famous individuals with multiple limbs, like Frank Lentini. The twins are listed by surname or — in its absence — their pseudonyms or nicknames. Other entries cover issues that conjoined twins and their parents confront as the twins develop, most notably separation surgery, but also questions about disability and identity.

By compiling fact and fiction about Siamese twins from the historical and medical records, this reference book brings into juxtaposition the carnival sideshow and the operating theater, the stage and the courtroom, medieval England and the contemporary United States. The book is not bound by time or place and the sources range from the writings of nineteenth century teratologists to the fictional musings of twentieth century authors. The information was compiled from medical literature consulted in museums and libraries, from the popular media including television documentaries and magazines, from the websites and organizations sponsored by the families of conjoined twins, and from correspondence with those who have operated on and photographed them.

The research is supplemented by illustrations and photographs reproduced from the special collections of universities, museums, and hospitals. The images exemplify configurations difficult to describe and allow the reader to attach names to faces that are so much like our own with bodies that are very different from ours (in some ways but very similar in others).

*Conjoined Twins* offers a rich human history of these individuals who arrive in tandem, the care they receive from their families and the medical community, and the legal, ethical, and popular thought that surrounds their condition.

Christine Quigley
*March 2003*

# INTRODUCTION

*"Not even Freaks have left reliable records of what it feels like to be what they are, avoiding publication as if words were an inappropriate medium for what their bodies so eloquently express."*— Leslie A. Fiedler

Tucked inside a file in the Mütter Museum in Philadelphia is a pencil drawing of a horse. Well-executed, but not remarkable … until you see that it was drawn by the fourteen-year-old hand of Giovanni-Batisto Tocci (1877–1940), a hand of his own though he shared a lower body with his conjoined twin brother Giacomo. One of many reactions to the necessity of sharing a body is pity, and in the case of the Toccis it is justified. They were deeply unhappy about their condition and it left them unable to walk, unlike their century-later counterparts Abby and Brittany Hensel (*b.* 1990). The Hensel family and other conjoined twins find pity and similar sentiments condescending and have expressed this view in interviews. Enough quotes have been gathered in this book to make a few generalizations, though not all conjoined twins are equally included (and some not at all). Those who have been the most vocal are the best represented. But others — like the Tocci brothers — say something by their silence.

Some twins are described in this book only in the form of vital statistics. The intimate anatomical details of others are described at length from published medical findings. In many cases, the families have chosen privacy, protected by pseudonyms and confidentiality agreements, and little has been reported. In a few cases, the disparity is due to sketchily recorded history. For instance, the depiction of the connection between the twelfth-century Biddenden Maids is misleading. On the other hand, nineteenth century doctors and pathologists left exhaustive details about the bodies of Siamese twins Chang and Eng Bunker (1811–1874) and biographers and chroniclers left volumes about their lives. The result is that the lives of some twins are easier to research than others, which is reflected in the length of the entry. Living twins have for the most part sought seclusion, as have the families and doctors of twins recently born or recently separated, except for the obligatory press conference or occasional interview.

In earlier times, one of the benefits of appeasing the curiosity of the public was that persons with unusual bodies, such as conjoined twins, could make a living and see the world in the process. This is best exemplified by the lives of Millie-Christine (1851–1912), who were born into slavery and later met Queen Victoria. The Scottish

3

Brothers (1490–1518) were actually raised in the court of King James IV. Lucio and Simplicio Godino (1908–1936) were exhibited to the public as children, but controversy surrounding their display drew the attention of their benefactor Filipino multi-millionaire Tecodoro Yanco. Today's conjoined twins and their families have the opportunity, through the media, to reach organizations offering financial assistance, caregiving networks, and informational resources. And there are other reasons to appear before the public. While Daisy and Violet Hilton (1908–1969) appeared on stage from the age of three to entertain audiences, the Hensel twins were featured on television on "Oprah" and "Dateline" and in *Time* and *Life* magazines not just as entertainment, but as living and happy examples that not all people have two arms and two legs and distinct bodies.

Text can only go so far in explaining the physical attachments of conjoined twins who vary from each other and so profoundly from the rest of us. Visual images in magazines and newspapers and on television force what the imagination may not want to allow. Photographs and video images of conjoined twins give viewers an opportunity to stare without being impolite. (Although Lori and Reba Schappell (*b.* 1961) have been quick to point out that mere manners have not stopped the stares and questions they have received when in public.) Reading their stories, including anecdotes about their lives, coupled with the intimacy of pictures in a book, promotes seeing conjoined twins as people, no different from the rest of us except for their physical make-up and the differences and difficulties that imposes.

Conjoined twins pose many questions by their bodies, ranging from whether their anatomy is favorable for separation to whether they should marry if they remain joined. For some twins, separation surgery is not an option due to the sharing of organs. And yet from an early age, many state — most of them

emphatically — that they would not want to be separated. Their condition of being joined to a twin is normal for them and we should expand our definition of what a normal body is, rather than make them conform to ours. The anatomy of other twins has prompted court action to determine whether separation that would knowingly result in the death of a "parasitic" twin is permissible. The controversy surrounding Jodie and Mary (*b.* 2000) is thoroughly covered in this book, as well as topics such as separation surgery. The subject of marriage appears as an entry cross-referenced to Rosa and Josefa Blazek (1878–1922), since Rosa claimed to have married, and Daisy and Violet Hilton, whose marriages were said to have been publicity stunts.

Over the centuries, conjoined twins have been seen as carnival attractions, omens, and medical anomalies. Corresponding entries in this book include freak, prodigy, and dicephalus, with the word "freak" explained in both its derogatory meaning and as it is embraced by writers such as Leslie Fiedler. Both the modern standardized terminology and the historical categories into which conjoined twins have been sorted are included. In addition, 150 pairs of twins are listed, most of them by last name. Surgeons past and present are also represented, as are hospitals like Children's Hospital of Philadelphia that are known for the separation of conjoined twins. Issues like disability and identity are discussed and the words of ethicists like Alice Dreger are taken into account. Fictional twins by Mark Twain, Vladimir Nabakov, and Katherine Dunn have a place in this book, as do Adolph-Rudolph and other fraudulent twins. Other entries cover relevant films, websites, and institutions. Classic and contemporary books, articles, and papers are listed and described in the bibliography.

Despite the help of alphabetized entries, it soon becomes evident when reading about conjoined twins that they do not fit in comfortable categories (not even the most basic "one" or "two"), which is why modern thinkers theorize that we find them so fascinating. Surgeons are also challenged and admit when separating twins like Stella and Esther Alphonce (*b.* 1999) that there is no defined plane of cleavage. Each pair of twins is different and the twins are markedly different from each other. Those who are not extensively joined can be relatively easily separated, depending on the organs involved, whether the blood supply is shared, and if there is adequate skin to close the wounds. Psychologists suggest that separation surgery be carried out at as young an age as is safely possible. But despite often contrasting personalities, conjoined twins retain an attachment after physical ties are severed. After separation, they do best when placed in the same crib.

Surgeons have been accused of coercing the separation of conjoined twins in all cases, despite the difficulties of cutting and teasing their bodies apart and the resulting deficits. The operation is considered "successful" if only a single twin survives. News stories engage in a kind of score-keeping in which the separation of Mary and Decontee Cole (*b.* 2000), which took a forty-member team eight hours, is compared to the separation of Ganga and Jamuna Shrestha (*b.* 2000), which took twenty-six members ninety-six hours. In fact, retired pediatric surgeon John M. Templeton, Jr., reassures us that the decision to separate conjoined twins is made on a case-by-case basis and only undertaken when anatomically warranted. The surgeons are acutely aware — more so than the public — that surgery is not always appropriate or even possible. Ruthie and Verena Cady (1984–1991), for instance, shared a single heart for seven years. The Hensel twins, though they each have a heart, share a single pair of legs and would be unable to rely on prosthetic limbs. As their father describes, they would be "half a body" each. Instead the parents have allowed the

girls to maintain their physical connection and therefore retain their integrity, mobility, and emotional health. By deferring the decision, the Hensels have put it in the hands of their daughters, which is what adult conjoined twins like the Schappells advocate. (Neither the Hensels nor the Schappells intend to be separated.)

In cases where separation is warranted, parents and surgeons look on the operation as a release: "We were able to free them from one another," says cardiac surgeon Marcello Cardarelli about the surgical separation of the Onziga twins (*b.* 2001). The Starks referred to the day their daughters Alexandra and Sydney (*b.* 2001) were to be separated as "Independence Day." Many families have made the decision to separate and "normalize" their conjoined twins, even to the point of reassigning gender to Win Htut (*b.* 1982) so that her twin Lin could retain the penis they shared. While some envision anger on the part of separated twins that they were not able to make their own decision about surgery, the mother of the Moon Creek twins (*b.* 2000) feared later recriminations from her children if she did *not* have them separated. In fact, the surgery holds more than immediate consequences. Alice Dreger (1998) asks about the emotional trauma Angela Lakeberg (1993–1994) would have had to face if she had survived, knowing that she was the reason for the deliberate death of her conjoined twin Amy during surgery. Hassan and Hussein Abdulrehman are grateful that they were separated, but Hussein reveals that he would never have forgiven his mother if his twin had died during the operation.

With today's level of technological achievement in the separation of conjoined twins, it's easy to downplay the risks of surgery. It's also easy to apply modern medical knowledge to historic cases and determine that Chang and Eng Bunker, for instance, could have been separated, though all of the surgeons they consulted during their lifetime recommended against surgery. In many parts of the world, it is typical to bring conjoined twins to the West for surgical separation. Fees are often waived by doctors and hospitals in the U.S. and Canada for the opportunity to exercise their experienced surgical skills on twins born in the Dominican Republic, Mexico, Morocco, Pakistan, Peru, and the Congo. The stories included in this book allow the comparison of conjoined twins across time and cultures and allows the reader to find similarities between pairs of twins who lived centuries and worlds apart.

There is no doubt that the history of conjoined twins is full of sadness. The deaths of the Alibert twins in the eighteenth century and the Finley twins and Ritta-Christina in the nineteenth century were brought on by exposure as a direct result of exhibit to the public. Masha and Dasha Krivoshlyapova (*b.* 1950) have been institutionalized their entire lives and were the subject of experiments by Soviet scientists for decades. Dao and Duan (*b.* 1990) were orphaned at birth in Thailand. Once world-famous, Daisy and Violet Hilton spent their final years as clerks at the produce counter of a North Carolina grocery store. And craniopagus twins Yvonne and Yvette Jones MacArther (*b.* 1949) died just a few months short of their college graduation. There are stories of stillbirths and twins that did not survive separation. But there are also more uplifting stories, like that of the Schappells, breaking out of institutionalized existence to live on their own. Cases like those of the Lakebergs and "Jodie and Mary," in which the subjects — complete with diagrams on the eve-

ning news — have become abstract, are tempered by stories in which the conjoined twins are as real as the children next door and, like them, are growing into their bodies, whether they have been separated or remain joined.

The causes of conjoined twinning remain elusive, but the twins are no longer billed as the "products of unwed mothers" or the result of "maternal impressions." The entry causes reviews the possibilities and explains the formation of conjoined twins. Statistics are provided under frequency and survival rates. What used to be thought of as "lusus naturae" (nature's sport) has become over the last few decades a medical challenge. In this book, ethics, legal issues, religious convictions, and the cost of treatment are discussed within the accounts of specific sets of twins. Also explained in context are the uses to which conjoined twins have been put in literature and the media to symbolize everything from simple sharing to divine wrath. After reading the stories, both good and bad, one cannot help but be struck by how normal these "abnormalities" are. As Alice Dreger confirms, "… a close reading of the many biographies of conjoined twins clearly shows that their lives are not necessarily horrible, unbearable, or even that unusual.… Some have even had positively boring lives worthy of the best of us.… I do not recommend that we romanticize conjoined twinning, but neither is it rational to condemn it outright as an unlivable, thoroughly miserable condition." Conjoined twins remain, however, very interesting to most of us.

# ENCYCLOPEDIA
# OF CONJOINED TWINS

**Abdulrehman, Hassan and Hussein.**
*Twentieth Century.*

Conjoined twin boys born in the Sudan in 1986 joined from the chest down. They shared many organs, but only three legs. They were separated at eight months by Dr. Lewis Spitz of Great Ormond Street Hospital in London. Each baby was given a leg and the skin from the vestigial third leg was used to close the incision. Hassan, the weaker of the two, was believed unlikely to survive the surgery. He is now the more outgoing of the two boys, who are in high school. They are very close and sleep in the position in which they were attached, but have no recollection of having been joined. They have been reported to suffer from nightmares in which surgeons attempt to reattach them and are said to be haunted by images of Chang and Eng Bunker. Each of the Abdulrehman twins uses a cane. They have had many surgeries and are left with some disability, but feel lucky and proud to have been separated. Interviewed on "Joined: The Secret Life of Conjoined Twins," they explain that they wouldn't want to have to live a life of compromise. But Hussein points out that if his brother had died during the surgery, he would not have forgiven his parents.

**Abortion.**

Today, termination of a pregnancy (therapeutic abortion) may be offered when an anomaly is present. Many families decline to abort conjoined twins, whether or not it is believed that they can be surgically separated. Other families do not have a choice, in cases where a pregnancy is spontaneously aborted or in cases where the baby is non-viable. Leslie Fiedler (1978) notes that malformed children have been dispatched at birth by exposure or ritual sacrifice among all ancient peoples. Rosamond Purcell (1997) points out that in earlier times midwives were the first to see monstrous births and many must have concealed them, whether they were miscarried or died at birth. One such burial was discovered in his yard by fifteen-year-old James Paris du Plessis, later servant to Samuel Pepys (1633–1703). Du Plessis described a stillborn male child buried in a box in the garden; it had two heads, similar to one he had paid to see at Marybone near London.

**Adolph-Rudolph.** *Nineteenth Century.*

Two young men who fraudulently exhibited themselves at the turn of the twentieth century as a pair of conjoined twins (Bogdan 1988).

**Aesop, George and Alex.**

A pair of fictional conjoined twins featured in *National Lampoon.*

**Agnasi, Valerrhea and Valeryn.** *End of Twentieth Century.*

Conjoined twin girls born February 7, 2000.

**Agunin, Fatima and Amina.** *Twentieth, Twenty-first Century.*

Twin girls born in Morocco joined at the lower back, sharing urinary and genital systems. They were brought from Ibn Sina hospital in Rabat to La Paz Hospital in Madrid. There they were separated at 21 months of age on February 14, 2001. The separation surgery involved fifty specialists and took twelve hours, followed by five hours of additional surgery to reconstruct their shared genital and urinary systems. After the separation, the twins were sedated and stable in the intensive care unit. Their hospitalization was expected to last four weeks, after which they would return to their parents in Morocco. At a press conference, Dr. Juan Tovar said, "It all ended as expected although the operation was very difficult." The girls did not share a heart or any vital organs. Surgeons believe they will live relatively normal lives and perhaps even be able to give birth, despite each being left with a single leg and kidney.

**Ahire Brothers.** *Twentieth Century.*

Male conjoined twins born at a private nursing home in Thane, India, on May 22, 1998, with a triplet sister. They weighed a total of three kilograms. The twins were attached from the throat to the navel and shared a liver. In addition, their hearts shared the same pericardium and they did not have a sternum. The babies were brought to Wadia hospital, where x-rays and other tests were performed. Because Wadia does not have a heart-lung machine, surgery was attempted two days after birth at the P.D. Hinduja National Hospital. The two surgical teams were headed by pediatric surgeon Dr. Ela Maheshmeisher and cardiac surgeon Dr. Nitu Mandke, who told the press, "Our initial impression was that we would have to sacrifice one of the babies, as they shared vital organs. But luckily, they had separate intestines, and both of them could be saved" (Siamese Twins Saved After 10-hour Surgery 1998). The twins were to remain in intensive care while they were weaned off ventilators. The operation lasted ten hours and their weight afterward was 1.7 kg and 1.3 kg. Both boys died after separation surgery.

**Alibert Twins.** *Eighteenth Century.*

Conjoined boys born September 19, 1706, to Catherine Feüillet and Michel Alibert in Vitry, near Paris. They twins were joined at the abdomen and lived until September 26, when the strongest one died and the other followed three hours later. Dr. M. Du Verney ascribes their death to the awkwardness of their swaddling, which resulted in a posture that cramped their intestines. He also noted that they were given cow's milk, which curdled in their stomachs, rather than being suckled. And lastly he points out the frequency with which they were unwrapped and moved about in order to display them to the public (Wilson 1993).

**Alphonce, Stella and Esther.** *Twentieth Century.*

Conjoined twin girls born in 1999 in Dar es Salaam, Tanzania, to Lucy Namangura. They were born by Cesarean section and their parents were not expecting conjoined twins. Pygopagus twins, they were joined at the hip and buttock and shared a single anus. They were taken to the Red Cross Children's Hospital in Cape Town, South Africa, to undergo separation surgery. The team was led by University of Cape

Town neurosurgeon Jonathan Peter and co-surgeon Dr. Graham Fieggan. If successful in retaining the function of all four legs, the surgery would be unprecedented. Unlike previous separation surgeries, both twins were viable and healthy babies, with all systems formed and functioning. In preparation for surgery, the twins were x-rayed from every angle to determine whether their spinal cords were fused.

The twins were separated at eight months of age in a fourteen-hour operation. There was no defined plane of cleavage in the fused portion of the spine, but instead a web of nerves and blood vessels in the lumbar and sacral area. Surgery was performed under a microscope and viewed on televisions inside and outside the operating room. First, colostomies were performed. Then the girls were parted from the back by dividing the bone and cartilage to reach the spinal cords. The surgeons stimulated the cords to determine their correspondence to the muscle function in the lower legs prior to dividing them, but the results were sometimes puzzling. Dr. Peter told the press, "But in one instance we stimulated an electrode to a thigh muscle only to see all four limbs moving! That really made me very nervous. In fact the electrodes were more of a hindrance than a help" (Spotlight falls 2000). The coverings of the spinal cords were then carefully sewn shut and watertight before the operation could continue, to avoid contamination and the risk of meningitis. General surgeons completed the separation, which involved reconstruction of the excretory and reproductive systems. The wounds were closed and the separated twins were taken to intensive care.

Dr. Peter noted that after the operation, "The highlight for me was walking into the intensive care ward the following day and seeing four little legs moving!" (Spotlight falls 2000). This confirmed that they had been successful at separating the spinal cord and retaining function. Heinz Röde, who par-ticipated in the surgery, explains on BBC2's "Conjoined Twins" that, "You cannot go through Africa in this ... situation. You will be outcast, you will become ... a monster, you will become a curiosity, you will become a showpiece." On the same program, Alice Dreger responds, "Conjoined twins tend to grow into a body that they're born with, the same way the rest of us do and so they're born into this body joined and they will develop an understanding of their lives as joined. Now that can be very difficult in a place like Tanzania, but I'd also have to ask the question would that be any more difficult than, for example, being paralyzed from the waist down, and is that a justified reason for going ahead with the surgery like that? These are very difficult cases and I'm not saying there's a simple answer, though we have to at least take into account what conjoined twins themselves would say." In Dr. Peter's opinion, "If you read about twins who haven't been separated, their lives are such a painful existence" (Spotlight falls 2000).

Doctors hoped that the Alphonce twins' colostomies could be reversed and didn't anticipate any ongoing problems. Their mother was glad to see them come through the surgery, convinced despite the reassurance of a neurosurgeon-translator that they would not come out of the operating room. In June 2001, the Alphonce twins returned to southern Tanzania, healthy, happy, and learning to walk. Stella has a weak heart, but is believed to be capable of having children of her own. They were to be transferred to the care of Dr. Joseph Shija at Muhimbili University College of Health Sciences in Dar es Salaam.

*See also* "Conjoined Twins"

**Anencephaly.**

Anencephaly, a condition incompatible with life in which a baby is born (or still-born) with parts of the brain and spinal cord missing and exposed, is associated with duplication of facial features.

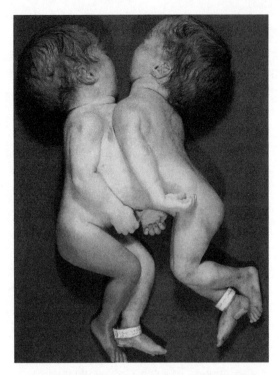

Lantern slide of teaching specimen of omphalopagus conjoined twins, probably photographed on the autopsy table. Courtesy of F. Gonzalez-Crussi.

### Anne and Marie. *Twentieth Century.*

Dicephalus twin girls born at the Academy of Medicine in Sofia, Bulgaria, in February 1981. They had two heads, two spinal columns, and two esophagi, but a single heart.

### Anomaly.

Conjoined twins are considered anomalies since they deviate from the natural order. The first citation of the word in the natural sciences is from 1646 (OED 2001).
*See also* Monster; Prodigy

### Aquila and Priscilla. *Seventeenth Century.*

Conjoined twin girls born on May 19, 1680, at Ile Brewers, near Taunton, England. They slept at different times, cried heartily, and were seen by upwards of 500 visitors a day. Their story was told in at least two broadsheets (Wilson 1993).

### Armstrong, Tay-lah and Monique. *End of Twentieth Century.*

Female conjoined twins born prematurely in Australia in April 2000 to Pacquita Armstrong and Shane Conyard. The babies were joined upside down at the back of their heads, a type of craniopagus twins not recorded in medical literature. Their union was detected at fourteen weeks of pregnancy by Gary Pritchard during a routine ultrasound and the parents were given options, but decided to go ahead with the pregnancy. The twins were born seven weeks premature. Tay-lah was operated on at four days of age to correct a narrowing of the main heart artery. She also developed renal problems and later developed cerebral palsy (Australian surgeons 2000).

The twins were separated at six months of age at the Royal Children's Hospital in Brisbane. Their parents, who were said to have signed an exclusive television and magazine deal, instructed the hospital not to comment on the operation, but a news conference was planned. A 25-member surgical team led by neurosurgeon Dr. Scott Campbell performed the twelve-hour operation on October 24, 2000. The team included anesthetists, neurosurgeons, plastic surgeons, pediatric and neonatal physicians, cardiologists and a cardiac surgeon, an obstetrician, nurses, and technicians. The surgeons had consulted with international colleagues and practiced on mannequins. "We knew the operation would be awkward because of the way they were joined. So we practiced with the dummies to make sure we could flip them over safely. We also practiced on the babies themselves, so there were no mishaps," said Dr. Campbell (Separating the Armstrong Twins 2001). They had built up the twins' immune systems and blood volumes to cope with the surgery, but there was still a 70 percent chance that one twin would die during surgery.

During the operation, surgeons separated bone and blood vessels. The babies shared brain fluid and the juncture of their skulls was close to a vital sinus, as Dr. Campbell explained:

> It was very complex anatomy because there was a hole between the two skulls and part of Monique's cerebellum was protruding through. There were major problems because the conjoined area is the part of the brain where the superior sagittal sinus and the left and right transfer sinuses are located. The blood flow builds up as the veins drain ... if you occlude any of the draining veins there, you can cause a stroke. If you cut them and they bleed, the patient can potentially bleed to death. But we were able to navigate our way through and preserve both twins' sinuses. It basically meant that we did not have to make a decision about which twins' sinuses to keep and we were able to treat them both equally [Separating the Armstrong Twins 2001].

The seven and a half centimeter wounds were closed with skin and fascia grafts from their thighs. Plastic surgeon Dr. Richard Thiele believes that there will be little scarring. Monique's surgery was finished first, followed thirty minutes later by Tay-lah's. They were taken to the intensive care unit and placed on ventilators, from which they were removed the following day. The surgeons announced that the operation had been a success and that the babies were in critical but stable condition, but there was still the threat of infection and leakage of brain fluid.

On October 30, 2000, Tay-lah underwent surgery at Royal Children's Hospital to repair a cerebrospinal fluid leak, after which the wound was resutured. She may also require more heart surgery and an anti-reflux operation. She is considered the weaker of the twins, but was in critical but stable condition. Monique was released from the hospital about four weeks after the separation surgery. Despite some feeding problems, she was progressing well.

### Astbury, Nicole and Chloe. *Twentieth Century.*

Female conjoined twins born at St. Mary's hospital in Manchester, England, in 1995. They were joined at the breastbone and shared a liver and bowel. They died five weeks later of an infection.

### Asuncion, Kayla and Kyana. *Twentieth Century.*

Conjoined twin girls born at Community Medical Center in Fresno, California, on August 30, 1999. They were delivered by perinatologist Dr. Douglas Helm by Cesarean section. The babies were connected at the abdomen and shared a liver and a single umbilical cord, a condition detected at thirty weeks gestation by ultrasound. On the same day, a fetal echocardiogram indicated that Kayla had a congenital heart defect that put her health in danger and resulted in an irritable disposition. After birth she cried often and scratched at her sister, who ignored her distress and slept peacefully in an isolette in the neonatal intensive care ward. The girls' parents, Lorlyn Bungacayo and Randy Asuncion, were interviewed during a hospital press conference in September announcing their surgical separation, which was performed at Valley Children's Hospital at the age of one month. Detailed maps of their anatomy were prepared by radiologist Dr. Michael Myracle. The separation surgery would relieve Kyana's heart of the stress of moving much of the twins' shared blood supply (Gathright 2000).

### Atkinson, Prisna and Napit. *Twentieth Century.*

Conjoined twins born in Thailand in 1953 and separated on March 29, 1955, in Chicago.

## Attard, Gracie and Rosie. *End of Twentieth Century.*

*Nobody, certainly not a child, can be required to act as permanent life support for another person.* — Dena S. Davis, Arizona State University

*It was the first time a British court had been asked to accelerate the death of one person in order to offer the chance of life to another. The court wrestled mightily with the choice, weighing morality and mortality, asking profound and searching questions of the doctors on one side, the parents on the other.* — Laura King (2001)

Pseudonyms "Jodie" and "Mary" were used by the British courts to protect the anonymity of these two female conjoined twins born in Manchester, England, on August 8, 2000, joined at the pelvis with a fused spine and a common aorta. Their parents Michaelangelo and Rina Attard, Roman Catholics from Xaghra on the Maltese island of Gozo, came to England to give birth when they realized the babies were joined and would need sophisticated medical care. An ultrasound at six months had revealed the girls were joined at the rump with each girl's legs resting on the other's belly (Reid 2000). After their birth at St. Mary's Hospital in Manchester, Gracie was bright and alert, but Rosie — believed to have suffered brain damage — was passive and dependant on Gracie for the circulation of oxygen and blood through their bodies. Rosie's heart and lungs were essentially nonfunctional. The doctors in Manchester estimated that there was an 80 to 90 percent chance that both babies would die within six months if they were not surgically separated, due to the burden on Gracie's heart of supporting both herself and her parasitic twin. A medical team from London concurred when asked to provide a second opinion.

The parents were opposed to the separation surgery, which would result in Rosie's death. Liam Holton, father of surviving separated twin Eilish, was sympathetic: "What those poor people are suffering at the moment is the cruelest form of psychological torture. They are having to let one of their children die so the other can live. There is no worse dilemma a parent could ever find themselves in" (Donaghy 2000). Through their lawyer, Simon Taylor, the parents issued a statement: "We cannot begin to accept or contemplate that one of our children should die to enable the other one to survive. That is not God's will. Everyone has a right to life, so why should we kill one of our daughters to enable the other one to survive? …. We have faith in God and we are quite happy for God's will to decide what happens to our two daughters." The question of whether the surgery should proceed was put before England's High Court, which decided on August 25, 2000, that Gracie's right to life was paramount and that surgery should be carried out. The surgery was tentatively scheduled for the second week of October, unless Gracie's condition significantly improved, in which case it would be delayed until the twins were three months old.

Separate attorneys represented the conflicting interests of the parents, the doctors, each of the twins, the public health service, and the government. Judith Parker, the lawyer assigned to represent Gracie, urged everyone to think of the surgery not as something to hasten Rosie's death, but as the restoration of Gracie's bodily integrity, which would — after separation — require only rectal and vaginal surgery. The parents argued that separation would not necessarily result in a normal life for Gracie and pointed out the hardship of caring for her in their isolated country. "We cannot see how we can possibly cope either financially or personally with a child who will have the serious disabilities that Gracie will have," they told the court. They worried that they would have to leave their daughter permanently in England so she could receive proper care. Alternatively, Gracie would receive substandard care in Malta and would be subject to a lifetime of discrimination because of her disability (Kaveny 2002). The family's convictions not to intervene were supported by the head of the Roman Catholic Church in London, Archbishop of Westminster Cormac Murphy-O'Connor, who agrees that no one may commit a wrong action hoping that good may come of it. They were also backed up by English law, in which there is no obligation for doctors to provide treatment to prolong life, even in a medically futile situation. Also in English law, however, the child's interest is paramount and takes precedence over parental consent (Reid 2000). Parker stated that Gracie had a 95 percent chance of surviving separation surgery, but only a 1 percent chance if surgery is delayed until Rosie dies naturally (Moseley).

The British judges could find no comparable cases of surgical separation without parental consent in Australia, South Africa, or Canada. The case raised strong moral, religious, and ethical concerns that resulted in public outcry, activist threats, and hate mail directed at the doctors. A spokesman for the Hastings Center, a bioethics research organization in Garrison, New York, categorized the question as "lifeboat ethics," in which any outcome is tragic, but said that most ethicists would be in favor of surgery if there is clear medical evidence that only one of the children could survive. Retired neonatal physician Keith Roberts, who pioneered separation surgery of conjoined twins in England, characterized the weaker child as akin to a congenital tumor that must be removed to assure the survival of the stronger child:

> Where the egg has not divided symmetrically, the lesser half is not a human being. It is more logical to think of it as a tumor, a growth which is sapping life. By giving it a name, these poor parents have created a situation where they think they are killing a baby by having the operation. But what they are calling Mary [Rosie] is really a tumor, and all that is being proposed is the removal of a tumor [Edge 2000].

There was no question that Rosie's life could

not be prolonged by artificial means or by a heart-lung transplant.

Catholic moralists were divided about whether the operation was impermissible because it counted as the intentional killing or mutilation of Mary (Rosie). If allowed on moral grounds, was the surgery merely morally permissible, or was it morally required because of its potential benefits to Jodie (Gracie)? (Kaveny 2002).

The Court of Appeal heard arguments on September 6, 2000, about whether doctors operating on the twins could be charged with Rosie's assault or murder and whether Rosie, unable to survive on her own, has a legal right to be protected from death. The Lord Justices struggled to answer these questions and to determine Rosie's status as a viable human being. Depending on the Court's decision, the parents had the option of appealing to the Law Lords, Britain's supreme court, or to the European Court of Human Rights. The case also had diplomatic overtones, since the parents brought their babies to England for treatment and British doctors suggested causing the death of one of them. Britain's Pro-Life Alliance offered the parents and twins a "safe haven" in Italy if they lost the appeal and chose to leave Britain (Reid 2000). On September 22, 2000, the appeals court ruled unanimously that the separation surgery should be performed to save the life of one of the twins. In their unprecedented opinion, Gracie's right to have the chance of a normal life outweighed Rosie's equal right to life because Rosie had no long-term chance of survival.

Lord Justice Alan Ward stated that there was an irreconcilable conflict between the best interests of each child that placed the court in an impossible position: "There is an irreconcilable conflict and the court cannot fully honor its separate duty to each child to do what is best for that child." The surgery was characterized as the removal of the fatal harm to Gracie presented by Rosie's draining her life blood and explained as an act of self-defense performed on Gracie's behalf. "The sad fact is that [Rosie] lives on borrowed time, all of it borrowed from her sister. She is incapable of independent existence. She is designated for death," he explained in his ruling. Lord Justice Brooke pointed out that their remaining conjoined might lead to Gracie suffering from cerebral palsy or excessive bleeding if her heart is not overwhelmed as early as doctors expect. "[Rosie's] conjoined existence therefore poses a serious threat to Gracie in more ways than one," he concludes. Ward warned that the decision in this unique case does not authorize the killing of a patient once a doctor determines that the patient cannot survive. Dr. Michael Wilkes, chairman of the ethics committee of the British Medical Association, agreed that the decision should not be viewed as sanctioned killing. But Dr. Richard Nicholson, editor of the *Bulletin of Medical Ethics*, objected to the court overruling the parents' wishes and allowing deliberate killing. In explaining the ruling, Lord Justice Ward wrote, "The parents' wishes do not persuade me that it is right that [Gracie] should be denied the enjoyment of a life for which she is well-equipped." On September 28, 2000, the parents of Gracie and Rosie announced their decision not to appeal the court ruling. A last-minute appeal by the Pro-Life Alliance to halt the surgery was rejected on November 3, 2000.

The surgeons operated on November 6, 2000, at Manchester's St. Mary's Hospital. The surgical team of twenty expected the operation to take up to fifteen hours. After the operation, which actually took twenty hours and did — as expected — result in Rosie's death, Gracie was breathing without the assistance of a ventilator and had begun feeding normally, with her parents at her side. Gracie was expected to remain in the hospital for many months and to undergo further surgery to repair a dislocated pelvic joint and to reconstruct the lower internal organs, the rectum, and possibly the vagina.

The parents agreed to provide exclusive interviews and photographs to *News of the World*, the *Mail on Sunday*, and Granada TV for what is reported to have been £350,000 (Boseley 2002). The money was to be put in a trust fund to pay for Gracie's continuing treatment, but the deal was still controversial. When word of their agreement with the media reached the court, a High Court judge lifted the ban on publishing the twins' real names (King 2001).

The case has been referred to by the court as "unique and unusual" and reporters note that few involved with it have gone unmoved. Even coroner Leonard Gorodkin coupled his clinical findings in Rosie's death with an expression of sympathy for the parents: "For them, the twins were two persons. They clearly had two daughters who they loved equally … I only hope that the love they clearly have for their surviving twin … will bring them pleasure and joy in the future, and will lessen the pain of loss" (Kind 2001). Rosie was honored with a large funeral and buried in Xaghra, Malta, on January 19, 2001. In June, Gracie was cleared by doctors to return home, although she faces additional reconstructive surgery. Her lower limbs, which were twisted at right angles when she was joined to Rosie, have been aligned but still have some deformity. Doctors, however, hope that she will be able to walk normally and bear children of her own (King 2001).

***See also* Jodie and Mary**

## Atypical twins.

Used to describe parasitic twins and conjoined twins that are intermediate between the various types (Spencer 1996).

***See also* Parasitic twins**

## Autopsy.

The first known autopsy in the New World was performed on conjoined twin girls in Santo Domingo in 1533 and confirmed that each child had a complete set of organs. The autopsy was conducted at the request of the priest who had christened them and was vindicated for having baptized them as two individuals (Smith 1988).

*See also* **Blazek, Rosa and Josefa; Bunker, Chang and Eng; Finley, Mina and Minnie; Gibb, Mary Rae and Margaret Stratton; Johanna and Melchiora; Lakeberg, Amy and Angela; Martha and Marie; Paré, Ambroise; Ritta-Christina**

**Autosite.**

An autosite is the term for the more fully developed conjoined twin who supports a parasitic twin.

*See also* **Parasitic twins**

**Aydin, Bashir.** *Twentieth Century.*

A male baby born to Fadine and Mahmut Aydin in Adiyaman, Turkey, with a fully developed head protruding from his abdomen. The head was removed in a five-hour operation, leaving Bashir normal except for the scar on his stomach. *The Sun* (March 31, 1992) exaggerated this parasitic twin, however, reporting that the head was being kept alive on a heart-lung machine, that it watched television (preferring "The Three Stooges"), and that it often showed emotion. After the surgery, Bashir was rumored to speak with the spirit of the twin that was removed.

**Baez, Yulissa and Yuli.** *End of Twentieth Century.*

Female conjoined twins born in Santo Domingo, Dominican Republic, on July 1, 2000. They were joined at the thorax and shared a heart. Doctors were unable to perform the separation surgery or to find a U.S. hospital to do so. Both girls died in August 2000.

**Banda, Luka and Joseph.** *Twentieth Century.*

*I really felt the weight of the world on my shoulders as I walked back into that operating room. I didn't have my $350,000 Zeiss operating microscope that I have at Hopkins or my $400,000 3-D wand or my lasers or my ultrasounds or any of that fancy equipment. I just had my loupes and a scalpel and faith in God, and I went in there and said, "Lord, it's up to you."*— surgeon Benjamin Carson about separating the Banda twins

Conjoined twins born in Zambia in 1997 to Joyce Banda, a mother of five. The boys were joined on the top of their heads and facing opposite directions. Their skull was described as one continuous tube, lacking any horizontal separation between one brain and the other, although the brains themselves were not joined (Bor 1998). The twins were taken to Ga-Rankuwa hospital in Medunsa, South Africa, in October 1997, and separated there on December 31, six weeks after tissue expanders had been inserted beneath their scalps. The team of twenty doctors and nurses was led by pediatric neurosurgeon Dr. Benjamin Carson, who learned about the twins when he was accepting an honorary degree at a local university and flew in from Johns Hopkins Medical Center in Baltimore at the request of surgeon Dr. Sam Mokgokong. In preparation for the twenty-eight-hour surgery, Dr. Carson practiced on a virtual reality device that created a three-dimensional replica of their brains from MRIs, including every detail of their complex shared blood supply. The operation involved separating numerous blood vessels, nudging the brains apart, covering the exposed skulls with tough cow membrane, and suturing the scalp closed (Bor 1998).

On BBC2's "Conjoined Twins," Dr. Carson describes the surgery: "...I knew from having done the virtual surgery before, that there was a plane and I remembered where the plane was so I began to tease in that direction and eventually the plane showed itself..." After nineteen hours of surgery,

Dr. Carson had the boys' heads separated three-quarters of the way, but was afraid they would bleed to death. He suggested leaving the twins partially linked for weeks or months to allow their brains to develop alternate pathways for blood. The plan was scuttled during a quick meeting, where it was decided that the hospital lacked the facilities to keep the boys alive in a partially divided state (Spitz 1999). Dr. Carson remembers, "After twenty-eight hours and after a point where we almost gave up again because the vascular anatomy was so complex, they woke up. Now one of them right in the operating room popped his little eyes open and reached up for the tube and tried to extubate himself. The other one was doing the same thing by the time we got to the intensive care unit. Within two days they were intubated, within three days they were eating, and within two weeks they were crawling around, neurologically intact, and it was just unbelievable."

The costs of the operation were borne by the Zambian government (Spitz 1999). After the surgery, Dr. Carson commented, "There have been about twenty-three attempts to separate such twins in the past. As far as we know, this is the first time anybody's been able to completely separate them in one operation — not only with both surviving but apparently with no deficits" (Bor 1998). Dr. Sam Mokgokong had participated in a similar surgery, but the twins had died; Dr. Carson had separated conjoined twins who were left with neurological deficits. The Banda twins would wear helmets for the next year to protect their heads from injury. Ten months after their separation surgery, the Banda twins were flown back to Pretoria's Ga-Rankuwa Hospital for a three-week stay during which complications (including a wound of Joseph's that would not heal) would be attended to by Dr. Mukgokong and surgeon Dr. Tackson Lambart. Unlike the Binder twins, the Bandas did not suffer from any neurological deficits after the separation.

*See also* **Binder, Patrick and Benjamin**

**Beaver, Fonda Michelle and Shannon Elaine.** *Twentieth Century.*

Conjoined twin girls born on February 9, 1980, by Cesarean section to fourteen-year-old Kim Beaver of Forest City, North Carolina. She was expecting twins, but did not know they would be conjoined until the day before their birth. The girls weighed a total of twelve pounds and shared a single pelvis, colon, rectum, and vagina. They each controlled one of the two legs. The twins were separated in 1981.

**Bengal, Two-Headed Boy of** *see* **Two-Headed Boy of Bengal**

**Bicephalus** *see* **Dicephalus**

**Biddenden Maids** *see* **Chulkhurst, Mary and Eliza**

**Bijani, Laleh and Ladan.** *Twentieth, Twenty-first Century.*

*Sometimes we have quarrels and disputes over various issues, but generally we have a good understanding and love each other.* — Ladan Bijani

Twenty-seven-year-old conjoined female twins born in Iran joined at the head. Their story and picture appeared in the Scottish media in March 2002. As they aged, the twins exhibited different personality traits. Laleh dislikes cooking, for instance, so Ladan cooks for both of them. They each graduated from Tehran University Law School. They underwent tests in Germany in 1996 to assess the possibility of separation, but surgery would be complicated by a shared artery supplying blood to the brain. The twins have been waiting for a chance to be surgically separated that would not jeopardize either of their lives.

*See also* **Schappell, Lori and Reba**

## Binder, Patrick and Benjamin.
*Twentieth Century.*

Conjoined twin boys born by Cesarean section to Josef and Theresia Binder on February 2, 1987, in Ulm, Germany. Their condition was discovered during an ultrasound. The twins weighed eight pounds fourteen ounces at birth. They were joined at the back of the head and shared the superior sagittal vein, the major vein that drains blood from the brain, in addition to skull and skin tissue. Transferred immediately to the children's hospital, the babies were taken home after five weeks. The Binders' German physicians consulted with surgeons at Johns Hopkins University Medical Center in Baltimore about separation. If surgery were not performed, the twins would be bedridden the rest of their lives (Clark and Hager 1987). Johns Hopkins assembled a team of seventy physicians — seven pediatric anesthesiologists, five neurosurgeons, two cardiac surgeons, five plastic surgeons, and dozens of nurses and technicians — and prepared for five months, including conducting three dress rehearsals. They equipped the operating room with a hinged table and two of everything else (Clark and Hager 1987). Four Johns Hopkins doctors flew to Germany in May 1987 to insert inflatable silicone balloons under the scalps of the boys to stretch the skin.

The Binder twins arrived in Baltimore on September 2, 1987. Surgery began on the morning of September 5, and the separation was performed by pediatric neurosurgeon Ben Carson. In his book *Gifted Hands* (Carson and Murphey 1990), he describes, "At the end of the five-month period, everything was so organized that at times it felt as if we were planning a military operation. We even worked out where each team member would stand on the operating room floor. A 10-page, play-by-play book detailed each step of the operation. We endlessly discussed the five three-hour dress rehearsals we'd had,

using life-sized dolls attached at the head by Velcro." The operation took twenty-two hours. After anesthetizing the twins, their heads were positioned and the neurosurgeons and plastic surgeons cut through the scalp and removed shared bone tissue. Heart surgeons Dr. Bruce Reitz and Duke Cameron opened the twins' chests to remove small pieces of pericardium, for later use. After opening the dura and separating the brains, the team encountered bleeding that was difficult to control because of the size and shape of the shared vein. The babies were attached to heart-lung bypass machines and their temperatures reduced to 68 degrees, bringing them into hypothermic arrest. Dr. Carson and Donlin severed the shared vein over the next twenty minutes and the twins were separated. *Newsweek* refers to the moment the boys were "untethered" (Clark and Hager 1987).

Carson and Donlin each fashioned a new sagittal vein for one of the twins from the pericardium previously removed, all within the one-hour time frame allowed for the bypass. Bleeding from all of the severed blood vessels ensued, furthered by the anticoagulant used to thin the blood for the bypass. The babies required transfusions of a total of sixty units of blood, some of it supplied by the American Red Cross. The hemorrhaging eventually stopped. The boys were next put into a barbiturate coma to slow down the swelling and their scalps were closed. They were maintained on Phenobarbitol and attached to life-support machines for two weeks so that their blood flow and respiration could be reduced and monitored during healing. They were CT-scanned periodically.

The Binders' hospital bill was estimated to top $300,000, which will be reimbursed by West Germany's health insurance program. The cost did not include doctors' bills, which were waived by all those participating in the surgery (Clark and Hager 1987). After the operation, the media were told that the boys had a fifty-fifty chance of survival. Subsequent surgeries (twenty-two of them) would insert a titanium mesh covering mixed with a paste of crushed bone where each boy had shared a skull and improve the closure of the scalps. Almost all of the post-operative emergencies were brought under control quickly except the respiratory arrest suffered by Patrick, who aspirated some food. He was resuscitated and, although no one knew how long he had been deprived of oxygen, he made a good recovery. The parents signed an exclusive agreement with *Bunte* magazine to report on the progress of the twins after they left Johns Hopkins. After the separation, the twins had severe neurological deficits that left them institutionalized (Bor 1998).

*See also* **Banda, Luka and Joseph**

## Binewski, Electra and Iphigenia.

Fictional conjoined twins in Katherine Dunn's *Geek Love* (1989). The narrator describes: "The girls were Siamese twins with perfect upper bodies joined at the waist and sharing one set of hips and legs. They usually sat and walked and slept with their long arms around each other. They were, however, able to face directly forward by allowing the shoulder of one to overlap the other. They were always beautiful, slim, and huge-eyed. They studied the piano and began performing piano duets at an early age. Their compositions for four hands were thought by some to have revolutionized the twelve-tone scale." "Elly" and "Iphy" performed in their family's carnival and were advertised as "Siamese beauties linked in harmonious perpetuity.... Twin musicians! Twin miracles!"

*See also* **Sexuality**

## Blazek, Rosa and Josefa. *Nineteenth Century.*

*When I lifted the covers to examine the patient, I found that she was attached to another woman, whose name is Rosa, at the ilium and back. I then realized that I had the Blazek (grown-together) twins to treat.* —Dr. Benjamin H. Breakstone, who treated Josefa for appendicitis in 1922

Female conjoined twins born with the assistance of a midwife in Skreychov, Bohemia (now the Czech Republic), on January 20, 1878. Rosa (Rosalice) and Josefa were the second and third of six or seven children. Labor was said to have lasted only fifteen minutes (Guttmacher 1967). Each child had a placenta and an umbilical cord. When their parents consulted the local witch, it was recommended that the children be deprived of food for eight days, but they survived and their resilience convinced the witch that they should remain alive. They were not nursed for the first month because they had not been expected to live; they were weaned at two years. The twins were joined in the lumbar region of the spine by a bony union that completely fused their pelvises. They had a single urethral opening and anus, but had two vaginas. Their circulatory system was shared. The girls had a limited area of shared sensation near their union, but it was reported that where sensation was shared, it was half as strong (Perlstein and LeCount 1927).

The Blazek twins were first examined by doctors at six months of age. It was reported that their heads were asymmetrical. Their vertebral columns formed a "V" and were united from the second lumbar vertebra. They had funnel-shaped chests and the union of their soft parts began at the level of the ninth thoracic vertebra. They had two labia minora with one well-developed clitoris. A clear roentgenogram was never made of the twins (Perlstein and LeCount 1927). The Blazeks began talking at age two, walking at four.

Their appetites and sleeping habits differed markedly, although later reports indicate more regularity. Rosa preferred sour and Josefa liked sweets; one liked beer and the other liked wine. The urge to urinate was experienced separately, while the urge to defecate was experienced simultaneously. While they had measles at the same time, only Josefa contracted diphtheria at age eight and only Rosa suffered from colitis. At twelve, both girls came down with chorea and both began menstruating one month before their fourteenth birthday (Perlstein and LeCount 1927). Other physical differences included the fact that Josefa had only upper molars, while Rosa developed them all. Rosa developed a bladder stone that had to be removed in 1906. The girls' personalities were also dissimilar, with Rosa active and Josefa quiet, though neither was quarrelsome. Rosa took the lead when they walked, with Josefa walking backwards. Both twins were said to have below-normal intelligence (Perlstein and LeCount 1927). Although several showmen applied for permission to exhibit the girls, their parents refused until they were thirteen. Reaching that age in 1891, they were examined by Dr. Marcel Baudouin and began their stage career in Paris which led to exhibitions around the world. They continued on the stage for thirty years, touring music halls and theaters throughout England and Europe, among them the Empire Theatre in Bristol. Between them, they sang and played the piano, violin, and xylophone. They spoke English, Russian, Polish, and German in addition to their native tongue.

Rosa and Josepha Blazek as they appeared in tights for their "ladies only" matinees. Courtesy of the Mütter Museum, College of Physicians of Philadelphia.

In 1907, Rosa reportedly married Franz Dvorak with her sister as bridesmaid, but other accounts suggest that the marriage was forbidden by their parents or the courts. Perlstein and LeCount (1927) state that Rosa had a sex drive, while Josefa did not, and noted that Rosa's body showed evidence of syphilis. Rosa supposedly gave birth to a male child named Franzel at the Prague General Hospital on April 17, 1910. It was said that they had applied for advice about an "abdominal swelling" to the surgical clinic, denying the possibility of pregnancy, but giving birth unattended a short time later. While only Rosa experienced labor pains, both sisters were able to nurse the baby (Guttmacher 1967).

The birth of Franzel brought the twins to the attention of American showman Ike Rose. He signed the sisters to an exclusive contract and promoted them, together with the child, until the outbreak of World War I. Rosa's husband was said to have been killed in the German army in 1917. After the war, the twins worked for a German showman for a year, after which Rose signed them to a three-year contract with the C.A. Wortham carnival in the U.S. When they were on their way to the Hamburg port to board the *Manchuria* for Massachusetts with their brother Frank and Rosa's son Franzel, Rosa was arrested over a dispute about a bill. Both women were found guilty and fined, Josefa afterward swearing out a warrant for false arrest. They set sail and arrived in Boston in February 1921, where they were met by reporters. They attracted more attention during their next two weeks in New York City, where they underwent a much-publicized examination by a group of twenty-five doctors.

In March 1921, they traveled to Philadelphia, making a two-week appearance for a reported $2,500 a week at the World's Museum billed as the "Grown Together Twins," followed by five days and nights on the stage of the Pilsbury Garden. In April, the Blazeks arrived in San Antonio, Texas, the winter quarters of the C.A. Wortham carnival. After a one-night appearance in San Antonio and a week-long stint in Fort Worth, the carnival began its route through the Midwest to Canada. During the tour, Rosa and Josefa would present themselves in revealing tights to "ladies only" matinees. At that time, the twins were reported to weigh a total of 210 pounds and to make their own clothes. At about the time the show reached Calgary, they were examined by a female physician who described their bony fusion as measuring forty inches in circumference and Josefa's curvature of the spine as causing her to walk with her heel raised. Josefa claimed to have a sweetheart with the

show, but said he had died of appendicitis in July.

During the winter of 1921, the Blazek sisters made appearances in Louisiana and Alabama. Their next stop was Chicago, which they reached by train on January 9, 1922. As a publicity stunt, the twins were taken to the American Hospital to inquire about separation. Examination by a team of doctors led by Max Thorek ruled that division would result in the death of one of the twins. They appeared on numerous stages in and around the city, but soon — possibly instigated by their brother — accused Ike Rose of pocketing most of their income, taking in some $1,200 a week and paying them only $200. They also asked the courts for an injunction to prevent Rose from advertising Franzel as "the son of two mothers." Rose defended himself by explaining the original contract terms, which included his provision of room and board, transportation, clothing, and a maid.

While still on tour, Rosa contracted influenza and three weeks later Josefa had an apparent attack of appendicitis (Perlstein and LeCount 1927). Doctors attributed it to her consumption of a lot of meat, when they had eaten little meat in their homeland (Breakstone 1922). In general, Josefa was constipated. Hospital chief surgeon Dr. Benjamin Breakstone took the opportunity to thoroughly examine the twins. He found with the aid of a rectal tube that Rosa's sigmoid emptied into the rectum about seven inches above the anus and Josefa's about four inches above the anus (Breakstone 1922). He diagnosed appendicitis and jaundice in Josefa and catarrhal jaundice (almost cured) in Rosa and ordered the Blazeks to the hospital, which they chose not to do. Two days later, on March 25, 1922, the twins were rushed to Chicago's West End Hospital, where they were diagnosed with jaundice. Josefa was in critical condition. She lapsed into unconsciousness after three days and her pulse weakened. Dr. Breakstone was prepared to attempt separation if one twin died. The twins' best interests were looked after by their lawyer J.L. Triska, who was busy executing their wills. Their fortune was said by their brother to total approximately $200,000 and to include a large farm in their homeland. On March 30, 1922, Josefa died after contracting pneumonia. She was followed fifteen minutes later by Rosa, who had also lost consciousness a few hours earlier. The twins were forty-four years old. Separation, which would have involved rebuilding part of the digestive tract and severing one of the legs, had been vetoed by Frank Blazek.

The death certificate was signed by coroner Peter Hoffman and the Blazeks lay in state at the John T. Chrastka funeral home on April 3, 1922. The same day, George W. Brady, a radiologist at the West End Hospital, revealed that their fused pelvises would have made natural childbirth impossible and that Rosa had

The Blazeks with Rosa's son. Courtesy of the Mütter Museum, College of Physicians of Philadelphia.

no scar from a Cesarean section. In Dr. Brady's opinion, the Blazeks had died of an intestinal obstruction that was difficult to detect because of their juncture. Because the women had died intestate an autopsy was mandated to determine their legal status and thus their heirs. This postmortem examination was conducted secretly by J.H.M. Otradovec and E.R. LeCount. They confirmed that Rosa was Franzel's mother (a claim that is still debated) and therefore he was entitled to her half of the estate. Meanwhile, it was being debated whether the es-

tate should be probated in America or Czechoslovakia. After Frank Blazek requested guardianship of Franzel, it was revealed that the Blazek sisters' estate totaled a mere $400. The rest of their fortune was presumably taken to Berlin by Ike Rose, who left the country after the twins' deaths nullified their lawsuits against him.

The Blazeks' postmortem examination also revealed that they had accumulated more than three inches of subcutaneous fat, that their outer breasts were larger and more pendulous than their inner ones, and that their vaginal canal was bifurcated. The exam also found Rosa's liver to be cirrhotic. Rosa and Josefa were embalmed with formaldehyde (Perlstein and LeCount 1927). They were thought to be buried in Chicago, but their death certificates indicate that their bodies were returned to Bohemia. The Chicago Historical Society has no record of their lives.

### "Body Doubles: Siamese Twins in Fact and Fiction."

A Spring 1995 exhibit organized by Laura E. Beardsley at the Mütter Museum, College of Physicians of Philadelphia.

### Bohemian Twins *see* Blazek, Rosa and Josefa

### Bosin, Eustasia (?) and Eustocia (?). *Twentieth Century.*

Conjoined twin girls born in Papua New Guinea in 1996. Separated in Australia in 1996.

### Bransfield Twins. *Eighteenth Century.*

Conjoined boys born (possibly stillborn) in London in 1781. The engraving by obstetrician Dr. Bland shows them to have two heads, four arms, two spinal columns, one sacrum, two legs, and one penis. Internally, they had two stomachs, two sets of intestines, one rectum, and one bladder (Harris 1892).

### Brodie, Rodney and Roger. *Twentieth Century.*

Born in 1951 joined at the head, but with separate nervous and circulatory systems. They were examined at the University of Illinois Medical Center in Chicago at six weeks of age to determine whether they could be separated. Preparation for the surgery took fourteen months, with the operation taking place on December 17, 1952. It took a twelve-person team twelve hours and forty minutes to separate the twins, with Rodney given preference. After both boys suffered spinal fluid leaks, Roger went into a coma and died on January 20, 1953. Rodney's skull was rebuilt in more than twenty subsequent operations. He appeared on a national television program sponsored by the American Medical Association in May 1953, followed by inclusion in *Life* magazine. Rodney left the hospital in December 1953. In May 1955, he suffered and recovered from a brain hemorrhage.

### Bryce, Alaina and Xela. *End of Twentieth Century.*

Conjoined girls born on October 18, 2000, by Cesarean section to Taluai and Adrian Bryce of Vancouver. They were joined at the abdomen and weighed a combined twelve pounds five ounces. The twins were successfully separated on October 31.

### Bunker, Chang and Eng. *Nineteenth Century.*

*No definitive record of the twins' life exists; their conjoined history was a confusion of legend, sideshow hyperbole, and editorial invention even while they lived.* — Darin Strauss (2000)

The "original Siamese twins" were born in Meklong, Siam (now Thailand), on May 11, 1811, the fifth and sixth of nine children born to a Chinese-Siamese mother named Nok and a Chinese father named Ti-eye. (In their native land, they were therefore always known as the Chinese twins.) They were delivered after an uneventful pregnancy with the head of one between the legs of the other (Bolton 1830, Harris 1874). Chang was the more delicate of the twins, though they were both said to have been feeble during their first six months, and they grew up in a place where their condition was considered an omen. In fact, King Rama II had ordered their death in an attempt to avert the disaster it heralded, but the sentence was

**Oil painting of young Chang and Eng Bunker by Irvine. Courtesy of the Royal College of Surgeons of England.**

But biographer Kay Hunter (1964) suggests that their names translate to "to tie strongly" and "pale, without flavor." At age six, Chang and Eng contracted smallpox on the same day and recovered simultaneously two weeks later. They were also said to have had the measles the following year. Two years later in 1819, they lost five siblings and their father to a cholera epidemic that swept through the region (Wallace and Wallace 1978).

The boys were joined from sternum to sternum by a three-inch cartilage that connected their livers and eventually stretched to four inches. They shared sensation only in the very middle of the band. "Deviations from the usual forms of nature are almost universally offensive; but, in this case, neither the personal appearance of the boys, nor the explanation of the phenomenon by which they are united, is calculated to raise a single unpleasant emotion," reads an 1829 description (The Siamese Twins 1829). When one of the boys fell, the other could pull him upright by the band (Drimmer 1973). They were said to have had their first full-scale fight with each other at the age of eight (Hunter 1964). After working for a local fisherman, the two bought a small boat and went into business for themselves. From the age of ten, they also became merchants, reselling at a profit goods that they purchased from the marketplace. Their business expanded to include raising and selling ducks and duck eggs, considered a delicacy. Because of their condition and their reputation as egg preservers, they were summoned by King Rama III to Bangkok at age fourteen and were given gifts by the king's wives. The king later (1827) sent them on a diplomatic mission to Cochin China, which involved transport by junk and by elephant, and a guard of 100 soldiers to protect them from the curious crowds, after which they

not carried out (Wallace and Wallace 1978). Bolton (1830) explains, "But afterwards hearing that they were harmless, and would probably be able to support themselves by labour, he allowed them to remain unmolested." For several months, the family was inundated by visitors who came to see the boys after hearing about their unusual birth. The twins' names have been popularly believed to indicate their positions in relation to one another and William Linn Keese made use of the idea in his poem about them:

Their names grew out of a family hitch,
How best to label t'other from which;
And we gather from this domestic plight
That Chang meant "left" and Eng
    meant "right"

THE SIAMESE BROTHERS.

Aged.18.

Drawn on Stone, & Published, by I. M. Baynes, 44, Burton Street, Burton Crescent; Printed, by C. Hullmandel.

Etching of Chang and Eng, age eighteen. Courtesy of Harvard Theatre Collection, Houghton Library.

children. All her work and efforts for the twins must have been based entirely on instinct, since there was obviously no source of medical or psychological advice available to her.... In fact, what their mother did was to give them ample freedom to make their own mistakes and profit by them, combined with a programme of training designed to help them to move about easily and take part in normal activities.

They were participating in just such an activity when they were "discovered."

When they were thirteen, they had been noticed by British merchant Robert Hunter, who spotted them swimming in the river and handling their rowboat. Hunter arranged a partnership with thirty-seven-year-old American

were liberally compensated (Wallace and Wallace 1978).

Kay Hunter (1964) gives much of the credit for successfully raising the twins to their mother:

> Although this woman of Siam never achieved any fame for herself, and her story is briefly recorded among the many jumbled little histories of her two famous sons, yet she deserves to rank as one of the unsung heroic "Mother Figures" of the world.... But remembering her background, which was uneducated and limited, and her upbringing of religious rites and superstition, her attitude towards her children's deformity was something of a miracle in its intelligence and perseverance. From the very beginning she set out to equip them for life by training them, as far as possible, to be like other

Captain Abel Coffin to split the profits from the display of the boys. He convinced their mother and the king to allow him to take the boys out of the country on a tour of the U.S. and Great Britain that would last two and a half years, by which time the boys would be twenty-one. Hunter told the king that the twins would be an excellent advertisement for the country, which was eager to increase its contact with the West (Drimmer 1973). Nok was promised a sum of $3,000, but according to Chang and Eng only received $500. The twins were to receive ten dollars a month plus expenses, a salary that was raised to fifty dollars after two years (Wallace and Wallace 1978). The twins left for the United States with Captain Coffin on April 1, 1829, arriving in Boston on August

Lithograph of Chang and Eng in 1839. Courtesy of the Southern Historical Collection, Wilson Library, University of North Carolina-Chapel Hill.

year by Dr. John Collins Warren of Harvard University Medical School who measured Chang's height at five feet one and a half inches and Eng's at five feet two inches, advised against separation, and suggested that the changes in their lives may bring about their deaths within a few years.

Bogdan (1988) calls the Bunker twins some of the nineteenth century's most studied human beings: "Almost from the moment they stepped off the boat in Boston they were probed, pinched, pictured, and pondered by physicians and other scientists presenting the spectrum of learned associations." Dr. Warren's findings were reported in the popular press and include a detailed description of the band between the brothers:

On examining them, however, they are found not to touch each other, the band which connects them being, at its shortest part, which is the upper and back part, about two inches long. At the lower frontpart of the band, which is there soft and fleshy, or rather like soft thick skin, as about five inches long and would be elastic, were it not for a thick rope-like cartilaginous or gristly substance, which forms the upper part of the band, and which is not above three inches long. The band is probably two inches thick at the upper part, and above an inch at the lower part. The back part of the band, which is rounded from a thickening at the places where it grows from each body, is not so long as the front part, which is comparatively flat. The breadth or depth of the band is about four inches. It grows from the

16, aboard his ship *Sachem*. Traveling with them as a companion was their young Siamese friend Teiu. They used the time to learn English. During the voyage, Captain Coffin noted that Chang was brighter but more irritable and Eng was quieter, more reposeful, with wider intellectual interests. The day after their arrival in the States, the first American newspaper article about them was published in the Boston *Patriot*. They were soon examined by Dr. Joseph Skey of the British Army, whose tests determined that waking one brother roused the other. They were examined more thoroughly that lower and centre part of the breast of each boy, being a continuation of the cartilaginous termination of the breast bone, accompanied by muscles and blood-vessels, and enveloped, like every other portion of the body, with skin, etc. At present this band is not very flexible; and there is reason to believe that the cartilaginous substance of the upper part is gradually hardening, and will eventually become bone [The Siamese Twins 1829].

It was stated that they usually had their arms around each other's neck or waist, whether they were standing, sitting, or moving. Their movements were described as strange, but not ungraceful or constrained, and to be initiated by a common will between the boys. Bolton (1830) wrote "...a remarkable consent or agreement is displayed without any apparent conference." William Linn Keese (1902) penned the following lines about their union:

This band extended from breast to breast,
And Chang and Eng was the firm expressed.
The business they did was a joint affair,
Like other copartnerships, each had share;
The only thing they could not divorce
Was the gristle that Nature held in force.

Hunter (1964) elaborates: "As opposed to their mental outlook, it must be assumed that in the case of their bodily movements they had become like two dancing partners who had grown so accustomed to a combined movement as a pair, and so trained to the impulses of the other partner that a simultaneous step or turn was inevitable. It was a conditioning of the mind rather than a compulsion of the spirit." They were referred to as "Chang Eng" and were said to weep bitterly whenever separation was mentioned. When Dr. Thomas Harris brought the subject up during his 1829 examination in Philadelphia, Chang tried to kick him (Schuknecht 1979). Dr. Warren identified the origin of the band from each boy's ensiform cartilage (The Siamese Twins 1829).

Under Captain Coffin's management, the brothers were publicly exhibited for the first time in Boston, being billed as "The Siamese Double Boys." Their appearances were well-attended and commanded premium prices of two to six dollars per ticket (Hunter 1964, Drimmer 1973). Twenty-eight-year-old James Webster Hale (d. 1892) was retained to look after the twins' welfare and assisted Coffin in renting a tent and advertising the exhibit, which was a financial success with a fifty-cent admission fee. Darin Strauss (2000) puts words in Eng's mouth: "Our first audiences fell into two halves — either they frightened easily, or they did not believe. And then they returned." The Boston *Daily Courier* raised questions about the twins' joined condition, including the ramifications of indicting and incarcerating one of the boys and the implications of one twin converting to Christianity. At their next stop in Providence, Rhode Island, the boys — possibly out of boredom at standing quietly on the stage during lectures about them — began to develop an act, performing acrobatics and feats of strength. They then boarded the *Chancellor Livingston* for New York City, arriving on September 18, 1829, and played to overflow crowds for three weeks. During this time, they were examined by Dr. Samual Latham Mitchell and Dr. William Anderson, both of Rutgers Medical College. They then performed for a week in Philadelphia. After their eight-week tour of the eastern U.S., Chang and Eng traveled to England on October 17, 1829, aboard the *Robert Edwards*, commanded by Captain Samuel Sherburne. One of them was said to have had a painful toothache during the journey (Bolton 1830). They arrived in Southampton on November 19. During their several months in England, they enjoyed great success. Their appearances began with a well-publicized private event at the Egyptian Hall in Piccadilly on November 24, to which many prominent British literary and scientific men were invited, among them members of the Royal College of Surgeons. Attendees included Sir Astley Cooper, anatomist Joshua Brookes, and Sir Anthony Carlisle, who later stated for the press that there was nothing disgusting or indecorous in the exhibition and that the twins "do not deserve to be regarded as monsters" (Hunter 1964).

To have money on hand for their expenses, and also to pay for a $10,000 insurance policy on the twins and purchase materials (molasses rum and corrosive sublimate) to preserve their bodies should they die, Captain Coffin signed a note payable to Peter Remsen and Company for $613.78 (Wallace and Wallace 1978). He paid the twins a wage of ten dollars a month. Because the twins had suffered from colds since their arrival in England, London physician Dr. George Buckley Bolton was selected to attend them regularly. Dr. Bolton describes treating them for coughs and sore throats, prescribing additional leather waistcoats and a leather coverlet to keep them warm. He noted that their eyes nearest each other (Chang's right eye and Eng's left) were the strongest and was said to have allowed some of his colleagues — including Dr. Peter Mark Roget of thesaurus fame — to conduct experiments on the brothers (Wallace and Wallace 1978, Hunter 1964). Dr. Bolton (1830) defends himself: "I have neither instituted, nor permitted to be made, any unjustifiable experiments upon these youths; considering myself bound, by professional responsibility, as well as by a sense of national justice, to resist all such improper proposals." Dr. Bolton recorded that Eng's tongue was consistently whiter than Chang's and that he was subject to occasional constipation. The twins took their meals together, but did not like to be observed while eating. They eat different foods at the same time, but neither will eat or drink what the other dislikes. Chang's stomach was more easily upset, but his bowels were regular. They were said to obey the calls of nature at the

same time, even when they were the result of medicine (Bolton 1830).

Chang and Eng were exhibited to the public at the Egyptian Hall for a half-crown admission fee in early December 1830; 2,000 of their patrons spent an additional shilling to purchase a sixteen-page autobiographical booklet authored by Hale. At that time, they were considered less well-developed for their age than their American counterparts. The right lateral curvature of Chang's spine and the stretching of the band over time were noted and it was confirmed that they had normal genitals, but that Chang and Eng were very modest about their examination. The Bunkers were described as "very cleanly and delicate … exceedingly affectionate and docile" (Buckley 1830). Dr. Bolton (1830) records that they helped each other dress and that they were both very fond of music and dramatic performances. He also credits them with great imitative powers. Having mastered the English language in a very short time with the help of a tutor (Hunter 1964), their reading tastes were history and poetry.

Chang and Eng appeared at Lewis' Great Sale Room and the Surrey Theatre. They were romantically pursued by a young woman named Sophia, who abandoned her attempts when she was told it would be bigamous to marry them both (Wallace and Wallace 1978). Their subsequent tour included the major cities in England, Scotland, and Ireland, including Bath, Windsor, Reading, Oxford, Birmingham, Manchester, Leeds, York, Sheffield, Liverpool, Glasgow, Edinburgh, Dublin, and Belfast. They returned to London on December 28, 1830. Altogether, they had been seen by more than 300,000 people, including Queen Adelaide (German wife of England's King William IV), Prince Esterhazy, Duchesses de Berri and Angoulême, the Duke of Wellington, and France's exiled King Charles X. They had also been presented to the British Royal Family. But biographer Kay Hunter (1964) cautions: "Chang and Eng Bunker were men of character and fanatical independence, and can never be lightly dismissed as freaks or show-pieces."

As they continued their performances, Chang and Eng perfected their act and were found to be wholly entertaining, not just curiosities at whom to gawk. Hunter (1964) elaborates: "The first shock of their appearance was beginning to wear off, and audiences were now accepting them as entertainers rather than as oddities. People were tending to forget that they were joined together, and were enjoying their shows because they were lively and amusing, which was what Chang and Eng wanted of an audience."

The twins left Great Britain from Portsmouth on Captain Moore's *Cambria* in late January 1831, having been prevented from touring in France for fear that they would deprave young minds and be harmful to pregnant women (Wallace and Wallace 1978). They arrived back in the U.S. on March 4, 1831, at which time their management changed. Having realized a substantial profit on his investment, Robert Hunter had sold his interest in the twins to Captain Coffin, though he stayed in touch with them for many years afterward (Hunter 1964). Coffin delegated their control to his wife Susan and friend Captain William Davis, Jr., with James Hale continuing as the twins' business agent (Wallace and Wallace 1978). They resumed touring at a wage of fifty dollars a month with an appearance in New York on March 15, 1831, followed by stops in large and small American cities, during which it is suggested that they may have had sex with prostitutes. Mrs. Coffin invested in a private buggy for the twins, a wagon for their baggage, three horses, and a hired man named Tom Dwyer, rather than allow the public a free glimpse on regular stagecoaches. They were arrested for assault in Athens, Alabama, when they scuffled with a doctor who tried to examine their band in front of the crowd; they were

fined $350, but the charges were dropped. They ran into trouble again during a respite in Lynnfield, Massachusetts, when they lashed out after being harassed by Colonel Elbridge Gerry and were forced to pay a fine of $200 (Wallace and Wallace 1978).

In October 1831, Hale quit and was replaced by his friend Charles Harris. Having reached the age of twenty-one on May 11, 1832, the twins — then in Pittsburgh — ended their arrangement with the Coffins, announcing that their contractual obligations had been fulfilled and that they were going into business for themselves. The twins alleged that Captain Coffin was not sharing his proceeds with them, though he claimed they were payable to their mother. While it is known that Coffin owed Nok an additional sum and that his wife confiscated some of Chang and Eng's belongings, there is no evidence that he defrauded or swindled the family (Wallace and Wallace 1978). The twins hired Charles Harris to continue their management and, through him, purchased the horse, carriage, and baggage wagon from Mrs. Coffin for $103. Tom Dwyer was replaced with a man named Thomas Crocker. Their first appearance on their own was in Buffalo, New York, in early June 1832. They toured New York thoroughly, followed by New Jersey, Pennsylvania, Virginia, and Ohio. Admittance was usually fifty cents. It was in New York that Captain Coffin caught up with them, tried unsuccessfully to convince them to rejoin him, and scolded and scuffled with them. Coffin then forced Hale to relinquish copyright of the biographical pamphlet about the twins, after which Hale wrote a new one, completed in May 1833 and sold at the subsequent exhibits (Wallace and Wallace 1978). That year they spent four months in and near Ohio, then went south for the first time, venturing with considerable financial success into Kentucky, Tennessee, Alabama, and Mississippi.

On January 14, 1835, the twins embarked for Cuba aboard the *Evaristo*, returning to Philadelphia aboard the *Edward* on April 9 after exhibiting and sightseeing. They were then shown in the Peale Museums in New York City and Albany, followed by a tour in Vermont. July found them in lower Canada for the first time. In October 1835, Chang and Eng returned to England aboard the *Resolution*, arriving in Dover on November 22, 1835. Crossing the English Channel on board the *Firefly* on November 24, they began a tour of France—from which they had previously been barred, Holland, and Belgium. When in Paris, a French surgeon performed an experiment that involved applying pressure to the band connecting Chang and Eng, causing them to faint from pain or fright (Wallace and Wallace 1978). They were described in several contemporary Parisian medical journals (Harris 1874). While in Holland, they stopped performing acrobatics as part of their act, but were still enthusiastically received, and even invited to the royal palace by King William. Arriving back in New York on August 7, 1836, aboard the *Francia*, they continued to tour large and small eastern and southern towns for an average admission price of fifty cents (Hunter 1964), often appearing at Peale's Museums in New York, Philadelphia, Albany, and Baltimore for extended engagements and for a time under contract with P.T. Barnum.

During their appearance in New York, they learned of the death of Captain Coffin on August 28, 1837, of fever. It was also in New York that they met physician Dr. James Calloway, of Wilkesboro, North Carolina, who invited them to visit the area in which they soon settled (Wallace and Wallace 1978). The twins retired from show business at age twenty-eight, retiring to Wilkes County, North Carolina. They adopted the last name "Bunker," but why they chose that name is not recorded. Some claim it was in honor of a well-liked family of that name; by another account it is a corruption of *Bon Coeur*; and according to Kay Hunter (1964) it was of-

fered by Fred Bunker who happened to be in line with them at the Naturalization Office. The Bunkers became naturalized U.S. citizens after filing their intent in Wilkes Superior Court in October 1839. They were said to participate in all elections (Daniels 1962). They were speculated to be worth between $40,000 and $60,000, but in fact had a savings of $10,140 (Wallace and Wallace 1978). They purchased 150 acres of land in the community of Traphill, about twenty miles northwest of Wilkesboro, along Little Sandy Creek on October 17, 1839. They attended church, sitting in a customized seat. The twins opened a general store, at the same time building up their supply of household equipment, but soon took up farming, buying two additional parcels of land during the next four years and building a two-story wooden house. They grew corn and other crops and raised livestock, including horses, cows, and pigs. They often quarreled bitterly, occasionally coming to blows, but referred to themselves in the first person and signed letters "Chang-Eng."

The two convinced members of the College of Physicians in Philadelphia to attempt separation surgery, having met two women they hoped to marry, and were only discouraged from going through with it by their fiancées. On April 13, 1843, in a double Baptist ceremony, Chang married Adelaide Yates and Eng married her sister Sarah Anne, although the relationships had outraged the community on moral grounds and threats and vandalism had been directed at the girls' father. David Yates also disapproved, but allowed them to marry at home rather than to elope. Adelaide and Sarah were accused of revolting against their strict upbringing and of seeking the notoriety such a union would bring. "The general attitude was one of surprise that the twins had not chosen a couple of circus freaks with whom to share their lives," writes Kay Hunter (1964). In his novel *Chang and Eng*, Darin

Strauss (2000) characterizes the ceremony: "Wilkesboro had put on its white shirt. It seemed there were more in Wilkesboro who were willing to celebrate a high-profile union than to try to prevent it by force. And so, a crowd of townsfolk was clustered around the house, decorated for the affair. Those not invited, especially the women, decided to throng in front of the first-floor windows, pushing and wrangling, peeking with their noses against the glass, hoping to be granted admission."

For nine years, the two couples shared a single house and a single bed. Within ten months of the wedding, Sarah and Adelaide each gave birth to her first child. Chang and Eng fathered a total of 21 children over the next 31 years. According to Kay Hunter (1964), they entered the babies' Christian names chronologically in the family Bible,

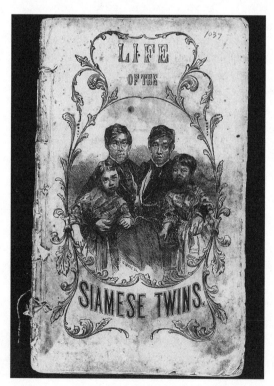

**Cover of Siamese twins' "true life" pamphlet, c. 1855. Courtesy of Becker Collection, Syracuse University Library, Department of Special Collections.**

without differentiating between the fathers. Eng and Sarah had a total of eleven children, listed in order of birth:

- Katherine Marcellus (*b.* February 10, 1844, *d.* 1871 of tuberculosis)
- Julia Ann (*b.* March 31, 1845, *d.* February 27, 1865, of unknown causes)
- Stephen Decatur (*d.* 1920, age 73)
- James Montgomery (*d.* 1930s in his 80s)
- Patrick Henry (*d.* 1938, age 88)
- Rosalyn (Rosalind) Etta (*b.* 1852, *d.* 1852, of burns from falling into the fireplace)
- William Oliver (*b.* February 1861, *d.* 1932)
- Frederick Marshall (killed in a barroom brawl, date unknown)
- Rosella Virginia (*d.* 1941, age 82)
- Georgianna Columbia (*d.* September 28, 1865, of burns from scalding water)
- Robert Edmond (*d.* 1951, age 85)

Chang and Adelaide had a total of ten children, listed in order of birth:

- Josephine Virginia (*b.* February 16, 1844, *d.* August 16, 1867, from a fall from her horse)
- Christopher Wren (*b.* April 8, 1845, *d.* 1932, age 88)
- Nancy Adelaide (*d.* 1874, age 26)
- Susan Marianna (*d.* 1922, age 72)
- Victoria (*d.* 1896, age 44)
- Louise Emeline (*d.* 1934, age 78), who was deaf
- Albert Lemuel (*d.* 1944, age 87)
- Jesse Lafayette (*d.* 1909, age 48, when struck by a bolt of lightning), who was deaf
- Margaret Elizabeth (*d.* 1950, age 87)
- Hattie Irene (*b.* September 12, 1868, *d.* 1945, age 77)

"I think bringing forth babies had almost become a contest to Sarah and Adelaide," writes Strauss (2000) in his novel.

In the summer of 1845, the two families purchased a larger house on a farm in White Plains near Mt. Airy in Surry County. The Bunkers were among the first farmers in the state to produce "bright leaf" tobacco and both Chang and Eng were known to smoke and chew it. In addition they grew wheat, rye, Indian corn, oats, peas, beans, and potatoes and raised milk cows, cattle, sheep, pigs, and fowl. Their orchard produced fruit and their hives produced honey and beeswax. To maintain their farms, the Bunkers owned both male and female slaves. Several slaves were purchased as children. By 1860, they had acquired a total of twenty-eight slaves and were rumored to have treated them harshly (Wallace and Wallace 1978). They were respected for killing a wolf that had terrorized the region (Daniels 1962). In addition to being known as gifted marksmen, the twins were excellent carpenters, building a larger house on their property and helping to construct the White Plains Baptist Church on a piece of their land. They were well sought-after by their neighbors for house-raisings because of their ability to lift a corner (Pancoast 1875). Chang and Eng were also greatly admired for their ability to handle horses, since they could drive a double team in perfect synchronization, one handling the front pair and the other the rear (Hunter 1964). They are also credited with inventing — out of necessity — the "double chop" method of chopping wood.

Chang and Eng chose as family physicians the brothers Joseph and William Hollingsworth. Dr. Joseph Hollingsworth described that their circulatory systems were separate, so that if one drank the other did not feel the effects and if one got sick the

Chang and Eng, their wives, and two of their children. Courtesy of the Circus World Museum, Baraboo, Wisconsin.

health of the other would remain normal. Together they weighed about 220 pounds. Their activities included hunting, fishing, playing checkers or cards, reading aloud, and playing the flute. They mastered the game of battledore and shuttlecock, precursor of badminton (Drimmer 1973). They were said to be expert in the handling of tools, plowing, shingling, and shooting (Allen 1875). They were said to enjoy company and to show great hospitality to visitors who were genuine and not just curious (Hunter 1964). Eng drank liquor in moderation, but Chang often drank to excess. According to one account, when Chang drank, Eng also became intoxicated (Pancoast 1875), but it is generally accepted that Eng was not affected in the short term. In 1848, they learned of the death of their discoverer Robert Hunter. On July 5, 1849, their manager Charles Harris died of tuberculosis. That same year they learned that their mother had died on December 28, 1847 (Wallace and Wallace 1978).

The twins returned to the stage out of financial difficulty. As youths, they had appeared in Asian dress to emphasize their exotic differences; now their costumes consisted

**Chang and Eng in later years. Courtesy of the Circus World Museum, Baraboo, Wisconsin.**

of suits and ties and their marital status was stressed (Bogdan 1996). They took their manager's advice to display their children and thus renew audience interest. For eight months in 1849, they arranged to be exhibited with two of their daughters (Katherine and Josephine) by Edmund Doty for a payment of $8,000. The tour was unsuccessful, possibly due to competition or overexposure, and was cut short after six weeks in New York. They received only partial payment and that only after several years. In 1852, the Bunkers bought a house in the village of Mt. Airy, North Carolina, into which Adelaide moved with the children of school age. Sarah remained at the farm (Wallace and Wallace 1978). The brothers embarked on a twelve-month tour of New England and Canada with a Mr. Howes in April 1853,

bringing along children Katherine and Christopher to the 130 towns in which they appeared (Wallace and Wallace 1978). In 1857, it was decided that each of the two families should have its own farm and farmhouse. They divided up the shared land and the slaves, with Eng retaining the original house at Traphill and the two brothers building another house a mile away for Chang and family. The twins spent three days in one household, followed by three days in the other, never varying from their routine regardless of the circumstances. Each twin was absolute master in his own house (Wallace and Wallace 1978) and their families stayed put while they switched residences (Hunter 1964).

Again in need of income to support their families, Chang and Eng decided to tour the West Coast, into which they had not previously ventured. They began with a short engagement with two of their sons (Montgomery and Patrick) at P.T. Barnum's American Museum in October 1860, but Barnum was said to have been resentful that he had not discovered the Siamese Twins and the twins found him to be stingy and exploitive (Wallace and Wallace 1978). Hunter (1964) notes that although he devotes pages to his other performers, Barnum hardly mentions the twins in his autobiographies. The twins and their boys boarded the *Northern Light* to Panama, crossing the isthmus by train and sailing from there to California aboard the *Uncle Sam*. They docked in San Francisco on December 6, 1860, and spent two weeks there before steaming north to Sacramento, where they performed for a single day on January 25, 1861. They had planned to travel to Siam for a reunion with their brother, but left for home on February 11, 1861, upon hearing that North Carolina might soon be involved in war. By the end of March they were reunited with their families and within a month the Civil War was underway. At its outbreak, municipal documents recorded Chang's worth at

$16,130 and Eng's at $18,850, with thirty-three slaves between them (Wallace and Wallace 1978). Of the two, Eng was drafted, but the claim was dismissed. The end of the war brought many losses to the Bunkers, including the deaths of two daughters in 1865. The twins lost money on loans they had made when the Confederate currency collapsed and they were forced to free their slaves or retain their services on salary.

In Fall 1836, Chang and Eng had allowed phrenologists O.S. Fowler and S. Kirkham to examine their heads. They were found to be strikingly similar in size, outline, and in the "minute development of nearly all the phrenological organs" (Fowler, Fowler and Kirkham 1840). In 1853, they were examined a second time and the results published in the *American Phrenological Journal*. The examiners found their heads to correspond remarkably and to exhibit both combativeness and benevolence, among other traits (Wallace and Wallace 1978). Over the years, the Siamese twins were the subject of artists, writers, and playwrights. These included Edward Bulwer-Lytton, whose book of verse *The Siamese Twins* was published in 1831, and Gilbert Abbott à Beckett (*d.* 1856), whose play *The Siamese Twins* debuted in London and was also staged in New York. Mark Twain also found them amusing, making them the subject of a humorous essay entitled "The Siamese Twins" in 1868 and drawing on their lives and those of the Tocci Twins for his 1894 novel *The Tragedy of Pudd'nhead Wilson*, which was later divided into the farce *Those Extraordinary Twins* and the tragedy of the original name. They were also the subject of a 1902 poem by William Linn Keese entitled "The Siamese Twins, A Chapter of Biography." In about 1865, Chang and Eng were photographed with their wives and two of their sons by Mathew Brady. As Pingree (1996) catalogs, "During their life—and after their death—Americans viewed, read and collected lithographs, newspaper articles, cartes de visite, satires, poetry, drama, photographs, novels, and cartoons regarding the twins, and even dressed as them for masquerade parties.

After the Civil War, the Bunkers had little choice but to return to show business, which they did over the next three years. Under the management of Simon Bolivar Zimmerman and his brother-in-law Henry Armand London, Chang and Eng—now age fifty-four—made several short tours in the Eastern and Midwestern U.S. Their appearance at the New England Agricultural Fair in Brattleboro, Vermont, in 1865 was described (Siamese twins in their own land 1874):

> ...they were exhibiting themselves with two of their sons. The fathers were beginning to show marks of age, Eng especially, who looked five years older than his brother. They had nearly forgotten their native language, and in lieu of the deep emotion they had formerly evinced in speaking of their country, they seemed now to care very little about it, and wound up the conversation by saying nonchalantly, "America is our home now; we have no other."

Manager Zimmerman was succeeded by Messrs. Shepherd and Bird and later by Judge H.P. Ingalls. While in Kansas, Chang became sick and lost some of his hearing. While in Ohio, they traveled for a short time with Millie-Christine (Wallace and Wallace 1978). Between tours another death occurred, that of Chang's daughter Josephine Virginia in 1867. In 1868, the twins appeared for three weeks at a newly renovated theater on Broadway owned by Barnum and George Wood. By 1969, their health had begun to decline and their eyesight to fail (Mould 1989). Chang's drinking had worsened. They decided to take up Barnum's offer to send them to Great Britain and Europe to tour and (to promote their exhibition) to seek the advice of surgeons regarding their separation. With daughters Katherine and Nannie, and manager Ingalls who had been retained by Barnum, the twins left Mt. Airy on November 28, 1868, stopped in Washington, D.C., to call on President Andrew Johnson, and arrived in New York to board the *Iowa* to Liverpool on December 5. Upon their arrival, they traveled to Edinburgh by train. There they first consulted physicians on Katherine's behalf and she was diagnosed with consumption. Sir James Young Simpson then sought out the twins and conducted several tests of their vascular union by trying to illuminate the band from behind (although it proved to be opaque) and by testing their urine (Harris 1874). After his examination, Simpson advised that surgery would be perilous (Wallace and Wallace 1978). Two weeks in Edinburgh were followed by two weeks in Glasgow.

On February 7, 1869, they moved on to England, where they toured extensively for six months and had another audience with Queen Victoria. Upon examination in London, they were also advised against separation surgery by Sir Henry Thompson, Professor Syme, Sir James Y. Simpson, Professor Nélaton, and Sir William Fergusson, who reported that although they obviously dreaded the day when the living would be tied to the dead, the large wound would result in a shock to their systems that could easily cause death (Hunter 1964). Harris (1874) called the examinations a scheme to secure free publicity and pointed out that they may have feared the suffering or possible fatal result of surgery, "but the excuses framed by them appear to have been largely based upon a want of appreciation of any happiness to be obtained by an independent existence, believing themselves to be quite as much in the enjoyment of it as those with whom they came daily into contact.... Had they been successfully separated in adult life, at their own request, we should have seen all their individual physical defects very prominently brought to notice." Harris (1874) was also doubtful that after their

years of adaptation they would be able to walk forward as individuals.

In London, Chang and Eng became friends with eccentric naturalist Frank Buckland (*d.* 1880). Buckland had sought them out, having heard about them from his father. He was a child when they had been brought to the United States and remembered tying the tails of two cats together to form "Siamese twins." Buckland, inspector of England's salmon fisheries, presented the twins with examples of conjoined salmon that are sometimes produced during artificial hatching. Of Chang and Eng, he wrote, "Although I have elsewhere read articles against the exhibition of the 'Siamese Twins,' I think our friends ought to go and see them, and this, not only because the twins are historical, nay even almost proverbial, characters, but because they are in themselves instances of a most rare and abnormal form of human life, which it is very improbable we shall ever see or hear of again in this generation" (Burgess 1967). The twins became very attached to Buckland, who entertained them many times and kept a photograph of them and their families in his album.

On April 26, 1869, the twins hosted a "Chang-Eng River Trip," a public cruise from St. Katherine's Docks to the Nore. Tickets were expensive, but refreshments were served and a lucky few would have the opportunity to partner with the brothers at whist. This excursion and other events were well-attended, but biographer Kay Hunter (1964) speculates about their audience's reaction to their now advanced age:

> No doubt some who had been brought up on the almost legendary twins were a little disappointed to discover that Chang and Eng were two elderly men, quite incapable of turning cartwheels and performing the feats of agility which an earlier generation had seen. But they were received with affection, like old friends who had been absent for too long, and other members of the entertainment

profession regarded them as "good troupers," which was the best possible commendation.

By the time Rudolf Virchow saw them in Berlin, however, Chang and Eng were being laughed at on stage and the renowned pathologist found their performance undignified and noted their contempt for the audience (Hunter 1964).

The twins left for Ireland on July 20, 1869, and departed for home from Queenstown on the *City of Antwerp* on July 30, docking in New York in mid–August and arriving back in Mt. Airy by August 15, 1869. They spent only five months at home, part of this time appearing at fairs in the Western and Northwestern states (Wallace and Wallace 1978). They then left for an ambitious European tour, this time with sons James Montgomery and Albert. They traveled aboard the *Allemagne*, which left New York on February 1, 1870, with a man named Wallace who had promoted them in England. They docked at Glückstadt, Germany, and made their way to Berlin by train. They were booked for three weeks at the Circus Renz, during which time they were examined by four German physicians, but they looked forward to meeting Dr. Virchow to seek his opinion on separation. After examining them in his office for more than an hour, Virchow reported that Chang was hard of hearing in both ears, but Eng was deaf only in the left ear. He advised against separation because of the shock it would pose to their systems and would risk it only upon the death of one of the brothers. Both by then were partially blind in their two anterior eyes, possibly from looking outward and obliquely (Gould and Pyle 1956). Their outer arms and legs were stronger and better developed than the inner ones (Harris 1874).

In June 1870, the twins steamed to St. Petersburg, Russia, and from there to Moscow by rail. While few records of their Russian tour survive, they are said to have met Czar Alexander II (Wallace and Wallace 1978). With their plans to exhibit in Austria, Italy, Spain, and France curtailed because of the impending war, they returned to Glückstadt and sailed for home on July 30. Seven days into the voyage, Chang had a stroke, which left him paralyzed on his right side. They arrived in New York in late August 1870, knowing that they would never travel again (Wallace and Wallace 1978). Chang's condition never improved and required that Eng support him physically for the next three years, propping a crutch under Chang's left arm and lifting Chang's right leg with a strap that he carried. In their homes, they were restricted to the ground floor. Chang's paralysis and his now total deafness made him more irritable than ever (Hunter 1964). Although they used to take sides in the disputes, Sarah and Adelaide now stood apart from the fraternal disagreements and took comfort in each other and their families (Hunter 1964). After a particularly bitter quarrel, they begged Dr. Hollingsworth to separate them. Chang was at this time worth $23,000 and Eng worth $7,000 (Wallace and Wallace 1978).

They died in North Carolina within three hours of each other at age 62 on January 17, 1874. Their death is believed to have been precipitated by the ride to Eng's house in an open carriage during very cold weather, despite Eng's objections to their adhering to their normal schedule. Chang's cough and chest pain had been diagnosed by Dr. Hollingsworth as bronchitis a couple of days earlier. They had also been thrown from a carriage in April of the previous year. According to the *Philadelphia Medical Times* (Chang and Eng 1874), Chang said to Dr. Hollingsworth several times during the last year of his life, "We can't live long."

On the eve of their death, Chang slept fitfully and experienced severe pain in his chest and difficulty breathing. He woke Eng twice, once to go out to the porch for some air and the second time to sit in front of a

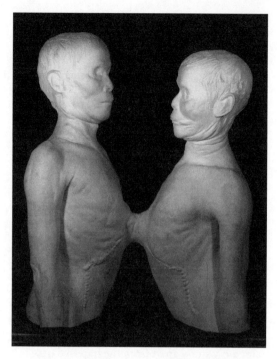

The plaster cast of the Bunker twins prepared by sculptor John Casani after the autopsy. Courtesy of the Mütter Museum, College of Physicians of Philadelphia.

fire, although Eng insisted they would be warmer remaining in bed (Hunter 1964). Upon checking on them early the next morning, Eng's son William discovered that Chang had died. The family found Eng very distressed and covered with a cold sweat. He made no further mention of Chang except to ask that the body be moved closer to him (Allen 1875). They rubbed his arms and legs at his request, but he fell into a stupor that lasted until his death a couple of hours later. According to his widow, Eng's last words were, "May the Lord have mercy on my soul." Adelaide and her children were summoned, as was Dr. Hollingsworth. The widows prepared the bodies of the twins so that neighbors could pay their respects and a clergyman performed the Last Rites the following day. Sarah and Adelaide initially objected to an autopsy, but Dr. Hollingsworth convinced them to allow him to preserve the bodies (by cooling them and en-

casing their series of wooden and soldered tin coffins in charcoal) until he could find someone in Philadelphia to perform a post-mortem. He was concerned that their graves would be vandalized and their corpses stolen.

A walnut casket with lining and handles was prepared for fifty dollars by S. Gauland (Wade 1962). William Augustus Reich furnished the tin coffin and describes his experience in a letter written presumably to a sister

> It was a sight the people that was there. It was a long time before I could get my foot in at the door so crowded.... The Siamese Twins is the greatest human curiosity in the world and who ever thought I would be the man to solder them up. I had to cut into 34 big sheets of tin to make the coffin have a notion to charge $20 do you think that would be about right?.... The Siamese twins were nicely dressed in black with slippers on I helped lift them in their coffin it was a strange sight.... It was the greatest job I ever done.... I'll send you a drop of solder that dropped on the coffin as I was soldering them up yesterday [Wade 1962].

Both of the twins left a will in which they bequeathed their property to their wives, with Chang making a special provision for his two deaf children. News of their deaths was relayed by the media, with a reporter from the *New York Herald* telegraphing his firsthand story from North Carolina on January 24, 1874. It was erroneously reported in London that the widows were willing to sell their husbands' bodies for $8,000 to $10,000, either to medical men or showmen (Wallace and Wallace 1978, Hunter 1964). Dr. Hollingsworth gave his opinion that separation, unless performed immediately upon Chang's death, would not have saved the life of his brother, since both were convinced that if one died so would the other (Wallace and Wallace 1978). Philadelphia doctor William Pancoast, who had inquired about the possibility of autopsy, was put in touch with Dr. Joseph Hollingsworth and the Bunker widows and it was decided by a group of physicians who assembled on January 26, 1874, that Dr. Pancoast and Dr. Harrison Allen should travel to North Carolina, examine the bodies, and preserve them until an autopsy could be performed. Dr. Pancoast felt that the twins owed their autopsy to science, having taken advantage of the best medical advice during their lives, often to garner publicity and without seriously considering separation. Pancoast (1875) explains:

> It was held to be a duty to science and humanity, that the family of the deceased should permit an autopsy. The twins had availed themselves most freely of the services of our profession in both hemispheres, and it was considered by many as a proper and necessary return, that at their death this *quæstio vexata* (the possibility of a successful section of the band) should be settled by an examination of its anatomical structure.

With permission of the Bunker widows, the doctors left Philadelphia on January 29 and arrived in Mount Airy on January 31, 1874, with a photographer, aid Dr. Andrews, and Dr. William Hollingsworth in the absence of his brother Joseph. With their legal advisor Robert S. Gilmer present, Adelaide and Sarah Bunker agreed that the bodies should be exhumed, embalmed, and examined, but denied permission for the band that connected the twins to be dissected, allowing only limited incisions on the posterior surface. A written agreement was drawn up and signed on February 1, 1874, specifying that the bodies would be removed to Philadelphia but would be returned to the family after the procedure. The coffin was recovered from the cellar, where it had been covered with several planks and a tumulus of powdered charcoal, and unsoldered (Chang and Eng 1874).

The tin coffin was taken to an upstairs room and the lid was unscrewed. Despite the fact that fifteen days had passed, the bodies — with the exception of some lividity, discoloration, and slight odor — were in good condition and were viewed by their widows (Chang and Eng 1874). The room was then cleared and the bodies of Chang and Eng were disrobed and photographed in a vertical position with close-ups of their union. Chang's body was found moderately emaciated with no rigor mortis. He measured five feet two-and-a-half inches in height. The superficial veins in the hands and feet were distended. The lips and the anterior abdominal wall were discolored. The genitals, particularly the scrotum, were swollen. Eng's body was spare, but moderately well-nourished, with slight rigor mortis. He measured five feet three-and-a-half inches in height. The left testicle was absent from the scrotum and later determined to have been retracted into the inguinal canal. The anterior abdominal wall was moderately discolored (Allen 1875). A midline incision was made on each and the aorta and the iliac arteries (Eng's right and Chang's left) were injected with a solution of chloride of zinc, a difficult process because Chang's blood vessels were in poor condition. The cut was widened and a decision was made: "Examination of the band through this incision convinced the Commission of the complex nature of the band, and suggested the suspension of a complete study of the parts until removal of the bodies to Philadelphia" (Chang and Eng 1874). The incisions were sewn up, the bodies were dressed and reboxed, and the lid of the tin coffin was resoldered. The party proceeded by wagon to Salem, North Carolina. There the bodies were dispatched by rail to Philadelphia, arriving on February 5.

The bodies were taken to the Mütter Museum and secured until a meeting of the College of Physicians of Philadelphia could be called. On February 8, 1874, the Fellows of the College agreed to underwrite the expenses of the trip and an additional $350 to have casts and photographs prepared, which would remain the property of the Museum. The original team began the dissection on February 10. Sketches were made by Hermann Faber and photographs of their suspended bodies were taken by M.P. Simons of Philadelphia. The autopsy continued the next day, during which the incisions made to reach the iliac arteries were extended six inches so that the abdomen could be opened. The doctors found the remains of the umbilical structures and noted that Chang's bladder was empty, while Eng's was distended. They noted that Eng's viscera had abundant fat. Chang's venous system was found to be engorged and Eng's comparatively empty. No examination of the lungs could be made because of changes caused by the embalming fluid (Allen 1875). The livers were removed, the peritoneal coverings dissected from the band, and the diaphragms exposed (Allen 1875). Through the incisions, the interior of the band could also be examined. It was found that the livers were connected by tissue in addition to blood vessels.

They had received permission to make the H-shaped incision in the back of the band. In the opinion of the doctors, separation of the twins may well have proved fatal. The risk would have been especially great as young boys, according to Dr. Allen (1875): "…an attempt at division of the band in early life would have been accompanied with more venous hemorrhage than at any subsequent period." Dr. Pancoast (1875), however, felt otherwise: "We are probably not sufficiently informed as to the condition of the twins in childhood to decide whether an operation would then have been justifiable. But it if ever was to have been performed, then was the proper time, before they had acquired their full mental and physical development." Shortly after the autopsy, Dr. Pancoast examined the question of whether separation would have been feasible. He remarked that the distress caused during the experimental application

of a ligature around the band showed that progressive tightening could not have been done safely. Dr. Pancoast did believe that the living brother should have been separated from the dead one, and that Eng would have been wise after his brother became ill to have engaged his surgeon to remain continually at his house (Pancoast 1875).

On February 18, Pancoast and Allen made a presentation of this "monster of a symmetrical duplex development" (in the words of Dr. Pancoast) to the College of Physicians and their illustrated report was later published in the *Transactions of the College of Physicians of Philadelphia* and the *Philadelphia Medical Times*. The doctors demonstrated the connecting band, which was nine inches in circumference (Allen 1875) and attached to each twin at the ensiform cartilage. In addition to cartilage, the band contained a hepatic and peritoneal pouch belonging to each of the men. Their bodies were turned over so that the posterior portion of the band could be observed and those present were allowed to inspect the bodies. The cause of Chang's death was suggested by Dr. Allen (1875) to be a cerebral clot, but this was unconfirmed because of the restrictions that prevented examination of the brains. It was surmised that the blood would have pooled in Chang's body, the blood loss resulting in Eng's stupor and ensuing death, though this was popularly attributed to fright. Worth Daniels (1961) offers his opinion: "…Chang's death was not due purely to the pulmonary edema. It was probably sudden as might occur with an abnormal rhythm. It appears to me that the diagnosis in Chang's case were: (1) Xiphopagic twin. (2) Generalized atherosclerosis. (3) Coronary atherosclerosis. (4) Myocardial infarction. (5) Congestive heart failure with pulmonary edema. (6) Arrhythmia, probably ventricular fibrillation" (Allen 1961).

The autopsy had been conducted in great secrecy, leaving newspaper reporters angry that the information was withheld from the public in favor of publication in a medical journal (Megargee 1897). At the insistence of sons Christopher and Stephen, the bodies — minus their entrails — were promptly returned to North Carolina. Two of the Bunker sons requested reimbursement from Dr. Allen for transport of the bodies from Salem to their home and it is not known whether any of the entrails followed (Wade 1962). Still fearing graverobbers, the family kept the casket in the cellar under charcoal for a year, after which they buried it in the yard (Wallace and Wallace 1978). The widows spent the rest of their lives in relative seclusion, with Sarah dying at the age of seventy on April 29, 1892, and Adelaide dying at age ninety-three on May 21, 1917.

Chang and Eng's joined livers can still be seen at the Mütter Museum. In 1968, the Museum allowed gastroenterologist Frank Brooks to examine the organs, conduct needle biopsies, and produce a histological report. In the report, the livers were found to be very poorly preserved, so that even with the use of special stains they could not be reasonably interpreted. The Bunkers' hearing loss was the subject of reexamination by otolaryngologist Harold F. Schuknecht in 1979. Ruling out infection and other remote possibilities, Schuknecht (1979) suggests that the muzzle blasts during hunting were the cause of their hearing losses at age 58. Chang had hearing loss in both ears, but Eng's hearing loss was greater in the left ear, which would have been protected from the sound of one of the shotgun blasts. The Mütter Museum also displays the plaster cast of the twins that was prepared by sculptor John Casani (d. 1898) after the autopsy, which shows Chang's marked spinal curvature. And on exhibit is one of the custom-made extra-wide wicker chairs they sat in. Life-size figures of Chang and Eng appear on stage at the Circus World Museum in Baraboo, Wisconsin (Fiedler 1978).

Chang and Eng's casket was exhumed from their farm in 1917 and buried inside the entrance of the cemetery of the Baptist Church in White Plains, North Carolina, upon Adelaide's death. The grave containing her remains and those of the twins is marked by a metal sign erected by the state and topped by a white granite headstone bearing the names of Chang, Eng, and both of their wives.

The Bunkers have been commemorated in many ways. The hundredth anniversary of their deaths was marked at the Mütter Museum by a display of photographs of the Rodriguez twins, who were being prepared for separation at Children's Hospital. The lives of Chang and Eng have also been brought to the stage. "Chang and Eng, the Musical," produced by Ekachai Uekrongtham and stressing themes of tolerance and interdependence, was performed at the Thailand Cultural Centre in March 2001. On July 27, 2001, the Chang and Eng Memorial Bridge was dedicated in North Carolina. Interest in the Bunker twins was revived recently in the United States with the release of the novelistic account of their lives, *Chang and Eng*, by Darin Strauss (2000). Ironically, "In and Chan" (as they are known in their homeland) were little known in Thailand until the past couple of decades. Local officials in Samut Songkram, forty-four miles southwest of Bangkok, had a statue cast in their likeness from broken bronze propellers donated by thousands of fishermen. Unveiled in 1994 in a ceremony presided over by Prime Minister Chuan Leekpai, the statue leaves natives of the country puzzled: since Thais are used to seeing statues for kings and royalty, they don't know if they're meant to pray or not. Local official Somyos Yeamprai hopes the memorial will become a tourist attraction and would like to complement it with a museum about the lives of the Bunker brothers (Khaikaew 1999). The statue has been visited by at least one Bunker descendant, but little patronage encouraged the town to secure a $150,000 government grant to surround the statue with a public park that was due to open soon.

The Bunkers left a long legacy. Their papers are housed at the Southern Historical Collection at the University of North Carolina. The Bunker Family Association of America was founded in 1913. Together, Chang and Eng had more than 200 grandchildren (Grosz 1996) and are thought to be survived by 2,000 descendants, about 100 to 150 of whom have regular family reunions. The reunions have been held annually since 1989, when Chang's great-grandson Milton Haynes of Raleigh, North Carolina, brought the descendants of the two branches of the family together. The first reunion was filmed by a camera crew from Thailand and drew about 170 people from all over the country.

### Bunton, Teresa Kay and Virginia (Ginny) Kate. *Twentieth Century.*

Female conjoined twins born August 9, 1956, in Elizabethton, Tennessee, to twenty-one-year-old Virginia Bunton of Butler, Tennessee, whose husband Raymond had died at age thirty-nine three months earlier. The girls were joined at the forehead. After reading about the birth in the Nashville papers, Representative B. Carroll Reece had the mother and twins flown to the National Institute of Neurological Diseases and Blindness (part of the National Institutes of Health) in Bethesda, Maryland. Their care was managed by Maitland Baldwin (*d.* 1970) at government expense, since their father had been a disabled veteran. On December 11, 1956, the twins were separated in a seven-hour surgery, which was the first successful separation of craniopagus twins. Having lost large amounts of spinal fluid, Ginny developed bacterial meningitis which left her with epileptic seizures controlled with Phenobarbital. At fourteen months, the girls left the hospital, but returned frequently for ex-

aminations and additional surgeries. With the implant of a steel plate in Teresa's skull unsuccessful, the girls protected the vulnerable areas of their heads with padding or plastic plates that they covered with their long hair. They attended public school for only a year and were then tutored at home until they graduated from Johnson County High School in Mountain City, Tennessee, on May 31, 1976. Six months earlier, Teresa had married and moved to Granger, Indiana, with Ginny remaining on the family farm.

### Cady, Ruthie and Verena. *Twentieth Century.*

*Mom, I wish my sisters weren't attached, so they could run faster.* — Maria Cady

Conjoined twin girls born April 13, 1984, in Durango, Colorado, to Marlene and Peter Cady, attached at the chest from the sternum to the navel. Three days before their birth, their mother had a disturbing dream in which she gave birth to two girls, but they were both being held in one arm (Cady 1987). The Cadys were expecting twins, but did not know they were joined until they were delivered. Marlene remembers her reaction while she was still numbed from the labor: "Oh, well, okay, let's just pull them apart. Just unsnap them or unzip them or whatever you do" (Cady 1989). Afterward she wondered whether working in a print shop with lots of chemicals or living in an area that had been mined for uranium had affected her unborn children. She explains, "But doctors don't know whether environmental factors could influence the formation of conjoined twins, and I feel that mulling over what might have caused it is a waste of time" (Cady 1989).

Shortly after birth, Ruthie and Verena were rushed to Denver for intensive care. Because they shared a three-chambered heart, Ruthie and Verena could not be separated. Doctors were convinced that even if one of the twins were given a heart transplant, separation would mean the certain death of one and a 90 percent chance of death for the other (Cady 1987). Based on their advice, the parents decided against surgery and took the twins home to their two-and-a-half-year-old sister Maria. The costs of their medical care soon exceeded $10,000, even after insurance and private contributions, since the Cadys needed a professional nurse and were on oxygen for the first four months of their lives. Their story was told in the local newspaper, after which they were offered help, including starting a fund on their behalf, donating baby formula, cooking and laundering for the family, caring for the twins, and taking their older sister on special outings. "The doctors had warned us that Ruth and Verena would attract a lot of attention," writes Marlene Cady (1987). She was grateful for the positive attention, but found others to be insensitive. One woman asked if Marlene displayed her daughters at fairs. She remembers, "It took me weeks to get over that thoughtless remark. But I was only more convinced of how important it is to share my beautiful girls with the world. I must show people that my daughters emanate love — that it is a blessing to be around them" (Cady 1987).

In addition to a heart, the twins shared a liver and part of their intestines. Their nervous systems were separate. They had a single, large navel. At the age of nine months, they were hospitalized with pneumonia and it was two years before they slept through the night (Cady 1989). Their mother notes that their mental development progressed normally, but that she had to teach them physical skills that her other daughter had learned on her own — things such as standing and walking unassisted. They began working with a physical therapist once a week at nine months and learned to navigate using a spina bifida walker. Once they began walking independently, "...they usually walk sideways. But sometimes, when one twin decides she wants something, she'll head straight for it, making the other walk backward. Then the other one may decide she wants to walk forward, and they will end up dancing around in circles until one gives in" (Cady 1987). Their mother regretted having to punish them both if one misbehaved. She adapted their potty chair so that one twin could use it while the other twin stood. In August 1985, the Cadys relocated from Colorado to Rhode Island. The move posed no problems, and was in fact beneficial, as their mother explains: "We found a family doctor who cared for the twins with compassion and insight — just as our doctor in Durango had. And now that we have moved to a lower elevation, the twins are able to breathe more easily" (Cady 1987). They visited the doctor once or twice a year and were on a daily dose of antibiotics, since they were more susceptible to infection because of their shared heart and their probable lack of a spleen (Cady 1989).

Doctors did not expect the twins to live for more than a year. The girls proved the doctors wrong, eventually learning to ride a tricycle, roller skate, ski, swim, and do gymnastics. They sang in the children's choir at Phillips Memorial Baptist Church and finished the first grade at Graden City School, after attending preschool and kindergarten. Before they started school, Marlene Cady was worried that the other children would make fun of them and wrote, "I guess I'll always have to teach other people how special my daughters are." As they grew older, the girls learned new ways to share, taking turns each day making decisions. Their desires to be a doctor and a nurse kept alternating. They dressed identically, but their personalities were distinct. Ruthie was the more domineering and enjoyed painting, drawing, and making things with her hands. Verena loved to eat and often made up physically for Ruthie's small appetite (Cady 1989). Verena softened Ruthie's temper and

Ruthie lifted Verena's spirits when she became worried about something. At the age of five, the Cady twins were featured in *People* magazine. The article indicated that they found it very upsetting when anyone asked about plans for separation surgery. Their mother cautioned, "We have to remember that it's not just a matter of separating them physically, but also psychologically, spiritually and emotionally. I don't know that the rest of us really have the capability to make that decision for them" (Cady 1989). About those who consider her daughters' lives tragic, Marlene writes, "I always tell those people that the only tragedy is in their interpretation of the girls' situation, because obviously Ruthie and Verena are happy kids" (Cady 1989).

Doctors revised their expectations in 1987, suggesting that Ruthie and Verena may live another ten years. Instead the Cady twins lived to the age of seven, dying on July 19, 1991, at their family cabin in South Kingston, Rhode Island. They had been on oxygen since January, but were restricted only by the 150-foot-long tube. Their mother, who characterized the twins as a perfect example of sisterhood and unity, described her last moments with Verena:

"She could feel that Ruthie was having trouble breathing because her lungs were right next to Ruthie's. She said, 'This is the time we're going to be dying.' She gave me a list of friends she wanted to give flowers to. She asked to be cremated because she didn't want to be in a box. She wanted to be free."

Ruthie died first and Verena followed fifteen minutes later. They were buried in Cranston, Rhode Island, on July 22, 1991 (Rhode Island Siamese Twins 1991).

## Campusano Frias, Jazmin and Nasmil.
*Twentieth Century.*

Conjoined twin boys born in the Dominican Republic on May 25, 1999, joined at the breastbone. They were separated at seven and a half months of age at St. Joseph's Children's Hospital in Paterson, New Jersey. The surgery divided their shared liver. They recovered well and returned to their native country.

## Cappello, Luigi and Angelo.

*The new lodger, rather shoutingly dressed but looking superbly handsome, stepped with courtly carriage into the trim little breakfast room and put out all his cordial arms at once, like one of those pocket knives with a multiplicity of blades, and shook hands with the whole family simultaneously.* — Mark Twain, "Those Extraordinary Twins"

The fictional conjoined twin brothers in Mark Twain's story "Those Extraordinary Twins." They are described as a "stupefying apparition — a double-headed human creature with four arms, one body, and a single pair of legs" and referred to as "that prodigy, that uncanny apparition that had come and gone so suddenly — that weird strange thing that was so soft spoken and so gentle of manner, and yet had shaken them up like an earthquake with the shock of its grewsome aspect" (Twain 1980). The twins were shown as tender toward each other, often feeding one another. Each twin was in control of their body for a week at a time. The story touches on a number of themes associated with conjoined twins, such as dominance, and has Angelo complaining, "Luigi, I often consult your wishes, but you never consult mine. When I am in command I treat you as a guest; I try to make you feel at home; when you are in command you treat me as an intruder, you make me feel unwelcome" (Twain 1980). Angelo also objects to being forced to endure Luigi's tobacco smoking and whiskey drinking. Like most conjoined twins, the two had different personalities and constitutions, with Luigi hardier, more assertive, and more masculine than Angelo. Another perennial theme raised in the story is whether the pair are one or two. Luigi says that there are advantages to their construction and that these include the purchase of a single railway ticket for both of them, which is not always the case: "Both of us get a bath for one ticket, theatre seat for one ticket, pew-rent is on the same basis, but at peep-shows we pay double" (Twain 1980).

Through the characters of Patsy Cooper and her daughter Rowena, Twain makes a number of observations, such as slight differences in their appearances, the ability of Luigi to take medicine for Angelo, and Luigi sustaining them when Angelo was unable to eat. The twins relate to the Coopers that they were orphaned and traveled for two years with a freak show.

In the story, the brothers are accomplished piano players and perform a duet. They delight in convincing someone that one of them is six months older than the other. They are soon brought up on charges of assault and battery against Tom Driscoll and retain David ("Pudd'nhead") Wilson to defend them. The jury is unable to determine which twin did the kicking that resulted in the lawsuit:

> We the jury do find: 1, that an assault was committed, as charged; 2, that it was committed by one of the persons accused, he having been seen to do it by several credible witnesses; 3, but that his identity is so merged in his brother's that we have not been able to tell which was him. We cannot convict both, for only one is guilty. We cannot acquit both, for only one is innocent. Our verdict is that justice has been defeated by the dispensation of God, and ask to be discharged from further duty [Twain 1980].

Since Tom Driscoll avoids it, the judge challenges Angelo to a duel; Angelo declines, but Luigi accepts in his place. During the duel Angelo and the judge both suffer superficial wounds before Angelo and his twin retreat. "If I had not run," says Angelo, "I might have been killed in a duel on the Sabbath day, and my soul would have been lost — lost" (Twain 1980). The rever-

ent Angelo goes through with plans to be baptized, but because of their recent notoriety, the event draws a crowd. Luigi is elected an alderman, but cannot sit on the board because his attached brother is not a member. At the end of the farcical story, the twins are hanged — the crowd intending to hang only Luigi.

***See also* Twain, Mark**

## Castillo, Luz (Lucy) and Millagro (Millie). *Twentieth Century.*

Female conjoined twins born on December 26, 1994, in the Dominican Republic, joined from the clavicle to the navel. Although surgery by Dr. Peter Altman and team revealed that the girls had two hearts, and the separation of their joined livers was successful, Millie stopped breathing on the operating table. She was revived and stabilized, but worsened and — despite additional exploratory surgery — died thirty-four days after separation in 1995 when she was removed from an artificial respirator.

## Causes.

Conjoined twins occur when the ova of identical twins do not separate completely. During the development of identical twins, the egg splits soon after fertilization. If the split is delayed until after the thirteenth day, the embryos do not completely separate in the womb and remain attached after birth. A more detailed description can be found in Rowena Spencer's paper "Conjoined Twins: Theoretical Embryologic Basis" (1993). Spencer concludes that there is no known process by which conjoined twins can be formed by *fission*, but there is firm evidence to support *fusion* in all cases. In other words, the embryos develop together, they do not unite after developing separately, as was believed in the nineteenth century and earlier.

Aristotle was convinced that conjoined twins resulted from two separate embryos coalescing in varying degrees (Gedda 1961) and argued that they were *lusus naturae*, or jokes of nature, not intended to terrify. Others' reasons for their development were similarly speculative. In the past, the development of conjoined twins has been attributed to God, the devil, maternal impressions, and the constriction of the womb during pregnancy. They were once considered portents of war and misery (Bondeson 2000). The early Christians considered them monsters that were signs of God's wrath, portents intended as warnings, or reminders that each birth was as miraculous as the original Creation (Fiedler 1978). While interest in their formation continues, interest in the reason for their existence has faded:

> By the second half of the twentieth century there is virtually no interest left in the discovery of reasons for the creation of monsters. The serious philosophical and theological debates are over; indeed, they had been lying dormant during the whole of the nineteenth century which was much more preoccupied with the classification, the scientific investigation, and of course the enjoyment and exploitation of its monsters. During the twentieth century, attention begins to be focused on the monster itself and its needs and desires [Wilson 1993].

Wilson (1993) points out that philosophy and medicine had finally diverged at the end of the nineteenth century and that the phenomenon of monstrous birth has become a medical one and — in the case of conjoined twins — a surgical and mechanical one.

The occurrence of conjoined twins has risen 33 percent in the last ten years because women are delaying pregnancy, which results — for reasons unknown — in the birth of a greater number of twins. Surveys have determined that the average gestation of xiphagus twins is thirty-seven weeks, with twins nine times more likely to deliver before thirty-seven weeks than non-twins. Unlike separate twin births, conjoined twinning has been determined to be unaffected by maternal age, ethnicity, and number of previous children. "Family history of conjoined twinning is also unrelated to producing conjoined twins, so genetic factors are not involved. Compounding the mystery is that no known environmental agents or traumas have been reliably linked to this type of twinning" (Segal 1999). Geographical studies pointed to unidentified environmental agents, since seasonal variation and living styles were unrelated to conjoined twinning; other studies focused on clusters by date. But Nancy Segal points out the inconclusiveness of the data to date: "The possibility of geographical, seasonal or temporal factors being associated with conjoined twinning is compelling, but incomplete reporting or chance events may explain the patterns and inconsistencies seen across studies" (Segal 1999).

***See also* Paré, Ambroise**

## Cephalopagus.

> *Imagine two profiles meeting on a median plane of fusion, as if two lovers would have wished to fuse while they embraced and their wish had been granted. The foreheads are fused, the noses have blended. Viewed frontally, two eyes can be seen, although each one is actually in profile. And this strange face repeats itself in the back — or is it the front?... The necks are fused into one, and so are the chest and abdomen. There are two hearts, but they are joined by a common aorta. Two mouths, but the intestines are shared. Human beings are supposed to have a front and a back, a top and a bottom. But when the front is also the back and the left is as much left as it is right, can we say that there is a top and bottom?*— anatomist F. Gonzalez-Crussi (1985)

Ventral union of the upper half of the body, from the top of the head to the umbilicus. There are two faces on opposite sides of a conjoined head, but one face may be quite rudimentary. Cephalopagus twins have four arms and four legs (Spencer 1996). Babies born with this extremely rare condition never survive.

There is a dry preparation of the skeletons of cephalothoracopagus twins on display

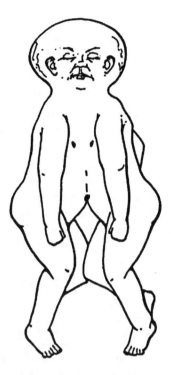

Diagram illustrating typical cephalopagus twins. Courtesy of Rowena Spencer and the W.B. Saunders Co.

at the Mütter Museum in Philadelphia. The back and top of the head are single, with duplication commencing at the base of the chin and cranium. So the bones of the face are single, but the skeleton is double below the head. The ribs and clavicles articulate with an anterior and posterior sternum. The pair were delivered on January 27, 1851, by Dr. Warrington of Philadelphia. The mother was twenty-eight and had two previous normal pregnancies.

During the delivery, the four feet presented first. The doctors attempted to retard the descent of one of the twins. Their pelvises and trunks descended and it was impossible for the doctors to get their fingers in between the small bodies. As they emerged, it was revealed that they were joined at the thorax. The arms and heads of the stillborn infant were brought out and the placenta followed in less than five minutes. The umbilical cord was said to be very thick. On the

back of the head was a symmetrical double-ear. The mouth was a single perfect cavity, with two tongues separated posterially by an irregular skin-covered mass thought to be a rudimentary cheek or lip. The baby had four nipples. Autopsy revealed a single liver and gallbladder. The twins had two hearts, but one was rudimentary and made up of a single chamber and vessel and the other had irregularities. Each trunk contained two lungs, two kidneys, and a regularly-developed trachea and set of bronchial tubes. There were two pharynges from which proceeded a single esophagus and stomach, then two sets of small and large intestines. The female genitals were perfectly developed internally and externally. The skeleton was prepared and dried, after which it measured thirteen inches. The skull had the frontal and parietal bones of a single head, but two occipital bones, four temporal bones, and two imperfect sphenoid bones (Warrington 1850–51).

**Cephalothoracopagus** *see* **Cephalopagus** (*and see* illustration on page 166)

## *Chained for Life.*

A 1951 film directed by Harry L. Fraser and starring Daisy and Violet Hilton as conjoined twins on trial for a crime of passion. The screenplay is based on Mark Twain's story, "Those Extraordinary Twins," but much of it is biographical. In the film, the girls are vaudeville stars encouraged to marry as a publicity stunt. As Dorothy Hamilton plans to wed crack shot Andre Pariseau, she dreams that she is not conjoined. She and her sister Vivian discuss separation, but Vivian is against it and the doctors are pessimistic that they would survive. The marriage license is denied in twenty-seven states on the grounds of bigamy. After they are wed, Andre deserts Dorothy and their marriage is annulled. Vivian kills Andre with the gun from his stage act. The story is narrated by the judge in the case.

In the publicity materials that were distributed with the film, theater owners were given several suggestions to increase ticket sales: a ballot to determine whether the audience would marry a Siamese twin, an essay contest to debate whether one twin should be held accountable for the other's crime, and a tie-in with the local dealer to promote Westinghouse's "twin-set" clothes washer and dryer.

*See also* **Hilton, Daisy and Violet**

## Chang, Chun-yi and Chun-jen.
*Twentieth Century.*

Conjoined twins born in China in 1977. Joined from the waist down, they shared three legs. Found abandoned, they were separated in 1979 at twenty-five months of age. In 1999, on the twentieth anniversary of their separation, they returned to Taiwan University Hospital, Chang Chun-yi in a wheelchair.

## Chang and Eng *see* Bunker

## Children's Hospital of Philadelphia.

In March 2001 surgeons at Children's Hospital performed the institution's fifteenth separation of conjoined twins. Dr. John Templeton, Jr., worked at the hospital from 1977 to 1995, during which time he and his colleagues pioneered separation surgery. Interviewed on BBC2's documentary "Conjoined Twins," he explained that they recognized early on that twins with a shared heart were going into heart failure and that the deterioration of the health of the smaller twin resulted in a drain on the larger twin. That prompted them in more than four cases to separate, leaving the heart tissue with the healthier twin and resulting in the weaker twin's death.

*See also* **Dao and Duan; Lakeberg, Amy and Angela; Taylor, Emily and Claire**

## Ching and Chang.

*And thus, our Twins were saved to flow*
*Thro' Time's far stream in rhythm and glory,*
*And inch by inch together grow,*
*The heroes of an English story.*
 — Edward Bulwer-Lytton (1831)

The names of the title characters in Edward George Earle Bulwer-Lytton's 1831 book in verse, *The Siamese Twins: A Satirical Tale of the Times.* The fictionalized lives roughly parallel those of the Bunkers and the twins encounter similar situations, including interest in their bodies by the public and by the medical community, the question of separation, and run-ins with the law.

## Chulkhurst, Mary and Eliza (Elisa).
*Twelfth Century.*

*The moon on the east oriel shone*
*Through slender shafts of shapely stone*
*The silver light so pale and faint,*
*Shewed the twin sisters and many a saint*
*Whose images on the glass were dyed:*
*Mysterious maidens side by side*
*The moonbeam kissed the holy pane*
*And threw on the pavement a mystic stain.*
 — *a poem found with old Biddenden*
 *Charity documents said to describe*
 *where they are buried*

Female conjoined twins believed to have been born in Biddenden in Kent, England, in 1100 A.D., joined at the hips or buttocks (probably pygopagus), although often depicted joined at the shoulders and hips. "[I]t may be that ... the Maids had four separate arms, and were in the habit of going about with their contiguous arms round each other's necks, and that this gave rise to the notion that these limbs were united" (Gould and Pyle 1956). Leslie Fiedler (1978) is less generous, suggesting that the legend grew up around the misinterpreted image of two unjoined women. The Chulkhurst twins are described in seventeenth-century legal documents as "two Maidens that grew together in their bodies" (Bondeson 2000). The "Biddenden Maids" are considered by some to be among the earliest documented cases of conjoined twins

Plaster casts of three wooden stamps for Biddenden cakes that were available in 1900. Courtesy of Jan Bondeson, M.D., Ph.D.

and by others to be a mere fable. While the story can be traced back for centuries, the names of the twins cannot (Bondeson 2000). It has been pointed out that their birth year is suspicious because their birth would have been considered an omen and 1100 is the year in which monarch William Rufus was found dead (Gould and Pyle 1956). According to popular belief, both died six hours apart in 1134 when the surviving sister refused separation surgery to save her life, remarking, "As we came together, we will go together." According to the local historical society, the twins expired as they were being carried on a litter to be cared for by the monks at Battle Abbey (*The Story of Biddenden* 1989). They were supposedly buried in their native village (Thompson 1968), but their grave has not been located (Bondeson 2000).

Mary and Eliza Chulkhurst have been commemorated for centuries at the church to which they bequeathed eighteen acres of land by the "Biddenden Maids' Charity": baking several hundred cakes stamped with their image and distributing them along with bread and cheese (and at one time beer) to the poor — and now tourists and specta-

tors — on Easter Sunday. One hundred years ago, the bread amounted to 540 loaves and the cheese totaled 470 pounds, plus some 300 cakes: "The impressions of the 'maids' on the cakes are of a primitive character, and are made by boxwood dies cut in 1814. They bear the date 1100, when Eliza and Mary Chulkhurst are supposed to have been born, and also their age at death, thirty-four years" (Gould and Pyle 1956). Once reputed to be a cure for stomach-ache when crumbled, the hard cakes are said to be more suitable for souvenirs and to keep indefinitely (*The Story of Biddenden* 1989). The ceremony was conducted inside the church until 1682, when rector Giles Hinton complained about the disorder and indecency; it was moved to the church porch until the end of the nineteenth century, when it was transferred to the Old Workhouse to the west of the church. Today the distribution is done from a window of the Old Workhouse, now called the White House, on Easter Monday morning. The Easter festival is organized by the Biddenden Parish council chair, who also administers the charity. The charity — which now also donates money, fuel, and health care throughout the year — has been

extended indefinitely since 1907 by com-
bining it with other local charities and by
selling the land, which now contains a development called the Chulkhurst Estate
(*The Story of Biddenden* 1989, Bondeson
2000).

**Clark, Margarete.** *Twentieth Century.*

Female with the body of a parasitic
twin protruding from her abdomen who
toured with the James Strates Shows.

**Climerio de Oliverra, Nadir and
Juraci.** *Twentieth Century.*

Female conjoined twins born in Brazil
on June 2, 1957. They share a renal and intestinal system.

**Cojoined twins** *see* **Conjoined twins**

**Cole, Mary and Decontee.** *End of
Twentieth Century.*

> The success of the surgery is an example of the
> experience and expertise of the entire staff at
> Columbus Children's Hospital. It was with the
> combined efforts of numerous departments and
> specialties — such as laboratory, respiratory care
> and radiology, among many others — that we were
> able to help these children. From the doctors and
> the operating room staff to the intensive care
> nurses — we can't thank them enough for making
> it possible to help these patients. — Surgeon-in-
> chief Dr. Donna Caniano

Conjoined twin girls born on June 4,
2000, in Sawee, Buchanan, Grand Bassa
County, Liberia, joined at the lower back.
Parents Emanuel and Anna Cole also have a
son and two other daughters. The babies
were born vaginally in the presence of a tra-
ditional birth attendant and taken to the
John F. Kennedy Medical Center in Mon-
rovia four days after birth. They shared an
anus, but their spinal cords were not fused,
so they had favorable anatomy for separation. The twins were separated in September 2000 during an eight-hour operation at

Children's Hospital in Columbus, Ohio, the
trip having been arranged by J.F.K. Medical
Center director Dr. S. Mohammed Sheriff.
Dr. Sheriff accompanied the twins, their
mother, and two nurses on the twenty-nine
hour journey to Ohio. Travel and other expenses were courtesy of KLM Airlines, an
anonymous American donor, the Health
Unit of the U.S. Embassy, and Liberian
President Charles Taylor. Surgery and services were donated by the surgeons involved
in the case and the hospital.

Upon arrival at the hospital, the twins
were admitted and given complete neonatal
screening and diagnostic tests to assess the
possibility of separation surgery. They
weighed a combined seventeen pounds two
ounces. After reviewing their central nervous, cardiac, pulmonary, gastroenterology,
liver, renal, genital, vascular, and skeletal
systems, doctors declared surgery advisable.
Skin expanders were inserted on July 7 and
saline injected weekly. Preparation for surgery began at 7:30 AM on September 11,
2000. Surgery began at 10:00 and lasted
eight hours. The forty-member team included pediatric surgeons, plastic surgeons,
urologists, orthopedists, anesthesiologists,
neurosurgeons, and nurses. The operation
was led by Dr. Gail Besner, who said, "We
are very pleased with the outcome of the
surgery. The truly wonderful part is we are
optimistic that Mary and Decontee will
eventually be able to go home and live
happy and healthy lives" (Conjoined Twins
Successfully Separated 2000). After the
surgery, they were listed in critical condition
but expected to recover completely. Recovery, including outpatient care, was estimated
to take two to three months. Lead pediatric
surgeon Dr. Gail Ellen Besner explained,
"They've never really seen each other, being
connected at the buttocks. But right now,
they're too tired. They're in side-by-side
cribs" (Gillespie 2000). They rested in separate cribs, but nurses hoped to reunite
them soon.

## Colloredo, Lazarus-Joannes Baptista.
### *Seventeenth Century.*

A male child born in Genoa on March 20, 1617, with a parasitic twin attached to his abdomen, as described by Gould and Pyle (1956):

> From his epigastrum hung an imperfectly developed twin that had one thigh, hands, body, arms, and a well-formed head covered with hair, which in the normal position hung lowest. There were signs of independent existence in the parasite, movements of respiration, etc., but its eyes were closed, and, although saliva constantly dribbled from its open mouth, nothing was ever ingested. The genitals were imperfect and the arms ended in badly formed hands.

Both heads were baptized; that belonging to the parasitic Joannes Baptista larger and having longer hair than that of Lazarus. Colloredo was examined and described by Bartholinus at age twenty-two. He was the subject of a 1637 broadside entitled "The Two Inseparable Brothers" that includes the following verses:

> The'imperfect once the small poxe had,
> Which made the perfect brother sad,
>   but he had never any,
> And if you nip it by the arme,
> Or doe it any little harme,
>   (this hath been tride by many,)
> It like an infant (with voyce weake)
> Will cry out though it cannot speake,
>   as sensible of paine,
> Which yet the other feeleth not,
> But if the one be cold or hot,
>   that's common to both twaine
> [Wilson 1993].

From the fall of 1637 until late 1639, Colloredo could be seen in London, followed by Norwich and Aberdeen (1642), Strasbourg (1645), and Basel and Verona (1645 or 1646). By the time of an examination in 1642, he was said to have married and fathered several children. Colloredo toured France, Germany, Italy, Spain, and later the British Isles (Bondeson 2000). He traveled with his little brother under a cloak when he was not on stage.

***See also* Parasitic twins**

## Colon, Cristal Paola and Paola Cristal. *Twenty-first Century.*

Conjoined twin girls born on April 10, 2001, to Ramon Colon and Mayda Marrero of Cayey, Puerto Rico, who had a one-year-old son. They were delivered by Cesarean section at New York's Columbia Presbyterian Medical Center after a difficult pregnancy. The Colons did not know of the twins' condition until seven months into the pregnancy. Together, the newborns weighed nine pounds three ounces and remained in intensive care after their birth. The girls were joined at the chest and abdomen and share a six-chambered heart and liver. Both sets of grandparents joined the family at the hospital. Their parents vowed to raise them as normal children, whether or not they could be separated. "If the decision is that they cannot be separated, well, that is the will of God.... Either way, we love them, and they will be raised like any normal child. The only difference is that they are joined a little, that is all," said their father, who described the girls to reporters as healthy and plump, with black hair. "They look wonderful," he said. "When I put a blanket over them they looked like they were sleeping together. You could never tell they are united" (Santiago and Gest 2001).

Unfortunately, Paola and Cristal died on Easter Sunday, April 15, 2001, of heart failure. Their mother described, "When I arrived at the hospital to see them, they were still alive.... I was holding them. They died in my arms" (Ferraro 2001). The cause of death was to be determined by autopsy, but was tentatively attributed to the malformed heart they shared. Had they lived, the parents may have had to make the agonizing choice to sacrifice one of the twins to save the other. Paola and Cristal lived for only five days.

## Conjoined triplets

So-called "triple monsters" were mentioned in the early historical literature as having been delivered stillborn, but have not been documented in contemporary medicine. Pregnancies have resulted in a pair of conjoined twins and a surviving singleton.

## Conjoined twins.

*Some sets of siblings adhere to their own ethics, like a society of two.* — Darin Strauss, *Chang and Eng* (2000)

According to the *Oxford English Dictionary* (2001), the first citation of "conjoined" to mean joined together, united, or combined is in 1570. Today, the word is preferred to "Siamese" when referring to joined twins. Gedda (1961) cataloged the possible symmetrical formations of conjoined twins based on their overall appearance: "teratoadelphia" (Λ-shaped), "teratopagi" (X-shaped), and "teratodymi" (Y-shaped). The terminology to describe the varying types of conjoined twins was standardized by retired pediatric surgeon Rowena Spencer in 1996. In general terms, *The New York Times* describes, "The conjoining can occur at many points of the body, and result in a variety of configurations, from a major sharing of brain, heart, liver or intestines, as well as external limbs, to the development of two nearly complete individuals connected only by a minor bridge of flesh on the torso" (Angier 1997).

Ironically, while the definitions and descriptions have been developed, the mind has a difficult time accepting conjoined twins because the brain is used to categorizing and they can't be accommodated in the existing categories. Conjoined twins are so profoundly similar to us and so pro-

foundly different at the same time, explains ethicist Alice Dreger, that our brains do cartwheels. Elizabeth Grosz (1996) articulates, "Freaks cross the borders that divide the subject from all ambiguities, interconnections, and reciprocal classifications, outside of or beyond the human. They imperil the very definitions we rely on to classify humans, identities, and sexes — our most fundamental categories of self-definition and boundaries dividing self from otherness." Allison Pingree (1996) adds, "For centuries, scientists, physicians, and philosophers in the Western world have been both plagued and fascinated by conjoined twins' confounding mathematics of personhood — the fact that they are both more than one yet not quite two.... As with other corporeal anomalies, the fleshy link between conjoined twins provokes a variety of emotional responses, from wonder to confusion, curiosity to pity, amusement to awe, and most of all, an intense desire to contain and interpret."

We may imagine their lives to be a living hell, but Dreger finds this view narrowly conceived. Still, Nancy Segal cautions that the condition comes with numerous emotional hardships for the twins and for their families: "Parents should provide extra care to the brothers and sisters of conjoined twins, especially if these siblings are ridiculed by others" (Segal 1999).

Some parents do not allow the media to release their names. The following anonymous conjoined births have occurred:

• Thoracopagus female twins born at Monmouth Medical Center in Long Branch, New Jersey, on September 15, 1977, weighing a total of eight pounds ten ounces. The twins were moved the following day by helicopter to Children's Hospital in Philadelphia where they were kept on oxygen in a special "warming bed" to combat their respiratory distress. They shared a common six-chambered heart which could not support both bodies, so lead surgeon C. Everett Koop obtained a court order authorizing the surgery that would result in the death of one of the twins. In fact, they went into cardiac arrest on October 7, but were stabilized. The seven-hour surgery was performed on October 11, 1977, by a team of nineteen doctors, nurses, and technicians. After the operation, the surviving twin suffered from liver and kidney problems and was found to have abnormally narrow blood vessels in her lungs. She underwent another surgery to locate the source of an infection, developed spinal meningitis, and died from septic shock on January 12, 1978. It was believed that although one baby had been dependent on the other for heart function, the other child had depended on her twin for liver functions. The parents refused to permit an autopsy on religious and emotional grounds. Orthodox Jews, they had consulted a number of rabbis before consenting to the separation surgery.

• Conjoined twin girls born on June 6, 1978, joined at the chest and abdomen. They were delivered by Cesarean section at St. Mary's Hospital in Hoboken, New Jersey, weighing six pounds fourteen and a half ounces. Referred to as Baby A and Baby B because their parents did not want to make public their identity, they were transferred to Jersey City Medical Center and evaluated for separation surgery. Before surgery was deemed possible, the girls died on July 4, 1978.

• Dicephalus female twins born on June 22, 1998, in My Tho, Tien Giang, Vietnam, weighing eight pounds six ounces. The twins had two heads, two hearts, two spines, one set of reproductive organs, one set of lungs, one liver, two arms, and two legs. At the father's request, the mother was not told of their condition. The babies were moved two days after birth to the children's hospital in Ho Chi Minh City.

• Craniopagus male twins born February 20, 1992, at Thomas Jefferson University

Hospital in Philadelphia. Birth was by Cesarean section and their combined birth weight was twelve pounds fourteen ounces. Their heads face in opposite directions. The parents were informed at eighteen weeks, but opted not to terminate the pregnancy.

### "Conjoined Twins."

An episode of the documentary series *Horizon* on BBC2 that aired on October 19, 2000. The show includes interviews with Lori and Reba Schappell and Masha and Dasha Krivoshlyapova.

***See also* Schappell, Lori and Reba; Krivoshlyapova, Masha and Dasha**

### Conjoined Twins International.

Will L. Degeraty, Director
Conjoined Twins International
P.O. Box 10895
Prescott, AZ 86304-0895
(800) 235-7918 w
(520) 445-2777 h
*dwdegeraty@excelonlin.com*
*www.familyvillage.wisc.edu/lib
_conjoined.htm*

An international support group for conjoined twins, survivors of conjoined twins, and families of conjoined twins. The association was founded in 1996 and is a nonprofit organization funded solely by donations. CTI is directed by Will L. Degeraty, the grandfather of separated conjoined twins Shawna and Janelle Roderick, and co-directed by Michelle E. Roderick, their mother. Conjoined Twins International provides support services (networking and counseling); education of parents, educators, and medical personnel (maintaining a lending library, engaging speakers, and offering a telephone help-line); and research (cooperating with ongoing medical research with the goal of providing more financial support). CTI publishes a quarterly newsletter. Most of the more than two dozen families that comprise the membership prefer anonymity. Among the doctors on the

Medical Consultant Staff are Pierpaolo Mastroiacomo, Professor of the Birth Defects Unit in the Institute of Pediatrics at Catholic University in Rome, and Rowena Spencer, retired pediatric surgeon of Tulane University and Louisiana State University Medical Center.

## Corbin, Myrtle. *Nineteenth-Twentieth Century.*

Born in Clebourne, Texas, Myrtle was double-bodied from the waist down. She had four legs and two functional vaginas. She was billed as "The Woman from Texas with Four Legs." She married and gave birth to five children, three from one uterus and two from the other.

*See also* **Parasitic twins**

## Craniopagus.

This term is used to describe twins united on any portion of the skull except the face and the foramen magnum. They

Diagram illustrating typical craniopagus twins. Courtesy of Rowena Spencer and the W.B. Saunders Co.

share the bony cranium, the meninges, and sometimes the surface of the brain. They are rarely symmetrical. The trunks are not united and the twins have four arms and four legs (Spencer 1996). Occurs in about two percent of conjoined twins (Segal 1999).

*See also* **Bijani, Laleh and Ladan; MacArther, Yvonne and Yvette Jones; Schappell, Lori and Reba**

## Dao and Duan. *Twentieth Century.*

*Dividing conjoined twins is not about equality or fairness.*— Stacy Keach, narrator of "Siamese Twins"

Female conjoined twins from Thailand whose story was featured on the Nova program "Siamese Twins," which in their case was an appropriate title. They were born on June 6, 1990, attached at the pelvis with three legs. Dao is weaker and smaller than Duan, who seemed to have better control at birth over the third leg. Orphaned they were sent to America by an international adoption agency to assess whether they could be separated. Their third leg was not growing beneath the knee so they would soon be unable to walk. They arrived in Philadelphia on April 20, 1993, to stay with David and Barbara Headley while they were examined at Children's Hospital of Philadelphia. The Headleys, who have two adopted Asian girls of their own, communicated with Dao and Duan mainly through sign language because the twins only knew a few words of English. They were examined by Dr. James O'Neill, who noted that they had a single anus. Dr. O'Neill set up diagnostic studies, imaging studies, and consultations. These included a CT-scan, which revealed that the spinal canals were fused just below the level of the sacrum — if the spinal cords inside were also fused, surgeons might not be able to separate the twins. An MRI soon indicated that the spinal cords were not fused. Radiology showed that each twin had a colon that joined above a common rectum and a single kidney that drained into a shared bladder. They shared intestines and reproductive organs.

Neurosurgeon Dr. Luis Shut decided it would be too dangerous to separate the twins' spines from the front, due to the risk of infection from bacteria in the body cavity. He decided to do the separation in two stages. In the first, the two spines would be sealed off and the sacrum would be partially divided. Because this would weaken their pelvis, the twins were confined after surgery. Containing the cerebrospinal fluid and determining which nerves go to which leg were the hardest challenges. After the four-hour surgery, plastic surgeon Don LaRossa inserted skin expanders. The twins were placed in a cast to prevent them from moving over the next three months while they grew enough skin to close the wound. During that time, Dao began to get weaker. Dolls were used to explain the operation to the girls, who were anxious about it.

The Headleys had grown attached to the twins. Barbara says, "When they first asked us to find a home for these children, they were just children, like strangers. They didn't have a personality, they didn't have anything. And since we've gotten to know them, I mean we really love them and we really care about them and want them to do well. And they think we're their parents." All of the care provided by Children's Hospital was pro bono. Doctors flew in from Thailand to observe the surgery. Dr. O'Neill assembled his team of surgeons, radiologists, anesthesiologists, urologists, and neurologists. During the surgery, the bladder was divided, with Duan getting the larger portion, but Dao's was expected to grow over time. The incision was made from the front, with surgeons dividing the twins system by system, reconstructing organs, and controlling the bleeding. The surgeons had to dissect major blood vessels, including the connected aortas. The colons were divided, with Dao's later pulled through the skin to make

a colostomy. Duan was given the third leg. The documentary about the twins explains that the blood and nerves that serve these organs are principally under Duan's control and that she had the best chance of using these parts successfully. The thin layer of bone left in the sacrum was divided. The twins were separated and the surgical team split in two. More than thirteen hours after surgery began, Duan's wounds were closed with an adequate amount of skin and she was out of surgery. An hour and a half after Duan, Dao joined her in intensive care.

Both twins were at risk of infection and hemorrhaging after surgery, so the first forty-eight hours were critical. Doctors also watched for signs that the new skin was healthy and that the wounds had not been closed too tightly, compromising the function of the internal organs and possibly impairing breathing. Soon after the surgery, Dao developed a serious infection and fever, but recovered in a few days. She needed extensive reconstruction surgery to her bladder and colon, but she has a complete set of reproductive organs. Ten days after surgery, the twins were recovering physically, but having trouble adjusting psychologically. On the Nova episode "Siamese Twins," Barbara Headley says:

> The two of them won't acknowledge each other. We've been trying to get them to communicate or at least say hello. Once or twice they did talk to each other. It was really brief. We haven't had a chance to put them and their beds together because of all the equipment and all that's on their beds, and it just wouldn't be right. And Dao has a fever and she [Duan] doesn't, so they don't want them to make each other sick. But basically they seem angry at each other. When Duan woke up from surgery, she asked where Dao was, and I showed her. When Dao woke up from surgery, it was like there was a phantom person. She woke up and was screaming and flailing her arm that was where Duan was. And she was pounding on the bed with her

arm screaming and turning in circles looking for Duan. So I came in the room and I quickly oriented her and showed her where Duan was and she was OK. But for about twenty-four hours she would just fling her arm over and hit the side of the bed looking for Duan.

At three-and-a-half years, they are among the oldest conjoined twins to be separated.

Barbara Headley observed that they came to terms with their separation within two weeks. They were put together in their own room once out of intensive care. After they were put in the same bed, they were able to see and touch each other and they hugged. Dao is said to have put on a lot of weight and the twins are the same height. Dao's appetite and personality are as strong as Duan's and she is independent and doesn't let her sister dominate her anymore. The twins celebrated their fourth birthday at the hospital, where they have won the hearts of all the doctors and nurses. Dr. O'Neill said, "When you undertake something like this, your goal is to see that you can, if at all possible, come out with two complete individuals who can take their place in society and be productive. I think the other physicians have identical feelings of great gratification in seeing these children grow and develop and behave like normal children. There's no better feeling one can have than seeing that." Dao was learning to walk with a prosthetic limb and faced additional surgeries to repair her urinary system. Duan also needed a prosthesis after the removal of the lower half of one of her legs, which was not growing. The girls have started preschool.

The Headleys decided to adopt Duan and Dao, knowing the huge responsibility. They planned to start a charitable fund to pay for the extensive medical treatment and rehabilitation that the twins will need and that the insurance company will not cover.

**See also** "Siamese Twins"

## DeAndrade, Maria Carmen and Maria Guadalupe. *End of Twentieth Century.*

*But when Norma DeAndrade saw them, she took them into her arms and their burden became hers.* — Robert Miller

Conjoined twin girls delivered by Cesarean section on June 5, 2000, in Veracruz, Mexico, to Victor and Norma Solis DeAndrade, who also had a twelve-year-old daughter. Norma was thrilled to know she was going to have twins, but she and her husband refused to accept the news that they weren't developing normally. When they could no longer avoid it, their spirits plummeted. Joined below the shoulder, their babies shared a torso and a single pair of legs. They had a single large liver, two lungs, three kidneys, three ovaries, one uterus, and what appeared to be two hearts in a single pericardial sac. Together, the girls weighed nine pounds. They were placed in isolation to save them from the stares of the other parents. They were the first pair of conjoined twins born at the Veracruz hospital, which had no idea how to care for them. The Mexican government provided the standard shipment of groceries, but would not help with medical care. Carmen and Guadalupe's health began to decline and they were often sick with bronchial infections.

Through friends, the DeAndrades heard about the organization Healing the Children NE. They contacted president Angeles Glick, who agreed to help after seeing photographs of the twins. She brought the family to New Milford, Connecticut, where they stayed with Healing the Children staff member Jakelin Rodriguez. The twins required a cardiologist, a nephreologist, a pulmonologist, a plastic surgeon, a physical therapist, and a speech therapist. Each twin controlled a leg, but they could not walk at one year of age. Their combined weight at one year was 22 pounds and they were said to be cognitively normal. Carmen is easy-going and "Lupe" is smaller and quicker to get sick, but more of a fighter. Their parents wanted both girls to survive, but their mother stated that saving one would be better than losing two (Miller 2001). The twins returned to Mexico in Fall 2001.

## de Conza, Mario and Beniamino.
*Twentieth Century.*

Conjoined twin boys born in Italy in 1992. Mario died during separation surgery in 1994.

## DeHoyes, Rodolfo and Jesus.
*Twentieth Century.*

Conjoined twin boys united back to back. They arrived from Riobonda in September 1940 at age eight. In December of that year, they were appearing at the Marine Hippodrome in Hattiesburg, Mississippi.

## Delivery *see* Pregnancy

## Development.

Conjoined twins result from a single fertilized ovum within a single placenta and are therefore always identical twins. It is believed that environmental and genetic factors are responsible for the failure of the embryos to separate after the thirteenth day of fertilization. There have been no recorded cases of conjoined triplets or quadruplets. In many cases, one of the twins is smaller and weaker, possibly as a result of competition in utero for nutrition. Conjoined twins fare best when they have strong support from their parents (Miller 2001).
*See also* **Causes; Conjoined triplets**

## Diagnosis.

The minimal diagnostic criteria for conjoined twinning is the fusion of some portion of monovular or monozygotic twins. Clinical diagnosis is based on physical ex-amination and, necessary in the case of visceral conjunction, x-rays and ultrasound techniques. Conjoined twins can also be diagnosed in utero by x-ray or ultrasound (Bergsma 1979). The first radiologic study of conjoined twins, which found that positioning them was particularly difficult, was performed in Rio de Janeiro in 1900.

## Diana Cristina and Leydi Johana. *End of Twentieth Century.*

Conjoined twin girls born September 9, 2000, in Medellin, Columbia, sharing a liver, pancreas, and part of their intestines. Together they weighed less than nine pounds and had other abnormalities, including four gallbladders. Diana Cristina died of respiratory failure on September 14, less than twenty-four hours after a sixteen-and-a-half-hour operation to separate them. The surgery was carried out at the Leon XIII Hospital by a team of twenty, headed by pediatric surgeon Jose David Garcia. The twin who died had been given better chances of survival than Leydi Johana, who was afterward listed in "delicate but stable" condition in the intensive care unit.

## Dicephalus.

Conjoined twins sharing a single body, each with a separate head and neck. They account for 11 percent of all conjoined twins. This group is further subcategorized: *dicephalus tetrabrachius* are divided above the waist, with two torsos, four arms, and two heads; *dicephalus tribrachius* have a single torso, two heads, and three arms (one of them often atrophied); *dicephalus dibrachius* have one torso, two arms, and two heads and necks. Dicephalus twins were considered in ancient times to be the most remarkable of the prodigies of nature. The condition is extremely rare and only four pairs of dicephalus twins have ever survived, according to historical record (Jussim 2001). As late as the 1960s, recommendations were published discouraging doctors from treating or resuscitating newborn dicephali, but instead allowing them to die. Many dicephali are viable, but only without surgical intervention: "There is good reason to doubt, based on both medical and ethical reasons, that surgical separation of dicephalus conjoined twins should be attempted at all, except in a situation in which one twin is clearly dying" (Bondeson 2000).

There is a cast of a dicephalic infant on display at the Mütter Museum in Philadelphia. The Mütter Museum also exhibits a wet specimen of a dicephalic male infant. The latter is a male fetus delivered at the Good Samaritan Hospital in Cincinnati in 1929 by Dr. J.E. Pirrung. The baby lived only a few minutes. One of the two heads had a complete unilateral cleft of the lip and palate. In 1934, Dr. Pirrung showed Dr. Robert H. Ivy the specimen preserved in a jar in the hospital museum. In the late 1960s, Dr. Ivy remembered the rare specimen and decided to find out where it was curated. Among other studies, he hoped to do X-rays that would show how the spine divided. By chance, he received a letter in 1969 from Dr. Byron E. Boyer who had been shown — and presented with — the specimen by Dr. Richard T.F. Schmidt. It had been located, along with a lantern slide of it, in Dr. Van Dalton's office after his retirement. New photographs and X-rays were made in July 1969. A report by radiologist Richard B. Mulvey describes a mummified male fetus of six to seven months' gestation. The lumbar vertebrae are wide and fused and merge into a single axial skeleton at the level of the sacrum (Ivy and Boyer 1970). Dr. Ivy and Dr. Boyer donated the specimen to the Mütter Museum in 1970.

See illustration on page 167.
*See also* **Parapagus**

## Diplopagus.

A general term for equal and symmet-

rical conjoined twins, also known as *duplicatas completa.*
*See also* **Heteropagus**

## Diploteratology.

An early medical term for the existing body of knowledge about conjoined twins.
*See also* **Teratology**

## Diprosopus *see* **Parapagus**

## Disability.

*Over the centuries the bond between conjoined twins has been viewed as a curse, curiosity, or a handicap. Today we are most likely to see such individuals as handicapped, probably as severely handicapped. The perceived severity of this handicap leads to ethical questions....* — J. David Smith (1988)

*There are good days and bad days — so what? This is what we know. We don't hate it. We live it every day. I don't sit around questioning it or asking myself what I could do differently if I were separated.* — Reba Schappell

*If you're sorry for someone it means you think they're worse than you and we don't think we're worse than other people. But we have to keep proving it because of the way we look.* — Dasha Krivoshlyapova

The popular belief is that conjoined twins have an impossibly difficult and regrettable life. But craniopagus twin Lori Schappell coaches, "Until we tell you it's difficult, assume it's not." Nancy Segal (1999) notes that curiosity about conjoined twins goes well beyond that raised by other physical and behavioral deviations, and states, "I believe our fascination with these pairs stems from witnessing their incredible tests of human coexistence at the extreme." Some would even go so far as to say that conjoined twins would be better off dying early. This was written of the nineteenth century Finley twins in the Trenton, New Jersey, *Daily State Gazette*: "They have the appearance of long life, but it is sad to reflect, while looking at the pretty and playful babes, what a comfortless and miserable existence their deformity would doom them to if they should live many years" (Besse 1874). More than a century ago, Mark Twain wrote of his fictional conjoined twin Angelo Cappello, "He had known no life but the combined one; he had been familiar with it from his birth; he was not able to conceive of any other as being agreeable, or even bearable. To him, in the privacy of his secret thoughts, all other men were monsters, deformities...." (Twain 1980). Gretchen Worden, director of the Mütter Museum, points out that many conjoined twins have functioned together for years: "'Is it a normal life?,' she asks. 'It depends on what your definition of normal is. But they can live very fulfilling lives'" (Miller 2001). Alice Dreger (1998) relates that many conjoined twins consider themselves better prepared than singletons for the rigors of the world.

Leslie Fiedler takes up the cause of those with physical deformities in his book *Tyranny of the Normal* (1996):

> I simply do not assume (indeed, the burden of evidence indicates the contrary) that being born a freak is per se an unendurable fate. As I learned reading scores of biographies of such creatures in the course of writing my book about them, the most grotesque among them have managed to live lives neither notably worse nor better than that of most humans. They have managed to support themselves at work which they enjoyed (including displaying themselves to the public); they have loved and been loved, married and begot children — sometimes in their own images, sometimes not. More often than not, they have survived and coped; sometimes, indeed, with special pride and satisfaction because of their presumed "handicaps," which not a few of them have resisted attempts to "cure."

In *Freaks*, Fiedler (1978) concedes that not all conjoined twins overcome their handicap: "Most of us choose to recall Chang and Eng rather than the more tragic Toccis or the Hilton Sisters, because it is possible, despite certain difficulties, to read their story as one with a happy ending."

Rowena Spencer (1993) reminds readers that conjoined twins are as likely — if not more likely — to have *other* physical abnormalities as the average baby:

> It should be noted that physical separation of the various organs and organ systems which are not directly involved in the union of conjoined twins does not protect them from all the malformations to which singletons are subject. All abnormalities that can occur may be found in conjoined twins, and it is reasonable to assume that the catastrophic disturbance causing the conjunction may result in other congenital malformations as well. Hence, the incidence of other anomalies is quite high in conjoined twins.

Looking at the larger picture, Dudley Wilson (1993) writes, "...philosophy and theology, with their emphasis on the problem of diagnosis, seem to be giving way to emphasis on the problem of care and personal involvement. Worry about the origins of the monstrous is giving way to worry about the practical problems of coping with their presence within society, and ways of integrating them into it."

*See also* **Abdulrehman, Hassan and Hussein; Hensel, Abigail Lauren and Brittany Lee; Holton, Katie and Eilish; Lincoln, Charity Mae and Kathleen Faith; MacArther, Yvonne and Yvette Jones**

**Dithoracic** *see* **Parapagus**

**Dorsal union.**

Twins joined at the dorsal aspect of the primitive embryonic disc, which does not involve the thoracic or abdominal viscera or the umbilicus.

*See also* **Craniopagus; Pygopagus; Rachipagus**

**Double monsters** *see* **Conjoined twins; Prodigy**

## Dragstedt, Lester R.

The surgeon who is credited with performing the first successful separation of conjoined twins in the U.S. in 1955. Died July 16, 1975, at age eighty-one.

## Drimmer, Frederick.

Frederick Drimmer was a professor at the College of the City of New York. He was the author of several books about people with physical deformities, written with compassion and characterizing "freaks"—including the Bunkers and other conjoined twins—as having both dignity and courage. His book *Very Special People* was an international bestseller. Drimmer died of a stroke after a long illness in Norwalk, Connecticut, on December 24, 2000, at age eighty-four.

## Dufour, Lou.

A carnival showman born in 1896 who initiated the display of deformed babies billed as being the result of immoral behavior and known as an "unborn show." He operated the "Scroll of Life" show at the New York World's Fair in 1939–40 and a show called "Nature's Mistakes." Dufour died in 1977.

*See also* Punks; Specimens

## Elizabeth and Catharine. *Seventeenth Century.*

The "United Swiss Sisters" were born in Huttingen, Basle, Switzerland, on November 14, 1689, to Clementia M. and Martin D. Baptized Elizabeth and Catharine, the girls were joined at the abdomen by a band consisting of xiphoid cartilage, umbilical vessels, areolar tissue, and skin. The band was an inch and a half in length, one inch in thickness, and five inches in circumference and had a very thick umbilical cord attached to its lower surface. The day after their birth, their parents consulted with surgeons regarding their separation. The surgery performed by Dr. Fatio was described by Dr. Emanuel König. The cords were separated and tied, and the band was perforated with needles and ligated tighter and tighter until it was fully divided in nine days (Harris 1874). Six months afterward, the twins were reported to be in good health, making this the first documented successful separation of conjoined twins.

## Emberson, Faith and Hope. *End of Twentieth Century.*

*Why deprive me of that minute chance for the babies?*—Denise Emberson

Female conjoined twins born at National Women's Hospital in Auckland, New Zealand, on May 2, 2000, to Bruce and Denise Emberson of Wairoa. The Embersons continued the pregnancy despite doctors' advice to terminate the birth at five months. They decided to let nature take its course. They told a reporter that all they wanted was for the twins to choose their time. "It's life—their life," said Denise. "Even if their life ends within me now … least that was their life" (Millar 2001). The babies repeatedly outlasted doctors' predictions during the pregnancy. At the hospital, a team was formed and led by Dr. Peter Stone. They learned that the girls shared a liver. Pediatric cardiologist Dr. Nigel Wilson determined that Hope's heart had only a single good pumping chamber and that the hearts were joined by a single wall, which might preclude separation. Denise made it clear that she wanted the twin with the stronger heart saved, but doctors warned that it might be impossible to save either twin. They encouraged Denise to enjoy her pregnancy. "We're prepared for the … short time that we'll have with the babies," says Bruce (Millar 2001).

The names the Embersons chose for their girls reflect their positive attitude toward the sobering situation. Denise explains:

We've given Faith her name because she is, what has been told to us by the doctors, the stronger baby of the two, and she's positioned on the left and always has been. And we've given the second twin Hope and her name was given to her, she's possibly the weaker out of the two and we have to have a lot of hope that she does pull through as well with her sister. And they are one.

Denise's husband and daughters were both hopeful and fearful as she entered the delivery room at almost full term. Denise herself was resigned: "Now having to almost surrender that fight for my babies and hand them into the world. Literally hand them into the world and, I've done my best with them" (Millar 2001). The hospital provided the family with tight security. The doctors doubted that the babies would be born alive, but a family pediatrician said they made steady progress after a forty-minute delivery. Birth was by Cesarean section performed by Dr. Rob Holmes, who was interviewed minutes later: "Went very well, very well. We were extremely relieved. Still have very, very grave concerns for their well being and so it's a little victory" (Millar 2001). It was four hours before Denise and her daughters were able to see the babies. The twins were joined face to face, had joined hearts, and shared a set of lungs, so separation would be unlikely. Their combined weight was four kilos.

The Embersons signed an exclusive agreement with New Zealand TV3's *20/20* program to tell their story (Holm 2000). Reporter Amanda Millar spent months with the Embersons during their pregnancy and pronounced it "overwhelming for me to be invited by the family to be at the birth of these two very special little girls" (Millar 2001). Tests after birth revealed that neither baby had a healthy heart. "What we're seeing in total is very, very complex end of the spectrum of congenital heart anomalies," stated Dr. Wilson (Millar 2001). Sadly, Faith and Hope survived only three days, dying on May 5, 2000. They died peacefully cradled in Denise's arms and surrounded by family. Their sister told them, "You are very beautiful girls. We all love you two brave, brave girls. You are both very special to us all. You are both in our hearts all the time. I love your black beautiful hair and eyes. I am proud that I have you two. You are my sisters." Said their father, "We had them for a short time. We're really grateful for that." Their mother said, "We're just going to live with memories of them. It was just amazing. We've only lost them in flesh, not in spirit, not in our hearts and our memories. It was beautiful" (Millar 2001).

## Epholothoracopagus.

Joined at the upper chest with a shared heart and two faces on a single head.

## Exhibition.

*When human oddities have been exhibited, persons from all stations of life have been willing to pay for the privilege of viewing.* — Ronald E. Ostman (1996)

The practice of exhibiting human curiosities for profit extends back at least as far as the Renaissance (Adams 1996). The live exhibition of conjoined twins to the public for a profit has often been condemned, but the twins and the show business community have countered that this allowed them the opportunity to make a living and therefore be independent, in addition to providing them the means to travel and meet others like themselves. In some cases, conjoined babies were kept under wraps except on stage to preserve their parents' income, since it was thought that people wouldn't pay for what they could see for free. Still, it is thought inappropriate to pay for the opportunity to observe a conjoined twin. Ethicist Alice Dreger points out the irony that such twins are unable to make a living today, despite the fact that many people with beautiful bodies get paid to exhibit them. Dreger

Cover of Millie-Christine's autobiographical *History and Medical Description of the Two-Headed Girl*, printed in 1869. Courtesy of Joanne Martell.

Advertisement of Millie-Christine by John Doris for the 1883 Inter-Ocean circus season. Courtesy of Joanne Martell.

(1998, 2000) points out that in the past, those with peculiar anatomies had a mutually beneficial relationship with the medical community. The doctors satisfied their voyeurism, increased the medical knowledge of the condition, and built their reputations; in exchange, the exhibitors received expert opinions, occasional medical treatment, and written testimonies to their strangeness. Today, unusual anatomies are displayed publicly on television and in the popular press, but do not receive the profit from such exhibition — in fact, their appearance via venues like talk shows is seen as pathetic and distasteful. Their exhibition to the medical community, on the other hand, is expected to be provided freely "for the good of humanity" (Dreger 2000). Not only are those

with unusual bodies denied any recompense for allowing their examination, those who do so are being asked to participate in the reduction of such anomalies: "It dawned on me how strange it would be, if I were a giant or a dwarf, or a conjoined twin or a hermaphrodite, to see my kind of people displayed so that my kind of people might dwindle in number," remarks Alice Dreger (2000).

Public exhibition of conjoined twins was made possible when superstitions subsided and any money gained from the display became seen as a small compensation for the burden for caring for such a child:

> …the attraction aroused by simple curiosity begins to assert itself and the spectator is motivated more by feelings of

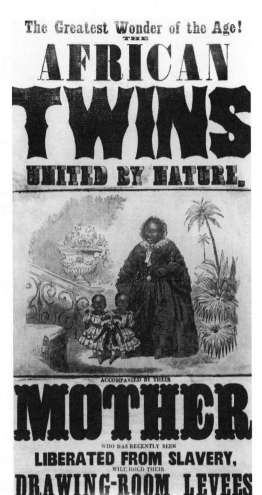

Advertisement featuring Millie-Christine and their mother Monemia. Courtesy of the North Carolina Division of Archives and History.

Advertising flyer for Millie-Christine's appearance at the Tremont Temple in Boston in 1869. Courtesy of the Dicksie Cribb Collection.

entertainment than of awe. At the same time, a belief in the commercial possibilities of the monster, which had always existed, increased. Indeed, a suggestion that the birth of a monster might well be a blessing consciously vouchsafed to a poor family by a benevolent creator was put forward ... [Wilson 1993].

James Paris du Plessis, a servant of Samuel Pepys who wrote and illustrated an unpublished history of prodigious births, includes descriptions of conjoined twins, one pair of which he exhumed in order

*Top:* Lithograph of Chang and Eng c. 1855 with vignettes of their home life. Courtesy of the Harvard Theatre Collection, Houghton Library. *Left:* Lithograph of Chang and Eng with vignettes depicting their lives at home in North Carolina. Courtesy of the Southern Historical Collection, Wilson Library, University of North Carolina–Chapel Hill.

to examine (since he was prevented by his family from getting a good look at it) and the other pair of which he paid to see at Marybone near London at the age of about fifteen (Wilson 1993). In a letter published in 1703, Charles Ellis complains of the high fee (300 Guilders) charged by John Ameston to see the bodies of his conjoined twin daughters; in another letter, Jacomo Grandi offered the father of female conjoined twins a great sum of money to obtain their bodies for dissection, but the man preferred to have them embalmed so that he could exhibit them (Wilson 1993).

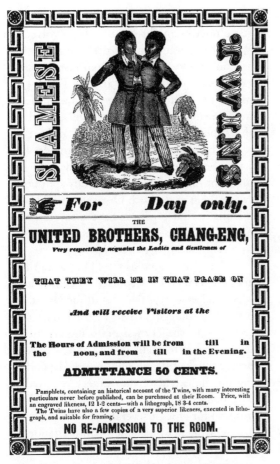

Handbill used to promote the Siamese twins. Courtesy of the Southern Historical Collection, Wilson Library, University of North Carolina–Chapel Hill.

The exhibition of stillborn specimens of conjoined twins has been done in both medical and carnival sideshow settings. Siamese twins were said to be especially popular at Coney Island (Stanton 1997). Lou Dufour's display of a "Real Two-Headed Baby" was featured at Chicago's Century of Progress exhibition in 1933 and 1934; during its two seasons, the exhibit broke all records, having admitted 15,225 paid visitors and grossing nearly $250,000 (Liebling 2001). The purposes of exhibition range from education to entertainment, but they are sometimes used to convey a moral message. Baby shows often condemned the dangers of premarital sex. Inside an "unborn show" a lecturer would deliver a talk that simulated a classroom and was illustrated with malformed fetuses — premature or aborted — in jars (Ostman 1996). The Chinese government arranges exhibits of deformed fetuses to reinforce the official policy of one child per family by implying that having more would result in abnormalities, including conjoined twins. Medically correct displays about the formation of conjoined twins may be seen in many of the world's medical museums, including the Mütter Museum in Philadelphia.

*See also* Dufour, Lou; Specimens; "World's Strangest Babies"

## "Face to Face: The Story of the Schappell Twins"

A 1999 A&E documentary about craniopagus twins Lori and Reba Schappell, including an interview with each of them, friends Herman and June Sonon, and ethicists Alice Dreger and Catherine Myser. The executive producers of the show are Linda Ellerbee and Rolfe Tessem and it was produced and directed by Ellen Weissbrod. The program shows footage of the twins recording the reactions of people in New York City to them in order to show what life is like through their eyes. And because their eyes face in different directions, Reba sometimes uses a camera to see what Lori sees without turning around. They are matter-of-fact about showing themselves in public, stressing that it is the public's fault if they have a problem with it. As Alice Dreger explains, the public may perceive their bodies as monstrous and infer that they live a monstrous life. The Schappell sisters do not want shielding and do not consider themselves vulnerable.

*See also* Schappell, Lori and Reba

## Facts About Multiples.

*http://mypage.direct.ca/c/csamson.*
An on-line encyclopedia of multiple

births that includes a section about conjoined twins.

## Fanning, Shannon and Megan.
### Twentieth Century.

*I remember thinking at the time how ridiculous the term "normal conjoined pregnancy" seemed. It was a real oxymoron.*— Larry A. Fanning, father of Shannon and Megan (Fanning 1995)

Conjoined twin girls born in 1994 to Larry and Sandi Fanning of Naperville, Illinois. Their doctor first noticed during the pregnancy that the girls shared an amniotic sac, which increased their risk for getting entangled in each other's cord. It was then determined that the twins were conjoined, apparently at the abdomen. Termination was offered, but the Fannings decided to continue with the pregnancy, monitoring closely and making decisions based on ultrasounds and other tests. "I found that it really helped when I utilized some of the same type of logic in my thoughts about the pregnancy as in my work duties. Not only did this tend to remove some of the emotional stress, but looking at the situation from a more technical standpoint helped me to analyze and better understand what was happening," writes their father (Fanning 1995). The girls were thought to share a liver and Sandi underwent five ultrasound examinations by her fifteenth week of pregnancy.

Their doctors at Lutheran General Perinatal Center encouraged the Fannings to consult a specialist regarding separation of the twins after birth. For the surgery they chose doctors at Children's Memorial Medical Center in Park Ridge, Illinois, who had been recommended and had participated in the separation of three other sets of conjoined twins. The Fannings relied on their faith to help them make the right decisions. The twins' father writes, "One of the things I prayed for was the ability to choose the best doctors and or the best hospital to perform the separation. We had heard some

stories about why some institutions and some doctors might want to be involved. We did not want anyone performing such critical surgery on our children just for the experience" (Fanning 1995). The Fannings met with the doctors from Children's Memorial prior to the birth, who explained the three possibilities. The twins could be joined by muscle and liver tissue and easily separated. They could share organs, which might or might not be successfully split between them or divided. One twin might be missing a vital organ or have a severe abnormality, in which priority would be given to save the healthy twin.

The Fanning twins were born at Lutheran General and transported to Children's Memorial as soon as their condition was stable. They underwent two to three days of testing. The surgery was performed by two teams of five to eight people and was expected to take three to eight hours, depending on the extent of the surgery required. The babies would have to remain in the hospital for at least several weeks.

During her pregnancy, Sandi attended a bioethics symposium on conjoined twins at Edward Hospital in their hometown of Naperville, which alerted the Fannings not only to the ethical and moral dilemmas involved in their case, but the financial issues involved in the care and separation of conjoined twins. Sandi and Larry Fanning considered themselves lucky that none of the friends and family they had confided in leaked the news of their expected conjoined twins to the media.

The Fannings' doctor at Lutheran General recommended at least thirty-four weeks' gestation. At thirty weeks, doctors began to suspect that one of the twins had a bowel obstruction. On March 23, the twins were delivered by Cesarean section and appeared to be more severely joined than anticipated. Their father stated:

> Shannon and Megan Fanning entered our world, more or less side-by-side,

arms around one another. They were so beautiful, so perfect, and both breathing on their own.... After getting cleaned up, they had resumed the position that must have seemed most comfortable and safe to them. They had their arms around one another. Not like they were dancing or hugging, but more like buddies. That scene will remain vivid in my mind for as long as I live.... It was to become the most definitive of all the photos taken. To this day, people seeing it for the first time usually have very little to say. That picture tells the whole amazing story [Fanning 1995].

In the womb, Shannon had been designated the feisty and more active one.

The girls were transported to Children's Memorial Medical Center as planned and their father joined them while their mother recovered at Lutheran General. Larry Fanning and family were given a tour of the facility and met the doctors who would be participating in the separation. On the morning of surgery, preparation began at 8 AM, but took several hours. The operation itself took more than two hours. It involved cutting through the abdominal walls, visualizing and separating the organs and blood vessels, and rerouting the intestines. Because of their partially shared circulatory system, it proved difficult to anesthetize the twins. Both had bowel obstructions, which were removed and repaired. Shannon was the first to emerge from surgery, covered with bandages, wires, and tubes. The girls began urinating within twenty-four hours of surgery, which was a good sign (Fanning 1995).

The Fannings were told that the next twenty-four to forty-eight hours were critical and that it would take seven to ten days before the operation could be declared a success. The girls could be released in four or five weeks. The twins' separation surgery would have to be followed by cosmetic surgery if, for instance, they wanted to provide each child with a navel or other similar features. After four and a half weeks at Lutheran General, Sandi was released and joined her babies at Children's Memorial. By Easter, Shannon's and Megan's condition had been upgraded from critical to serious and they had been extubated, but Megan was reintubated when she took a turn for the worse and experienced a seizure. An EEG and CT-scan were administered to determine whether she had fluid on the brain or a burst blood vessel, but the tests were negative and the seizure was deemed spontaneous (Fanning 1995).

In the third week after surgery (April 12), Shannon had a setback: a possible bowel obstruction that required close monitoring. Megan then required another radiograph to determine why her central line was leaking. Tests revealed that Megan, who had already been diagnosed with a heart murmur, could have a blood clot in her vein (Fanning 1995). Both of the girls were still being fed by nasogastric tubes, but their central lines were removed. In the fourth week, the babies weighed more than four pounds each. Their parents were allowed to take them home on April 21 and their father put his feelings into words:

> They would be leaving the safe solitude of the hospital room for the more hectic, less technically supportive atmosphere of their nursery at home. We hoped the change would only temporarily prove unsettling. We believed the support we could supply from the heart and the soul would at least match what they had previously received from monitors and other electronic equipment [Fanning 1995].

After they returned home, the Fannings received help from friends and family, ranging from babysitting to cooking to running errands. The feeding tube was removed from Shannon first. Both babies were baptized into the Roman Catholic church on June 11, 1994. As an Afterword to his book *Separated Angels*, Larry Fanning (1995) gives readers an update: "As time passes, the story of Megan and Shannon, and their unusual birth, begins to fade. They are now one year old; both are healthy and strong. Except for the scars on their tummies, and the lack of belly buttons, they cannot be distinguished from other twins of a similar age. They each have their own distinct personality. Shannon is still the feisty one, and now outweighs her sister. Megan is more gentle and loves to cuddle." In 1996, the Fannings were featured on an episode of Kathy Lee Gifford's CBS series "Miracle Babies."

*See also* **Holton, Katie and Eilish; Lakeberg, Amy and Angela; Media attention**

### Fetus in fetu.

The occurrence of an imperfectly formed fetus entirely within the body of its twin. The phenomenon has been documented recently in a six-month-old in Java in September 1992, a four-month-old in Saudi Arabia in August 1994; a fifty-nine-year-old in China; and a four-year-old in Nepal. The phenomenon is distinct from teratomas, or demoid cysts, that contain skin, central nervous tissue, teeth, glands, and other dermal tissue (Fiedler 1978).

*See also* **Parasitic twins**

### Finley, Mina and Minnie. *Nineteenth Century.*

*All ranks and classes visited them, and the greater portion of visitors admired their beauty, intelligence, and loveliness, many saying that they were the most beautiful children that they had ever beheld.* — Dr. H. Besse (1874)

Female ischiopagus tripus twins born in Peru township, Morrow County (by another account Warren County), Ohio, on October 12, 1870, to Joseph and Ann Eliza Finley. It was the fourth birth of their thirty-three-year-old mother, who is described as having a massive frame. Labor and natural delivery were completed a half hour before the doctor arrived and the twins were reported to weigh a total of twelve and a half pounds. The twins shared a single umbilicus and placenta (Townsend 1870). They had two heads, two arms, a single pelvis, and three legs. The had a single anus and a single set of genital organs between a normal set of legs that projected at a right angle from the body. A third double-leg on the opposite side terminated in a club foot with eight imperfectly formed toes. "This child or children, when lying on their backs may be described as forming a cross; that is, the body or two bodies united, with a head at each end of the common body, forming one straight line, and the two sets of legs projecting at right angles from the body form another straight line," described their doctor H. Besse (1874). It is disputed whether the babies had a single placenta and umbilical cord, both of normal size, or a pair of each. Upon examination, Besse determined that they had separate bladders.

Mina and Minnie are featured and depicted in Besse's book *Diploteratology*, in which Dr. Ralph M. Townsend writes, "Each end of the trunk is formed of a perfect thorax with its contained viscera, then comes the swell of the belly, and the children insensibly grade into one another" (Besse 1874). The book reprints mention of the twins in the contemporary newspapers including the Trenton, New Jersey, *Daily State Gazette*, in which they were described as bright and beautiful, with remarkably fine-shaped heads. One twin was weak and the other robust (Gould and Pyle 1956). The plumper baby was described (Besse 1874) as looking more content. The girls had different heart rates (the pulse of one beating six times faster to the minute than the other upon examination) and their circulation and respiration were independent (Besse 1874). They shared intestines, but were said to have good digestion. They were thought to have a single continuous spine, but Dr. Ralph M. Townsend wrote that upon closer examination they seemed to have two J-shaped spines arranged end-to-end (Besse 1874). They slept and ate at different times and suffered only from the usual ailments during their infancy. Their mother first nursed them both (which she could do simultaneously for the first few weeks), but soon gave her own milk to the smaller one and fed the larger one from a bottle. One child did not feel when the other was pinched and their attention could be stimulated separately. Their doctor described, "...when one of the children awoke, the arms as well as the perfect leg belonging to, or nearest the head of that child, began to move ... while either one had partial control of the double leg" (Besse 1874). A contemporary description from the *Ohio Statesman* reprinted by Besse (1874), stated that the two normal legs "are gifted with an ordinary amount of kicking ability."

Shortly after the birth of the twins, their parents were coerced by a Mr. Brown into signing a contract to take the twins on tour for fifty dollars per month, an agreement they soon broke (Besse 1874). Instead, the Finleys welcomed visitors to their farm and charged them an admission fee of fifty cents to see the double-child, which was presented resting on a pillow on Mrs. Finley's lap. Dr. Besse (1874) reprints a story from the *Mt. Vernon* (Ohio) *Banner* defending the exhibit:

> And here we may remark that instead of finding anything to condemn in this, we think it is every way praiseworthy and proper; for, if Mr. and Mrs. Finley made a "free show" of their double-baby, their house would be constantly so over-crowded with visitors as to endanger the health, if not the lives both of Mrs. F. and her marvelous offspring. By charging a moderate admission fee, however, the crowd is kept away, and such a sum of money will be realized as to enable the parents to properly take care of and provide for the curious freak of nature which has been placed in their charge by the will of Providence.

Their parents also increased their income by selling hundreds of photographs of the babies. The *Zanesville* (Ohio) *Courier* pre-dicted the twins would make a fortune for their parents; the *Pittsburgh Daily Dispatch* reported that they were paid five hundred dollars a week to appear at Burneli's Museum (Besse 1874).

On May 18, 1871, the twins were the subject of a scientific examination and lecture by Dr. F. Getchell at Jefferson Medical College. They were displayed in a crib on a revolving table and were found to laugh and cry at the same time. The demonstration — attended by Dr. William Pancoast and other physicians and scientists — had been arranged with Robert F. Simpson, the manager of the New American Museum at which the Finleys were appearing. Pancoast (1871) recorded that "each one defecates separately, as can be seen by the reddening of the face and the straining of the abdominal muscles of one while the other is tranquil." Two months earlier, in March 1871, Dr. Besse had become the agent of the five-month-old Finley twins, traveling with them and looking after their health. He exhibited the twins at the following locations, some of which drew more than one thousand visitors a day: American House, Columbus, Ohio; Preston House, Newark, Ohio; McIntire House, Zanesville, Ohio; Burneli's Museum, Pittsburgh; Robinson House, Pittsburgh; Brant's Hall, Harrisburg, Pennsylvania; Aulenbauch's Hall, Keystone House, Reading, Pennsylvania; New American Museum, Philadelphia; American House, Trenton, New Jersey; Greer Hall, Bull's Head Hotel, New Brunswick, New Jersey; Arcade Building, Lafayette House, Elizabeth, New Jersey; Library Hall, City Hotel, Newark, New Jersey.

At this last stop, in July 1871, Minnie became deathly ill with "cholera infantum," but recovered in a few days, leaving Mina unaffected until several days later.

In July 1871, Besse took the twins, their parents, and their nurse Carrie Robinson by steamer from New York to Boston. During the trip, Besse (1874) describes how he acceded to the wishes of the crew: "...by special request of some of the officers, we gave a short lecture and free exhibition in the magnificent parlor of the boat, with which that vast crowd seemed filled with wonder." They arrived in Boston on July 18, 1871, but upon arrival at the Temple House the children died. Minnie, who had begun vomiting nearly a week earlier, went into convulsions and stopped breathing in the afternoon. Dr. Besse (1874) writes of the brief revival that ensued and the death of Mina that followed:

> She was dead to all appearance, without a struggle, and looked as if sleeping pleasantly, in which condition she remained for one hour and forty-five minutes, when she commenced gasping for breath, and artificial means was resorted to restore respiration. This gasping continued at short intervals until 7:15 when she gave the last gasp. After this Mina, who had been perfectly well, to all appearance, until Minnie stopped breathing, showed signs of uneasiness, and continued sinking very rapidly and died at 8:15, just one hour from the time that Minnie gave the last gasp for breath. They both died very easy, and looked as if going into a pleasant sleep and never gave a struggle, and now they are quiet and lovely to look upon in death as they always were in life. The two souls have passed from the one body to the God that gave them this truly wonderful and curious body.

About twenty-four hours after death, Dr. Besse and his colleagues in Boston had a plaster cast made of the Finley twins that is still on display at the Mütter Museum in Philadelphia. The body was then injected with preservative fluid by Dr. F.S. Ainsworth and Dr. C.B. Porter. Although they were said to have distinct circulatory systems, it is recorded that the fluid "passed very readily from the aorta of the largest child into all the vessels of the smaller" (Besse 1874).

Although it has been reported that an autopsy was not allowed, a post-mortem examination was conducted thirty-eight hours after death by the doctors who embalmed the body. The results, presented before the Boston Society for Medical Improvement by Dr. Calvin Ellis on July 24, 1871, revealed that the spines were continuous at the lower portion and united with the fully developed pelvis. The lungs were more subdivided than usual and both livers had a number of supplementary lobules and fissures. Only a single bladder was found and the kidneys were reported to be larger than average. Three cysts were found in the abdomen. The twins had one uterus and a single pair of fallopian tubes and ovaries. The small intestines were fused and measured thirteen feet three inches in one child and seven feet ten inches in the other, leading to a single twenty-five-inch large intestine. The fused leg was shown to consist of a femur, two tibiae, and two fibulae. The spines were determined to be fused at the first sacral vertebra. The body measured twenty-nine inches in length. Dr. Ellis writes, "No more complete examination of the skeleton could be made, as the body was removed" (Besse 1874).

After the autopsy, the body of Minnie and Mina was placed in an alcohol-filled casket with windows through which it could be seen. The casket was taken home by the parents and the girls were buried. A verse in *Diploteratology* includes the stanza, "A mother's care is no more needed/To allay the rising moan;/And though she has to leave them,/They can never be alone" (Besse 1874).

### Foglia, Giuseppina and Maria Santina. *Twentieth Century.*

Born in Italy in 1959 joined at the base of their spines. Separated in Turin at age six. "Am I really myself?" asked Giuseppina after the operation, commenting to her sister, "You're so far away!" (Wallace and Wallace 1978)

### Foscott (Foscote), Fair Maidens of. *Unknown date.*

Female conjoined twins whose portraits, commented on by Samuel Pepys in 1668, can still be seen in the Norton St. Philip Church in Somerset, England (Bondeson 2000).

## Freak.

*Perhaps, then, the very word "Freak" is as obsolete as the Freak show itself, and I should be searching for some other term, less tarnished and offensive. God knows, there are plenty: oddities, malformations, abnormalities, anomalies, mutants, mistakes of nature, monsters, monstrosities, sports, "trange people," "very special people," and "phenomènes." "Monsters" and "monstrosities" were until very recently the standard terms used in medical treatises on the subject, and "monster"is the oldest word in our tongue for human anomalies.* — Leslie Fiedler (1978)

*"Freak" is a frame of mind, a set of practices, a way of thinking about and presenting people. It is not a person but the enactment of a tradition, the performance of a stylized presentation.* — Robert Bogdan (1996)

The word "freak" is a voluntary sign of nonconformity for some and an intolerable slur for others, writes Rachel Adams (1996). To think of it another way, "freak" is a category invented by communities unable to arrive at more imaginative ways of accommodating the great range of human physical variation (Adams 1996).

In the context of unusual bodies, the word is offensive to some people, but was the preferred term in the amusement industry — even by the exhibits themselves — until the end of the 1930s. "Human exhibits were not offended by the term because they did not take the nouns people used to refer to them seriously. Their main concern was to make money. Any designation that facilitated profit was acceptable," Robert Bogdan points out (1996). Leslie Fiedler (1978) titled his book *Freaks*, while pointing out that the name is rejected by the physiologically deviant humans to whom it has been applied because it reminds them of their long exclusion and exploitation by "normal" humans. Elizabeth Grosz explains why she uses the term in her writing: "Like a series of other negative labels ('queer' comes most clearly to mind), it is a term whose use may function as an act of defiance, a political gesture of self-determination. For this reason I prefer it to euphemistic substitutes: it makes clear that there are very real and concrete political effects for those thus labeled, and a clear political reaction is implied by those who use it as a mode of self-definition" (Bogdan 1996).

*See also* Monstrosity

## Freak Show.

"Freak shows," the formally organized exhibition of people with alleged physical, mental, or behavioral difference at circuses, fairs, carnivals, and other amusement venues, was once an accepted, popular, and lucrative practice in the United States. There is no record of these shows being attacked as offensive until well into the twentieth century. Today, they are on the fringe of society, seen by many as crude, rude, and exploitive. The few remaining freak shows are only the seedy vestiges of a once gala practice" (Bogdan 1996).

*See also* Exhibition

## *Freaks.*

*For pure sensationalism "Freaks" tops any picture yet produced. It's more fantastic and grotesque than any shocker every written.* — From a review of the film by Louella Parsons

A 1932 film directed by Tod Browning and suggested by the Tod Robbins story "Spurs." It was poorly received at the time, with theater owners canceling bookings and members of the P.T.A. and other organizations registering their protest (Fiedler 1978). The film was banned outright in Great Britain and was removed from distribution by MGM. Since its re-release in 1962, *Freaks* has reached the status of a cult classic. It begins with the words, "Never again will such a story be filmed, as modern science and teratology is rapidly eliminating such blunders of nature from the world." But Rachel Adams (1996) explains that the epigraph was not

THE STORY OF THE LOVE LIFE OF THE SIDESHOW

DWAIN ESPER PRESENTS

FREAKS

LOUELLA PARSONS *SAYS—*
FOR PURE SENSATIONALISM "FREAKS" TOPS ANY PICTURE
YET PRODUCED. IT'S MORE FANTASTIC AND GROTESQUE
THAN ANY SHOCKER EVER WRITTEN

EXCLUSIVE FOREIGN DISTRIBUTION CONTROLLED BY
EXCELSIOR PICT. CORP.
NEW YORK 19, U.S.A.

**Poster ad for *Freaks*, 1932. Courtesy of Becker Collection, Syracuse University Library, Department of Special Collections.**

added until distribution rights were sold to Dwain Esper in the 1940s: "Although the frame-up praises the accomplishments of 'modern science' for 'eliminating such blunders from the world,' this was never a position endorsed by Browning's version of the story, which is uninterested in pathologizing the freaks by describing their conditions in medical terms. Instead, its critique is directed at the social context that discriminates against the disabled, turning them into targets of laughter or abuse."

The story line involves the midget Hans falling in love with trapeze artist Cleopatra, who contrives to marry him for his money. After they wed, Cleopatra and her strongman lover begin poisoning Hans. The other freaks in the circus become suspicious and, following their "code," kill the strong-

man and mutilate Cleopatra, who then becomes the star of the freak show as a chicken-woman. The irony of the film is that rather than humanizing the freaks, it sets them apart and "reinscribes physical difference as a thing to be feared" (Hawkins 1996). Described as having their own code of ethics hints that the freaks have resorted to violence before and carrying the code out at the end of the show undermines the earlier "progressive" nature of the film in which the freaks are portrayed as harmless children and are shown behaving normally at home. In fact, turning Cleopatra into a freak as punishment for her immorality and greed plays into the idea of physical abnormalities as the visible sign of some hidden monstrosity, rather than the idea that freaks are merely accidents of nature as stated in the beginning of the film. The end attempts to undo some of the damage, but Hans' harmlessness comes at the expense of his being depicted as a baby rather than a man (Hawkins 1996). Among the stars of this revenge drama are conjoined twins Daisy and Violet Hilton; they used their own names, though the twins in the original script were named "Rosie" and "Mamie" (Adams 1996).

*Freaks* had a profound effect on its viewers, including Leslie Fiedler, who called his book of the same name a belated tribute to the film and its director, and Diane Arbus, who viewed it again and again as she began her photographic documentation of social marginality (Adams 1996). The film and Arbus' photographs allow viewers an extended gaze that allows them to overcome their initial shock of the extraordinary body and invest the freak with human qualities (Adams 1996).

***See also Chained for Life***

## Freeman, John Nelson and James Edward. *Twentieth Century.*

Conjoined twin boys born in Youngstown, Ohio, in April 1957. They were separated and known to be living in 1978, with John having settled in Kinsman, Ohio, and Jim having served in the Army.

## Frequency.

*The notoriety surrounding conjoined twins' deliveries masks their rarity.* — Nancy Segal

Conjoined twins occur once in every 40,000 to 100,000 births, but only once in every 200,000 *live* births. Their scarcity may be due to spontaneous abortion. Among those delivered at term, 40 to 60 percent are stillborn and 35 percent survive only one day. The newborn survival rate varies between 5 and 25 percent, although not all pairs survive the first year and beyond (Segal 1999). An average of one pair of every 200 delivered identical twins are conjoined and they are more often female than male. The ratio is M3:F7, according to Bergsma (1979). There are some forty live cases of conjoined twins born each year in the U.S. (Wallis 1996). There are fewer than a dozen pairs of conjoined twins currently living in the U.S. and, according to the BBC, probably fewer than a dozen *adult* pairs living in the world today.

The prevalence of conjoined twins is higher in Africa and India than in the rest of the world.

> Although this accident of nature is rare, world population rates mean it may happen far more often than we suppose. Experts agree that the incidence of conjoined twins is around one in 50,000, but 60 percent die before or during birth so the true incidence is more like one in 200,000. With 140 million babies born worldwide each year, that works out at 700 conjoined twins annually, or two pairs a day somewhere in the world. Perhaps the reason we don't hear more about them is that 90 percent of all babies are born in the Third World (where conjoined twins are genetically more likely to occur) [Edge 2000].

In their paper "Epidemic of Conjoined Twins in Southern Africa?," Bhettay, Nelson, and Beighton (1975) suggest that an environmental agent may precipitate the development of conjoined twins. They point out that five sets of conjoined twins were born in southern Africa in the first half of 1974 — three sets in Capetown hospitals alone. Bhettay et al. studied photographs and radiographs of the abnormal infants. Their very tentative hypothesis is a nationwide infectious epidemic or other diffuse factor:

> We suggest that conjoined twinning may be the result of the interactions of an environmental agent and a latent genetic predisposition, acting at a crucial stage of fission of the embryo [Bhettay et al. 1975].

The researchers note that the incidence of conjoined twins is probably under-reported, since many are stillborn and most surveys include only live births. Bergsma (1979) compares the occurrence of .06/1,000 live conjoined births in India and Africa to the rate of .004/1,000 live births in Europe and the Americas.

Conjoined twinning remains a rare condition: "Whatever the etiology of conjoining may be, it is certainly not a new dominant mutation" (Bhettay et al. 1975). Dudley Wilson (1993) found underreporting to be the norm historically, too: "Many more cases have never been recorded, often because they took place among the upper classes of society where such births were commonly either concealed or quietly disposed of."

*See also* Survival rates

### Galyon, Ronnie and Donnie.
*Twentieth Century.*

Born on October 28, 1951, in Dayton, Ohio, at eleven and a half pounds, the Galyons were rejected by their mother and raised by their father and stepmother Mary. The twin boys are joined at the chest and stomach and have four arms and four legs, but only a single navel, bladder, rectum, and penis (Hall 1991). They spent the first twenty months of their lives in the hospital undergoing a battery of tests and were not believed to be educable. The boys learned to walk at twenty-nine months. They have participated since childhood in many activities, including baseball (at which Ronnie is better), hunting (with Donnie being the better shot), swimming, and fishing.

Ronnie and Donnie's father managed their exhibit to the public as children, since the boys were hounded by the curious anyway. He allowed the boys to be observed through the window of a trailer. Carnival patron Jeff Langley (1997) remembers:

> I saw them twenty-five years ago when they were on display with the Bill Hames Show. A large picture window allowed a good view of the living room of Ronnie and Donnie's trailer, but the room was empty when my friends and I looked in-

side. Soon, we heard the sound of a buffalo stampede pounding against the floor of the trailer. Ronnie and Donnie came rumblin', bumblin', stumblin', fumblin' into the living room. They wore tiny T-shirts cut off to expose their connection at the abdomen. They turned to watch TV, paying no attention to us.

The twins later toured with a circus, mainly in Mexico and South America, and were said to have large numbers of female admirers. Ronnie and Donnie have two Social Security numbers and two voter registration cards, but only a single passport. Ronnie is described as good-natured, allowing the crankier Donnie to get his way. They were reported to have the occasional fist fight (Langley 1997). They sleep on a double-bed, with Ronnie, the bigger of the two, on the bottom. They have seven siblings and regret not being able to drive.

The Galyons currently rival the Krivoshlyapova sisters as the oldest living conjoined twins. They are retired from show business and live in the Midwestern U.S., where they live on their own in a house they purchased with their earnings. They did appear on an episode of Jerry Springer in 1996 or 1997, where they discussed their childhood, their family, and their current life. When asked if they would like to be separated, the twins have explained that they were born this way and understand that they will die together. They hope to outlive Chang and Eng Bunker. The Galyons keep the location of their home from the public, since they have been both vandalized and harassed.

*See also* Krivoshlyapova, Masha and Dasha

### Garcia, Gabrielle and Michaela.
*Twentieth Century.*

*It's a sad thing to see my children go through this, and to see my wife go through this, but you have to remain strong.*—Angel Garcia

Conjoined twin girls born at Loma Linda Medical Center in California, in February 1998, to Karen Crowe and Angel Garcia of Barstow. Delivered by Cesarean section at almost 38 weeks gestation, they are joined side to side (parapagus) and share a single pair of legs, as well as a single lower intestine, kidney, bladder, and possibly lower spine. Their condition was revealed by ultrasound at thirteen and a half weeks, but their mother declined an abortion. As she put it, "I'm not going to play God. If God takes my babies, that's up to him. I had to give them a chance of life, whether they are crippled or not. Either they will survive or not" (Rare Conjoined Twins Born 1998). The hospital released a statement that once the survival of the twins was assured, they would be evaluated and surgical separation deferred for three to six months. Neonatologist Dr. Gerald Nystrom explained the difficulty: "The biggest internal problem is that the two have a single, centrally located kidney. Because it appears to be large and structured more like it was trying to be two kidneys, there was a possibility that the organ — and therefore the girls — could be separated. However, if kidney separation were to fail, perhaps both babies would die" (Rare Conjoined Twins Born 1998). They were separated at eight months of age.

## Gender.

*United twins are never of different sexes, and all illustrations to the contrary are creations of the imagination, in which the old writers were fond of indulging.* — Dr. Robert P. Harris (1892)

Conjoined twins are always identical twins, so they are therefore the same gender. In at least one case of separation surgery, a single penis was given to one twin while a vagina was created for the other, resulting in separated twins of different genders. And in a case of conjoined twins born in 1957, confusion was caused by pseudohermaphroditism in one of the twins (Segal 1999). But claims by a male like Laloo that his parasitic twin was female were made just to heighten publicity. The premise of conjoined twins of different genders has been employed fic-

tionally for centuries. Leslie Fiedler (1978) refers to a sixteenth-century broadside about legendary twins "John" and "Joan." Fiedler also points out that journalistic accounts of female conjoined twins, more often than male, are laden with terms of endearment that betray a curious kind of affection.

*See also* **Htut, Lin and Win; Laloo**

## Gérard Brothers. *Eighteenth Century.*

Conjoined boys born in Beauvais, Oise, France, with two penises and no anus. They were autopsied and found to have two esophagi leading to a single stomach, liver, and set of intestines. They had one bladder, but two urethra (Harris 1892).

## Gibb, Mary Rae and Margaret Stratton. *Twentieth Century.*

*They are two of the nicest people you ever met in your life.* — Dr. Frank Lahey

Female conjoined twins born in Gloucester, Massachusetts, on May 20, 1912, to John R. and Margaret H. Gibb. They became known as the "Holyoke Twins" and were joined at the base of the spine above the buttocks. They partially shared a circulatory system and had a single anus, but had two vaginas. The girls both had brown hair and blue eyes, but distinct personalities, with Mary more easy-going and Margaret a worrier. Margaret was described as thin and Mary as stout. Margaret was the conversationalist of the pair, whose nicknames were "Maggie" and "Puddin." The girls did not share illnesses or transmit physical pain to each other. Their parents decided against separation surgery when the twins were three. They were tutored at home until age twelve. At thirteen, they were exhibited for one day by Dave Rosen at Coney Island, New York, but the impresario was charged with employing minors. "Rosen avoided trouble by successfully arguing that the girls were still under the custody of their father. While they did return home for awhile because

**Mary and Margaret Gibb with their mother. Photo courtesy of the Mütter Museum, College of Physicians of Philadelphia.**

they were shamed by the publicity of their possible separation, they eventually returned" (Stanton 1997). Their father launched their vaudeville career the following year (1927) and always saw to it that they exercised to keep in shape. The twins sang, danced, and played the piano, famous for their "Seein' Double" act. They performed at G.B. Ten Eyck's Gaiety Theater in Trenton, New Jersey, in November 1927; in Loew's theaters for two years under the management of Terry Turner; and on the Keith circuit for four years.

In August 1928, Mary and Margaret were rumored to be considering surgical separation, possibly because Mary had a suitor. They were admitted to New York's Park West Hospital, where the surgery was to be performed by chief surgeon Francis P. Weston. Three days later, amid a clamor of publicity and leaks of confidential information, hospital director Harold M. Mays called off the operation and the sisters never again pursued it. In 1930, they boarded the ocean liner *Majestic* for a European tour, garnering some publicity by attempting to sail on a single passenger ticket, a request denied by the White Star line who based their decision on the number of meals they would consume. The American Guild of Variety Artists similarly decided that each twin had to pay union dues. They appeared in France, Belgium, and Switzerland. In 1933, the Gibb sisters participated in Robert Ripley's "Believe It or Not" Odditorium at the Century of Progress Exposition in Chicago. From 1934 to 1941, the Gibbs toured with the Cole Brothers circus, the Ringling Brothers and Barnum & Bailey circus, and the United Shows of America carnival. It was while appearing with the latter in 1936 that they had a double date with their male counterparts, the Godino brothers, who died later that year.

They were billed as the only American-born joined-together twins in the history of the nation and signed autographs "America's Siamese Twins." In 1942 at the age of twenty-nine, the Gibb sisters returned to Holyoke, where they opened the Mary-Margaret Gift Shoppe at their home on Portland Street, where they lived with their widowed mother. They sold cards, novelties, vases, gifts, and baby clothes they made themselves. They retired in March 1949, afterward spending their time watching television, knitting, and playing cards. Mary grew heavier and was shorter than her sister. Margaret had surgery for a kidney stone in 1946 and for an abdominal tumor in 1953, both operations being performed by Dr. Frank Lahey at New England Deaconess

Hospital in Boston. The Gibb twins died within two minutes of each other at Holyoke Hospital on January 8, 1967, at the age of fifty-four. Their physician Dr. John Appel reported that death was due to cancer which had begun in Margaret's bladder and had spread to both girls' lungs, as confirmed by autopsy. They also suffered from hypertension and heart disease for ten years. At the twins' request, their bodies were not separated after death. Pathologist H. Paul Wakefield was able to observe small connected arterial branches, but did not do a microscopic examination of the connected tissue. The bodies were released to the Alger Funeral Home and were buried in Holyoke's Forestdale Cemetery in a custom-made coffin.

## Gionti, Maria and Lucia. *Twentieth Century.*

Conjoined twin girls born in the U.S. on August 3, 1998. They lived only two days.

## Godino, Simplicio and Lucio. *Twentieth Century.*

Born on the island of Samar in the Philippines in 1908, the boys were joined at the back by a strip of cartilage. They were brought to the U.S. for exhibition as the "Samar United Twins" before they were ten years old. Louis Sullivan of the American Museum of Natural History examined the twins on July 31, 1918, after the Society for the Prevention of Cruelty to Children questioned their display in Coney Island without a proper guardian. Sullivan reported in the *American Journal of Physical Anthropology* that the twins were intelligent, active, and well-educated, with a good command of the English language. Lucio was considered the leader and Simplicio the follower (Drimmer 1973). The guardianship controversy resulted in the Godinos' adoption by the commissioner of the Philippines to the U.S., multi-millionaire Tecodoro (Teodore)

The Godino twins as young boys. From Sullivan, L.R. 1919. "The 'Samar' United Twins." In *American Journal of Physical Anthropology* 2: 23. Reprinted by permission of Wiley-Liss, a subsidiary of John Wiley & Sons, Inc.

Yanco. Under his care, they continued their education in the U.S. and at home and developed their interests in tennis, golf, roller skating, and swimming. Yanco built a gymnasium for them on his estate and engaged the finest Eastern artists to give them musical training. They learned to play four or five musical instruments and to speak five languages. They later learned to ride a motorcycle and drive a car. In fact, they each had a car with the steering column on the respective side, but Lucio had the better arrangement, since in the Philippines the cars passed each other on the left as in England.

The twins headed a band of fourteen native instrumentalists called the *All Filipino Band*, that toured around the world, including the U.S. The press reported their popularity with women, noting the amount of fan mail they received and the mobs that

Lucio and Simplicio Godino with their wives. From Newman, H.H. 1931. "Differences Between Conjoined Twins." In *Journal of Heredity* 22: 201. Courtesy of Oxford University Press.

besieged them backstage and at their hotels. They were described as well-educated, cultivated, urbane gentlemen and reporters credited their popularity to their charm and engaging personalities, rather than their wealth. When they reached the age of twenty-one, they married Filipino sisters Natividad and Victorina Matos in Manila. When they returned to America with their wives, the four became a headline act on vaudeville. In what may have been played up as a publicity stunt, Lucio was arrested for traffic violations in 1929, but the charges were dropped rather than punishing the innocent twin. The Godino brothers roller-skated as part of their act (Kobel 1959) and a photograph of them in the rink appears in Luigi Gedda's *Twins in History and Science*. They were also the

research and pictorial subjects of a 1928 paper about identical twins by H.H. Newman.

In 1936, Lucio was admitted to a New York hospital with pneumonia. Simplicio showed no symptoms, but did have a premonition as he lay in the hospital two weeks later. He described it to reporters: "I was drowsing, not expecting anything, when all at once a feeling came over me that I can't describe. It was just a — a sensation ... I leaned over to speak to Lucio about it. As I did so, I touched his body. It was cold. I rang the bell. When the nurse came I told her my brother was dead" (Drimmer 1973). After Lucio's death, surgeons separated Simplicio within the hour and declared the operation a success. Simplicio seemed to be improving and was in good spirits, but died eleven days later of what was revealed to be spinal meningitis.

## Gonzales, Bessie and Doris.
*Twentieth Century.*

Craniopagus conjoined twin girls born in Honduras on September 23, 1995, to Doris Gonzales Quiroz. Preparation for separation began that winter and included five surgeries to separate thousands of blood vessels and a small amount of brain tissue. Shunts were planted to drain their shared vena cava. Skin expanders were inserted and filled to help close the incision. A week before the planned date of the surgery, Doris had heart failure, but the separation went ahead, led by Dr. Marion Walker. The twins were separated in September 1996 at Primary Children's Medical Center in Salt Lake City, Utah, weighing twenty pounds each. Additional surgeries and physical therapy will be necessary and the effects of possible brain damage may surface. Until bone grafts are performed to complete their skulls, the twins must wear helmets to prevent brain injury.

**Great Ormond Street Hospital.**

Britain's "center of excellence" for separating conjoined twins. Separations have almost become routine for Dr. Lewis Spitz and Dr. Edward Kiely. Dr. Spitz says, "My colleagues and I have accumulated experience of conjoined twins at Great Ormond Street.... Surgical separation of conjoined twins is a major undertaking. It requires careful and meticulous planning, involving two completely separate and dedicated teams of specialists, nurses and ancillary staff" (Edge 2000).

*See also* Abdulrehman, Hassan and Hussein; Holton, Katie and Eilish; Mc-Donnell, Niamh and Aoife; Smith, Natasha and Courtney

**Grown Together Twins** *see* **Blazek, Rosa and Josefa**

**Guadalupe Sisters.** *Twentieth Century.*

Female conjoined twins born in Mexico in 1998.

**Hall, Ward** *see* **"World's Strangest Babies"**

**Hansen, Lisa and Elisa.** *Twentieth Century.*

Twin girls born to David and Patricia Hansen on October 18, 1979, in Ogden, Utah, joined at the top of the head. They were quickly transported to Salt Lake City, where a fund was established to help defray medical bills of roughly $1,000 a day. They were separated on May 30, 1981, at the University of Utah Medical Center, with as many as eleven doctors working on them at one time. Dr. Stephen Minton described the moment of separation: "There was an exhilarating feeling of accomplishment. I was extremely excited at that moment" (Beecham 1979). Neurosurgeons said they were able to separate the brains easily, but could not yet assess possible brain damage. Both twins survived the sixteen-and-a-half-hour operation.

**Hartley, Daniel Kaye and Donald Ray.** *Twentieth Century.*

Conjoined twin boys born at the James Whitcomb Riley Hospital in Indianapolis on December 12, 1953, by Cesarean section to Mrs. Cecil Hartley of Washington, Indiana. It was her fifth pregnancy and the twins were issued a single birth certificate, but were each baptized. The boys had two heads, four arms, two spines, two hearts, and two stomachs. They shared a single fused pelvis, a common intestinal tract, a single set of lungs, and one pair of legs. Separation was considered, but ruled out. Daniel had a harelip, a poor appetite, and bad circulation. One of the twins showed signs of developing intelligence, but the other didn't (Edwards 1961). Bondeson (2000) writes, "The parents were poor, but nevertheless refused all the intrusive attempts from the media to capitalize on the twins." The Hartleys turned down an offer of $1,000 a week to exhibit the twins. By the age of two months, the boys were living at home, but in 1954 at the age of four months they developed pneumonia and died.

**Helen and Judith** *see* **Hungarian Sisters**

**Hensel, Abigail Lauren and Brittany Lee.** *Twentieth Century.*

*Abigail and Brittany hop into a waiting car. Inside, Mom gets two kisses and one hug.* — Kenneth Miller (1996)

Dicephalus female twins born in Minnesota on March 7, 1990, to Mike and Patty Hensel. Initially, the Hensels were shocked, but that feeling was followed by acceptance and absolute devotion (Miller 1996). The twins have two heads, two arms (a third vestigial arm was removed at four months), and two legs. They are able to coordinate their movements even though each controls one side of the body, so they are able to walk, run, swim, ride a bicycle, and shuffle cards. They found learning to ride a bike hard because of the balance required — pedaling together came naturally. The girls refer to themselves as individuals and have very distinct personalities, which their parents encourage. "I don't have two heads," declares Abby (Miller 1996), the twin on their left. At the same time, they often speak and act in unison and give indications that they can read each other's thoughts. Their teacher Connie Stahlke always gives the twins the option to work individually or to collaborate, but they each take their own tests and do not cheat even though they could do so easily. They have stated emphatically from an early age that they do not intend to be separated (Miller 1996).

They were delivered by a team of eight and none of the medical staff were expecting conjoined twins. Doctors dismissed Mike's hearing two heartbeats at one point and reason in hindsight that the girls' heads must have been aligned on the sonogram (Wallis 1996). Because of the breech position, a Cesarean section was performed. The doctors in the delivery room were taken aback: "We all stood in silence for about thirty seconds. It was extremely silent," recalls Dr. Joy Westerdahl (Wallis 1996). Two birth certificates were completed, but both read "first" as the order of birth. The twins were transported to the nearby children's hospital, where their aunt Sandy Fiecke acted as a surrogate for Patty, who remained bedridden with high blood pressure at the community hospital where she worked and gave birth. Sandy held and fed the girls, while Mike relayed the news to family and friends: "It's pretty hard to explain to your folks how the kids were put together," he said (Wallis 1996).

Mike and Patty were stunned at first, then depressed for a time wondering about the babies' health and whether they would be able to care for them. Their worries vanished and their optimism returned the first time they bathed the twins. Their pediatrician Dr. Joy Westerdahl explains that they are two people above the waistline and one below (Miller 1996). Their daycare provider Nancy Oltrogge helped the girls learn to walk at fifteen months and remembers, "They were a little wobbly because they were top-heavy. But once they got it. they just took off" (Miller 1996). No one instructed them about who should move which foot when. "They knew what to do," says Oltrogge (Wallis 1996). If they were to be separated, they would be unable to walk, since they could not support prosthetic limbs. And their would be other costs, as their father describes: "They'd be in surgery for years, suffering all the time, and then they'd have half a body each" (Miller 1996). Dr. Benjamin Carson of Johns Hopkins Children's Center agrees, "It would make them invalids.... And there would be major emotional and psychological trauma. They've grown together. That's their way of life" (Miller 1996). Wallis (1996) points out that the twins' smiling faces and apparent good health seem a rebuke to the current medical trend of attempting to surgically separate ever more complex conjoined twins, even if one has to be sacrificed.

The girls' condition is extremely rare, one of only four sets of surviving twins in recorded history sharing an undivided torso and two legs (Miller 1996). The Hensel twins have two hearts, two stomachs, three lungs, and a single set of organs below the waist. They have a long narrow region of shared sensation along their back (Wallis 1996). Their health is generally good, but they have suffered from pneumonia in Brittany's lung and a kidney infection. Abby can take medicine for Brittany, who tends to get more colds. The twins are pleased that they only need one set of vaccinations (Wallis 1996). Their tastes are different, so Brittany supplies their body with calcium, since Abby doesn't like milk. Their temperaments are very different, but they don't seem to have developed the oppositional personalities for which other conjoined twins were known (Wright 1997). Abby has a voracious appetite and is more of a leader. Brittany is more reflective and academically quicker (Miller 1996). It was reported in *Life* magazine (Miller 1998) that Brittany is more artistic and better at spelling, with Abby better at math and more aggressive.

But their lives require constant cooperation, since disagreement about where to go leaves them unable to move and misbehavior by one gets both of them sent to their room. They make decisions by flipping a coin, taking turns, or allowing their parents to make a ruling (Jussim 2001). Their unique coordination is a mystery, even to their physician Dr. Westerdahl, who asks, "How do they coordinate upper-body motion like clapping hands? I don't know if we can ever answer that" (Wallis 1996). "The paradoxes of the twins' lives are metaphysical as well as medical. They raise far-reaching questions about human nature: What is individuality? How sharp are the boundaries of the self? How essential is privacy to happiness? Is there such a thing as mental telepathy?" (Miller 1996). Wallis (1996) reports that the twins love to share a joke and reasons, "A puckish sense of humor is one of their best tools for contending with all the other sharing they must do day in and day out — a sharing of a more profound and intimate nature than most of us can imagine." The girls experience hunger and the urge to urinate and sleep separately. Abby takes the right-hand parts and Brittany the left during their piano lessons.

Abby and Brittany are growing up in a small town in the Midwest on twenty acres of land with dogs, cats, five cows, and a horse (Miller 1998). They have a brother DaKota (two years younger) and a sister Morgan (four years younger). "They are lucky not only in that the random conjunction of their inner organs happened in a way that made them fit for prolonged life, but also in that they were born into a particularly harmonic family in a small rural town," writes Bondeson (2000). They attend a Lutheran school with sixty-seven students (Miller 1996). Their teacher uses them as a model of teamwork. Though the city in which they live in Minnesota is undisclosed to maintain their privacy, these twins have appeared on *Oprah* and *Dateline* and have been featured in *Time* and *Life* magazines. In December 1994, surviving separated dicephalous twin Eilish Holton visited the Hensels with her parents and the meeting was taped for ABC's *20/20* (Wallis 1996). Miller (1996) writes, "…these little girls are a living textbook on camaraderie and compromise, on dignity and flexibility, on the subtler varieties of freedom." Freedom and privacy will be hard to come by as they enter their teenage years. Their father describes, "They won't have the same chances as other girls. They're goodlooking and it will be tough on them" (Miller 1996). In 1998, they photographed their favorite people and things for *Life* magazine. These included their parents and siblings, their favorite outfits, the family pets, their bicycle, the computer, eating watermelon, lying in the sun, and playing baseball. It would have been difficult to carry out their early career ambitions: Brittany wanted to be a pilot and Abby wanted to be a dentist, although Miller (1998) reports that both girls want to be doctors. The girls' lives are happy ones and their family reminds everyone not to feel sorry for them. "I just want people to know that they're two separate kids with their own personalities," says their mother. "If they had to be put together, I think they were put together perfectly" (Wallis 1996).

### Heteropagus.

A general term for unequal and symmetrical forms of conjoined twinning, also known as *duplicatas incompleta*. Includes parasitic twins.

***See also*** **Diplopagus; Parasitic twins**

### Hilton, Daisy and Violet. *Twentieth Century.*

*Headliners for three decades, Violet and Daisy Hilton have triumphed over hate, adversity and a goldfish-bowl existence to reach the top of their profession. They are not only beautiful but extremely talented, play numerous musical instruments and dance and sing.* — Advertising copy for the Hilton Sisters' appearances to promote *Chained for Life*

Conjoined twin girls born in Brighton, England, on February 5, 1908, weighing approximately six pounds each. Their union was said to be fleshy and cartilaginous, allowing freer movement as they grew. Surgery was deemed risky and wasn't performed. The pygopagus twins were reportedly sold at two weeks of age to the midwife Mary Hilton by their unmarried twenty-one-

Violet and Daisy Hilton, "United Twins." Courtesy of the Circus World Museum, Baraboo, Wisconsin.

year-old mother Kate Skinner. According to the twins, she repeated throughout their childhood, "Your mother gave you to me. I'm not your mother. Your mother was afraid when you were born and gave you to me when you were two weeks old. You must always do just as I say" (Hilton and Hilton 1996a). They entered show business before they were three years old, appearing at circuses, carnivals, and fairs. They were accompanied by Mary whom they called "Auntie," her successive husbands whom they addressed as "Sir," and Mary's daughter Edith. Models of the "Brighton United Twins" were displayed at Stewart's Waxwork in Edinburgh. By the age of five, they had toured Germany and Australia, and at age eight were brought to the U.S. to appear in the Johnny Jones Exposition Shows in Orlando, Florida.

In their biographies, the Hiltons claimed they had been shown no affection as children and had been physically and emotionally abused, although they had received an education and training in music, voice, and dance (Bogdan 1988). Auntie saw to this, although she refused to consider separating the twins, since this would take away her livelihood. In addition, Mary Hilton's third husband Mr. Green told them, "She'll never hit your faces. The public will not be so glad to pay to look at little Siamese twins with scarred faces" (Hilton and Hilton 1996a). In fact, they were kept from view of the public except when they were on exhibition (Hilton and Hilton 1996a). They were not allowed to play with other children and were often examined by doctors. They described, "How we loathed the sight of a hospital and the very bedside tone of a medical man's voice! We were punched and pinched and probed until we were almost crazy, and we always screamed and scratched and kicked" (Hilton and Hilton 1996a). By the time they were fifteen, the Hiltons were among the highest paid nightclub and vaudeville performers. As teenagers, the girls continued to wear

**Violet and Daisy Hilton with saxophones. Courtesy of the Mütter Museum, College of Physicians of Philadelphia.**

As Auntie aged, they were managed by Edith and her husband Meyer Rothbaum (calling himself Meyer Meyers), who encouraged them to take up the saxophone and ukulele. When Auntie died, the twins did not grieve but did regret and fear that they were now at the mercy of the Meyerses, who claimed Edith's mother had willed them the twins (Bogdan 1988). Because the twins had tried to run away during the funeral, the Meyerses never let them out of their sight, threatening to put them in an institution if they misbehaved. Meyer Meyers launched Violet and Daisy into a vaudeville tour in the mid–1920s, when they were teenagers. On the vaudeville circuit they met Bob Hope, Eddie Cantor, Bing Crosby, Sophie Tucker, and Harry Houdini. Their performances brought in as much as $5,000 a week.

The two had differing personalities, with Violet more passive than the independent Daisy (Drimmer 1997). As the twins explained, "…we are believed to share identical thrills, pains and even diseases. The truth is that we are as different in our reactions as day and night. I, Violet, often weep over something which makes my sister chuckle. I had whooping cough a year and half before Daisy. We did not even catch the measles from each other!" (Hilton and Hilton 1996a). It was only after prolonged suffering — such as from a headache — that any pain was experienced by the other twin. The biographical booklet sold at their performances portrayed them as orphans of an English Army officer and indicated that the Meyerses were their aunt and uncle. According to the story, their mother had died a year after their birth and their father had fallen in battle in Belgium.

long curls, bows in their hair, and identical childish dresses (Drimmer 1997). Though their shows were bringing in thousands of dollars, they only had seventy-five cents between them.

The sisters spent twenty years singing, dancing, and playing the violin, piano, and clarinet. Robert Bogdan (1988) said, "…the Hilton Sisters were presented as attractive, engaging celebrities who were exceptionally talented, charming, happy, and normal in every way except for one physical inconvenience: in their case, being born joined at the buttocks…. Although their presentation downplayed the difference that made them an attraction — their attachment — and flaunted their normal attributes, for their patrons as well as the rest of society their difference was what defined them."

Violet and Daisy Hilton, seated. From Newman, H.H. 1931. "Differences Between Conjoined Twins." In *Journal of Heredity* 22: 203. Courtesy of Oxford University Press.

Their later autobiography contained smaller inconsistencies, such as the claim that Daisy had blond hair and green eyes and Violet had dark hair and hazel eyes. The souvenir booklet listed their hobbies, which were said to include cooking (they were reported to be vegetarians), sewing, playing sports (tennis, golf, handball, swimming, and boxing), raising pets, attending the theater, reading books, and conversing. Daisy wrote with her left hand and her writing sloped to the right; Violet was right-handed and her writing leaned to the left. The autobiography described Daisy as impulsive, imaginative, and talkative and Violet as quiet and more cautious (Hilton and Hilton 1996a). Their agent characterized Daisy as a romantic and Violet as a realist (Myers and Oliver n.d.).

One thing they both agreed on was the need for privacy. Violet offered (Wallace and Wallace 1978), "…we had learned how not to know what the other was doing unless it was our business to know it." She explained in further detail, "It is as though some Power, greater and stronger than ourselves, has given us this inner harmony to compensate for our being forced to live constantly as an entity. And that harmony has been with us through the years — a harmony that has amazed many who have known us" (Hilton and Hilton 1996). It was Harry Houdini who suggested to the twins that they make the best use of their imaginations. They moved and lived in harmony with each other. Their agent described, "Their movements are rhythmic. There seems to be a subtle telepathy between them. When Daisy steps, Violet steps too. Their physical conduct is graceful; there is no physiological confusion, no clumsiness of procedure" (Myers and Oliver n.d.). In fact, their physical connection was described in their *Souvenir and Life Story* as giving them much freedom of movement:

> For instance one of the girls may lie down in bed while the other is sitting up. There is not now no matter in what position — and there never has been since birth — the slightest pain in the region about the connecting strip. It affords the girls neither the slightest discomfort in itself nor in relation to their movements.

When they were not on tour, they lived a life of isolation in a $75,000 mansion in San Antonio, Texas, that had been designed by Frank Lloyd Wright. The home had been purchased by Meyers with the money the twins had earned, but they were forced to do the housekeeping whenever they were there (Hilton and Hilton 1996a). While on tour, they finally convinced Meyers to provide them with a private room, but were still not allowed suitors. They longed for companionship over the years and noted, "So much happened during those sad years when the audiences of the world believed us cheerful and carefree…. It wasn't easy to laugh while our hearts ached and yearned for freedom and love" (Hilton and Hilton 1996a). They received gifts and love letters from admirers as they toured the U.S., Europe, Central America, India, and Egypt, but Violet is quoted by their agent as wanting something special:

> In various cities where we have played, people have brought us many different kinds of vegetables, such as cucumbers, turnips and even watermelons, which have grown together. These have all been very interesting and we appreciate very much the thoughtfulness of those who have presented these oddities to us, but we would much more prefer to have a live "twin" pet [Myers and Oliver n.d.].

Instead, they had to be content with their Pekinese dog and some twenty cockatoos. They did convince Meyers to give them diamond bracelets, which they hoped to one day use in lieu of cash. They toured on the Marcus Loew circuit and the Orpheum circuit.

Their appearances were preceded by booking agent William Oliver, who saw to the advance publicity, including supplying suggestions for news articles and advertising tie-ins (for cars, shoes, restaurants, etc.) and publicity photographs to accompany them. Oliver's "Advance Campaign," distributed before their tour suggested that theatres in which the girls were to appear work with local newspapers to host events such as twin parties and matinees for children. Oliver offered venues an exclusive engagement, with the twins seen publicly only on introduction to the mayor, visits to the hospital, and "run-ins" with local law enforcement (for instance, refusing to pay two train fares). No medical examinations were to be permitted. In the promotional literature, Oliver billed the Hiltons as "The only living Siamese twins in the world," and described them as "charming entertainers of magnetic and pleasing personalities, who will captivate everyone,"

**Violet and Daisy Hilton on point in their ballet costumes. Photo courtesy of the Mütter Museum, College of Physicians of Philadelphia.**

reminding their promoters "that there is nothing repulsive nor objectionable in the appearance or performance of these sweet girls." Oliver's wife-to-be felt otherwise.

An autographed picture they gave Oliver, signed "with love," resulted in their being sued by his fiancée for $250,000 for supposedly alienating his affections. The allegation, which was dismissed, brought them to the office of lawyer Martin J. Arnold and it gave them the opportunity to confide in him about their situation, which they characterized as slavery. Arnold had them picked up from their music lesson later that afternoon and put them up in the St. Anthony Hotel until their own case was brought to trial a few days later in San Antonio's Nineteenth District Court. During these first few days of freedom from Meyers, Violet

and Daisy listened to the radio, read newspapers and magazines, used the telephone,
ate and wore what they wanted, had their
hair done, had cocktails, and smoked cigarettes (Hilton and Hilton 1996b). The twins
finally gained their independence at age
twenty-three, in 1931. Judge W.W. McCrory
awarded them their freedom, dissolving the
contracts they had been coerced to sign and
Meyers' guardianship (Drimmer 1997). Of
the $2 million they estimated they had earned
during their careers, they were awarded
$67,000 in bonds, $12,000 in cash, and
$20,000 in personal effects (Hilton and
Hilton 1996b).

The court decision had been followed
by a fuller social life, including rendezvous
with Daisy's suitors, Mexican musician Don
Galvan and later bandleader Jack Lewis, both
of whom proposed. Violet dated English
boxer Harry Mason and later became engaged to orchestra leader Maurice Lambert,
but their request for a marriage license was
denied on moral grounds in New York and
twenty other states despite their appeals. The
refusals cited "morality and decency" and "a
matter of public policy." *Time* reported that
Manhattan officials, represented by corpo-
rate counsel William C. Chanler, stated, "The
very idea of such a marriage is quite immoral
and indecent. I feel that a publicity stunt is
involved" (Pygopagus Marriage 1934). The
cities of Marion, Ohio, and Charles City,
Iowa, sent telegrams offering to allow the
marriage, but the offer was never taken up.
Allison Pingree (1996) reasons, "The power
behind the image of Daisy and Violet was
that they were both permanently single because they were permanently doubled. They
were already each other's 'other half.'"

The Hilton sisters appeared in Tod
Browning's controversial film *Freaks* in 1932.
During the shooting at the MGM Studios,
they were observed at the commissary by a
drunken F. Scott Fitzgerald, who was working as a screenwriter. When they picked up
the menu and one asked the other what she

Violet and Daisy Hilton wearing muffs. Courtesy
of the Mütter Museum, College of Physicians of
Philadelphia.

was going to eat, it unnerved Fitzgerald to
the point where he rushed outside to vomit.
His visceral reaction to the twins and their
fellow freaks was echoed by others on the
lot, and the entire cast of the film was forced
to eat at a special table outside the commissary (Adams 1996). The employees at the
studio would have been further horrified to
learn that the script called for a camera shot
of the twins' junction and a scene in which
it is evident that Daisy and Violet experience each other's erotic sensations (Adams
1996).

Violet and Daisy continued their career
under their own direction and billed their
act the "Hilton Sisters Revue." They continued to play musical instruments, and in
addition performed ballet and acted in
sketches (Drimmer 1997). They were depicted on the sheet music of the songs they
sang, including "I Wanna Go Where You

Go-Do What You Do, Then I'll Be Happy"
by Cliff Friend and "Me Too. Ho-Ho! Ha-
Ha!" by Harry Woods, Charles Tobias, and
Al Sherman. Their promotional literature
listed them at a weight of 166 pounds and a
height of four feet nine inches. E. Burke
Maloney, who interviewed them in 1934
when they were touring with the Sells-Floto
Circus, offers the following description:

> They were about twenty-five, with
> auburn hair and rather pretty in an ane-
> mic way. They had dabs of rouge high on
> the cheekbones and each mouth was a
> dash of vermilion. They were joined at
> the sides, just above the hips, and when
> they walked they were awkward and not
> pleasant to see. They had fielded the
> same questions so often all over the world
> that they gave answers almost before the
> question was finished [Maloney 1978].

Dancing partner James Walker Moore
did receive official permission to marry Violet and the ceremony — which their agent
promised would be a great publicity stunt —
was held at the Texas Centennial Exposition
in 1936 before 100,000 guests, but the marriage was later annulled. On September 17,
1941, Daisy wed dancer Harold Estep (stage
name Buddy Sawyer) in an unpublicized,
but still well-attended ceremony in Elmira,
New York, but he deserted her ten days later
and she filed for divorce.

In 1941, Robert Saudek published a
paper in which he compared the twins' handwriting. Saudek (1941) notes that although
their environment was necessarily much
more similar even than identical twins, their
handwriting was not. Daisy wrote slopingly
and with less pressure. Violet's writing was
more even and balanced. The size of the letters varied along with the writing angle. But
Saudek also observed several similarities and
comments on them: "Over against these differences there are a number of similarities,
e.g., considerable similarities between the
short and tall letters, wide spaces between
words and lines, speed, great diversity of
original letter formations, but above all a

certain instability of the linkage types. Such
similarities cannot be accidental; nor does
common schooling come into consideration
in this connection, since the handwriting of
each sister deviates extremely from the pen-
manship model of their school" (Saudek
1941).

The Hiltons again turned their attention to work but when their popularity fell
off Violet and Daisy settled in Miami and
in 1955 opened the *Hilton Sisters' Snack Bar*,
which was unsuccessful. They are also said
to have owned a hotel in Pittsburgh (Drimmer 1973). They returned to the stage via
the carnival circuit and acted in their second
movie: *Chained for Life* (1951). They made
their last public appearance at a North Carolina drive-in in 1962 when *Freaks* was re-
released. Their agent left them stranded and
broke, so they stayed for a couple of weeks
in a Monroe, North Carolina, hotel before
renting a place at Tanzy's Trailer Park. They
asked Charles Reid for a job at the nearby
Park-N-Shop. He agreed to hire them if
they stopped wearing so much make-up,
growing their nails, and dying their hair
(Tomlinson 1997). After Reid remodeled the
produce counters to form them into a "V"
and provided his new employees with red-
and-white checked shirts, Violet and Daisy
worked the 8 AM to 4:30 PM shift for seven
years. They moved into a house owned by
the Purcell United Methodist Church and
refused photographs and interviews, even
declining to speak with an Illinois expert
on conjoined twins who arrived in 1967.
They were active in the church, but preferred to attend the men's Sunday school
class, either because women asked them too
many uncomfortable questions or because it
was held on the ground floor (Tomlinson
1997).

The Hiltons died January 4, 1969, at
age sixty-one after contracting the Hong
Kong flu. Their bodies were found by a
neighbor lying on a heat grate in the hall-
way of their house. They had left no will,

no diary, and no apparent survivors (Bogdan 1988). The only unusual thing their employer found when cleaning out their house was an entire dresser filled with pocketbooks, each containing three or four dollars. Funeral arrangements for the Hiltons were made through the Hankins and Whittington Funeral Home and they were buried in a single casket at Forest Lawn Cemetery in Charlotte on January 8, with family and coworkers present. They share a tombstone with a Vietnam veteran named Troy Thompson and their epitaph reads, "Beloved Siamese Twins."

On May 3, 1994, a group of items associated with Daisy and Violet Hilton was auctioned by Christie's; the lot included an x-ray photograph, a postcard photo of the twins as infants, two adult publicity photos, and news articles announcing their birth and death. The twins are today the subject of the musical "Side Show."

***See also Chained for Life, Freaks!,*** **"Side Show," "Twenty Fingers, Twenty Toes"**

## Holton, Katie and Eilish. *Twentieth Century.*

> *Not only did we want to give them individuality and independence, but we felt we had to do it because the children were living a charmed existence in our little happy family which we knew couldn't last. We have a lovely memory of those three-and-a-half years with them together.*— Liam Holton

Dicephalus girls born in Dublin, Ireland, on August 24, 1988, to Liam and Mary Holton of Donadea, County Kildare. The Holtons did not know the twins were conjoined until the day before their birth. They accepted the babies completely as soon as they saw and touched them: "Although Liam acknowledges fears prior to the twins' birth that he and wife Mary would not be able to accept them, he adds, 'When we saw them and held them that just evaporated away…. Our emotions were just taken over

by the joy of seeing the little children alive and wanting to be held like all newborn babies'" (Myser and Clark 1998). Mary, however, was wary of how to hold them without hurting them and apprehensive about forming too close a bond in case they didn't survive. The family lived in a small village outside Dublin and the girls were treated by physician Patrick Deasy. They hoped for acceptance in the community and were not angry or bitter, viewing Katie and Eilish as normal children in a unique situation.

Katie and Eilish had very different personalities, with Eilish the more reserved. The twins were described in television documentaries, including an episode of ABC's *20/20* in the early 1990s and *Discovery Journal* on the Discovery Channel more recently. Joined at the chest, abdomen, and pelvis, they had a shared thoracic cavity and lower body, with a short third arm between their heads. Technically, they were classified as thoraco-omphalo-ischiopagus bipus twins. Although physical therapy improved their mobility as babies, they weren't expected to walk for some time because of their "top-heavy" condition. They appeared healthy and surgery was not pursued, although it was known that Katie had a heart malformation. Tests showed that each child had a heart, a set of lungs, and a separate spinal column. They shared a bladder and liver, a single set of kidneys, and much of the large intestine. In fact, the girls never learned to walk and continued to shuffle across the floor, meaning they were later confined to a wheelchair.

In the summer of 1991, Liam and Mary contacted hospitals in London, Toronto, and Philadelphia to inquire about separation surgery. Although the twins were more severely joined than any others that had been successfully separated, the mortality rate for the surgery drops significantly after the first few months of life. In December 1991, Dr. Lewis Spitz of the Great Ormond Street Hospital in London evaluated the twins and agreed to perform the surgery, since the chances were good that both girls would survive. The parents pointed out to interviewers that this was not a sacrifice surgery, in which one of the twins would be given a chance at a normal life at the expense of the other — they had equal chances of survival. In December 1992, the twins were brought to London to begin the three-month preparation for the surgery, including the insertion of tissue expanders. Katie and Eilish began losing weight and had to be tube-fed for the week before the surgery. They were prepared for the separation psychologically by rehearsing with two dolls adapted to look like them and attached by Velcro. On April 1, 1992, at age three, the girls underwent separation at the Great Ormond Street Hospital in a sixteen-hour operation. Katie survived for only three days after the operation, succumbing to heart failure. In possible sympathy, Eilish had also suffered a coronary arrest but recovered.

Eilish remained in intensive care for four weeks. Her massive wound was as painful as a third degree burn. She was in physical pain, but was also emotionally drained. Dr. Spitz was interviewed about the surgery on BBC2's "Conjoined Twins" and said, "Following separation Eilish was clearly devastated that her twin had disappeared and for one year after surgery would not talk to me." She was released from the hospital after four months. Eilish was at first quiet and withdrawn, but soon began to take on some of the playful qualities her sister Katie had exhibited. She began to laugh more, even though she had been the serious twin, prompting their parents to note that Katie remained with the family in spirit. She spoke of Katie occasionally, but as if she were an imaginary friend to chat with in the car on the way home from school (Donaghy 2000). "She has always had a strong sense of survival more than a sense of loss. She has come through so much, it's only natural that she would. From early on, she took a great

command of herself. She is very matter of fact about what happened and that has helped her but she is also very determined. We have never put any barriers in her way because she only would have shattered them," says Mary Holton (Donaghy 2000) about her daughter Eilish. The family visits Katie's grave every Sunday and sometimes wonder what she would be like if she were alive. "But there is no point in dwelling on the past," say their parents. "We just try to live in the here-and-now and we think in years to come that Eilish will appreciate the decision we made" (Donaghy 2000).

The Holtons do not regret their decision, explaining that they might have lost both of the girls because of Katie's weak heart. Although they wouldn't have operated if they had known the outcome, they would make the same decision knowing what they had (Donaghy 2000). During the separation, Eilish was given the vestigial arm, of which she was expected to gain some use with therapy. Doctors believed she would experience some liver and kidney problems. While the parents had been open with the media about the surgery for the good of medical science, they asked for privacy after it was over. The twins were the subject of two films produced by Mark Galloway for BBC's "First Tuesday" series: *Katie and Eilish: Siamese Twins* and the short follow-up, *Life Without Katie*. Eilish took her first steps at the age of five with the use of a prosthetic limb (Bondeson 2000). She flew to Oklahoma City to be fitted for a prosthesis at age six and was walking unaccompanied within six weeks. She named the new limb after her sister (Donaghy 2000). In December 1994, Eilish and her parents visited the Hensel twins and their family.

In October 1999, Eilish Holton received a Indigo National Children's Day Bravery Award, after being nominated by her sister Claire. Claire writes, "I nominated Eilish because she had major surgery to separate her from her conjoined twin sister Katie, who died four days after surgery. Eilish spent seven months in hospital when she was three and a half years old. She wears an artificial leg and despite frequent hospital visits she is still a normal eleven-year-old" (Indigo 1999). The Holtons and the families of the other nine award recipients attended receptions in their honor in Dublin, appeared on television, and accepted the awards presented by Irish President Mary McAleese. Eilish, Ireland's only surviving separated conjoined twin, recently celebrated her twelfth birthday. She gets along well with her friends and her four siblings, Claire, Therese, Mairead, and her younger sister Maeve, who has in some ways helped to replace Katie (Donaghy 2000).

See also Hensel, Abby and Brittany; Separation surgery

## Holyoke Twins see Gibb, Mary and Margaret

## Hospital for Sick Children.

This hospital in Toronto, Ontario, Canada, had separated seven sets of conjoined twins by mid–1996. Among these were twin boys (whose names were not released) born on April 23, 1996, joined at the diaphragm and chest and separated on May 1, 1996.

See also Htut, Lin and Win; Jamal, Hira and Nida

## Hospitalization.

*Operating room nursing for conjoined twins is technically, organizationally and functionally complicated and complex. It's much more than taking care of two patients.... The procedures, therefore, must be a synchronous operation.*— Winifred A. Betsch and Margaret T. Reford at the Dallas Convention of Operating Room Nurses (March 1975)

Both the birth and the separation of conjoined twins requires sometimes extensive hospitalization. Depending on the anatomy and positioning of the babies, the mother may be hospitalized prior to the delivery, which is usually by Cesarean section. The twins may need immediate surgery to correct any life-threatening anomalies. They may then undergo thorough testing to assess their suitability for surgical separation. While the attention associated with a separation operation is often focused on the lead surgeon, the surgeon gives credit to the coordination of the surgical team, which includes doctors, nurses, and medical technicians. They work together to prepare the patients for surgery, which often requires preliminary surgeries — for instance a surgery to insert tissue expanders. The surgery itself may last hours, followed by extensive recovery, possible reconstructive surgery, and follow-up care. Some pairs of conjoined twins unfortunately die before they leave the hospital or are permanently institutionalized, but the majority are discharged and raised by their families.

## Htut, Lin and Win. *Twentieth Century.*

*No, we agreed all the time because we don't want to see them conjoined together. It is a hard life. It is very hot in Burma and they live under fan always. And when one want to stand up the other fall down. The hands are also confused with each other. They have no independence. We are feeling sorry for them every time we saw them.*— Nyi Htut about the decision to separate his children

Male conjoined twins born by Cesarean section in Mandalay, Burma (now Myanmar), on February 18, 1982, to Nyi Htut and his wife Tin Tin Myint. The boys shared a liver, urinary tract, intestines, pelvis, and a single set of genitals. They had two heads, four arms, and three legs. Together they weighed eleven pounds four ounces. Six days after their birth, they were sent 450 miles away to the Rangoon Children's Hospital. For the next five months, Nyi Htut kept the details of the birth from his wife — telling her nine days after the delivery that the twins were joined, but not severely — and kept her at home to prevent her from seeing accounts of the twins in the Burmese newspapers (Coping 1984).

In Rangoon, the twins were noticed in July 1983 by Alan Conn, a doctor with Toronto's Hospital for Sick Children who was on an Asian lecture tour. The Canadian International Development Agency underwrote the $100,000 medical costs, KLM Dutch Airlines provided transportation for the twins and two guardians, and the twins were escorted to Toronto in July 1984 for separation surgery. The parents remained in Burma with their newest baby, but were brought to Toronto in September at the expense of the city's Sutton Place Hotel. A team of forty-three assembled for the operation and rehearsed three times, using dolls to choreograph their movements as the surgery progressed. The team, led by chief surgeon Dr. Robert Filler, included two general surgeons, two orthopedic surgeons, two plastic surgeons, two urologists, five anesthetists, sixteen resident surgeons, and fourteen nurses, many of whom donated their services. On July 28, 1984, the babies were anesthetized. Dr. Barry Shandling remembers, "They were wired up like astronauts. There were tubes and wires coming out of them like a bunch of spaghetti" (Hluchy 1984). The incision began and initiated what Dr. Filler characterized as a "symphony." Their liver, urinary tract, pelvis, and intestines were divided over the next twelve hours and they were stitched up over the following five. The removal of the vestigial third leg provided enough tissue to close Lin's abdominal wall; silicone rubber and synthetic mesh were used to cover Win's wounds (Hluchy 1984).

Lin, the livelier child — and the one considered more masculine by Burmese standards, was allowed to keep the male genitals. A vagina was constructed from a section of colon for Win, but it was acknowledged that the child would never be able to have a full sexual response and would of course be unable to bear children. She would have to begin taking female hormones at puberty. During the surgery, Lin required six blood transfusions. Win required ten and later experienced internal bleeding, which brought her back to the operating room the following day. Lin was the first to feed himself after the surgery, with Win being fed through a stomach tube until her digestive system healed. Win underwent additional surgery to correct a club foot. During their recovery in the hospital over the next year, each child was fitted with a prosthetic leg at the Ontario Crippled Children's Center, so that they could begin to learn to walk. Ironically, the nurses who cared for the twins saw them as more deformed and handicapped *after* the surgery than before it took place. Although Dr. Robert Filler doesn't think their separation from each other will be an issue, the twins' nurse Alison Miller noted that they know the whereabouts of each other at all times and believes that being apart will be very strange for them (Aikenhead 1985). Their father described how they fought when put near each other, which he ascribed to their being afraid of being joined together again (Coping 1984). Lin rejoined his parents in Burma in July 1985, with Win returning in the fall of that year.

***See also*** **Gender; Separation surgery; Sexuality**

**Hungarian Sisters.** *Eighteenth Century.*

Helen and Judith were born in Szony, Hungary, on October 26, 1701, joined in the lumbar region of the spine, back to back. Helen was delivered first as far as the navel, followed by Judith in reverse order, with the labor characterized as difficult. Their emotions, inclinations, and appetites were not simultaneous. Helen was described as the more active and intelligent, with Judith — who became hemiplegic at age six, but later recovered — characterized as delicate and depressed. They became singers and linguists and were exhibited in England, Holland,

Germany, France, Italy, and Poland. The girls were seen in London in 1708 by James Paris du Plessis, who described them in his book *History of Prodigies*:

> They were brisk, merry, and well-bred; they could read, write, and sing very prettily; they could speak three different languages, as Hungarian, Low Dutch, and French, and were learning English. They were very handsome, very well shaped in all parts, and had beautiful faces. Helen was born three hours before her sister Judith. They loved each other very tenderly.

In May 1708, a scholarly description of the Hungarian twins was read before the Royal Society. Although he mocked "monster-mongers" in one of his novels, Jonathan Swift was one of the first patrons to observe Helen and Judith and commented that seeing them causes many speculations and raises an abundance of questions in divinity, law, and physics (Semonin 1996).

Helen and Judith were placed in the convent of the Nuns of St. Ursula in Presburg, Hungary, at age nine and remained there for the rest of their lives. The twins were examined by many eminent physiologists, psychologists, and naturalists, including Buffon (*d.* 1788). They were immortalized in verse by Pope and by some lines composed by a Hungarian physician (Gould and Pyle 1956):

> One urine passage serves for both;—
>     one anus, so they tell;
> The other parts their numbers keep,
>     and serve their owners well...

It is recorded that they had a single vulva, but two vaginal canals. They began menstruating at different times and intensities at age sixteen. Their intestinal tracts ended in a single shared rectum. William Pancoast (1871) describes their union as from the "second vertebral elements of the sacra to the end of the coccyges" and points out that their interior union established a direct communication between their two hearts, thus pro-ducing "a great community of life and functions." They each contracted measles and small-pox at the same time, but were affected in different degrees. Their case was debated during their lifetime. Contemporary medical men believed surgery to be too risky, but advised immediate separation if one twin were to die. Some suggested that the main objection to the twins marrying was the possible propagation of monsters. When Judith died at age twenty-two in 1723 (on February 23, according to Bolton 1830) due to "cerebral and pulmonary affections," Helen collapsed and followed almost immediately (Gould and Pyle 1956, Smith 1988, Wallace and Wallace 1978, Bondeson 2000, Martell 2000). They were buried together at the convent where they spent most of their lives (Guttmacher 1967).

## Ibrahim, Ahmed and Mohamed.
### Twenty-first Century.

*But doctors acknowledge that the surgery to separate them could kill one or both of these bright-eyed, lively boys, or cause brain damage that might cripple them, physically and mentally—in essence, trading one lifelong disability for another just as profound.*—Denise Grady

Craniopagus twin boys born in a remote village 500 miles south of Cairo, Egypt, to Sabah Abu el-Wafa in July 2001. Ahmed and Mohamed were brought to a hospital in Cairo shortly after birth and spent their first year there. They were brought to Medical City Dallas Hospital in June 2002 to be assessed for separation surgery. They are staying in an apartment under the care of two Cairo nurses, Wafaa Dardir and Naglaa Mahmoud, and arrangements are being made for their father to join them, while their mother remains in Egypt with their brother and sister. The visit was arranged by craniofacial surgeon Dr. Kenneth Salyer, who finds their condition "horrendous" (Grady 2002). The babies in their joined state cannot sit, stand, or crawl and they are unable to see each other's faces. Their crib has not been outfitted with a mirror in case the surgery is performed and results in the death of one of the twins. Together they measure five feet long and must be picked up by two people.

The boys share some tissue and several blood vessels in their brains, but often nap at separate times. Other than their conjoined condition, they are normal and healthy. Doctors confront both the ethical dilemma posed by the risks of surgery and the question of whether it is fair to spend up to two million on their care when the same amount — spent on food, vaccines, or sanitation — could potentially save many more lives (Grady 2002). The costs will be borne by the hospital and by the World Craniofacial Foundation, a charity created by Dr. Salyer. Although Dr. Salyer has not separated craniopagus twins, he has reconstructed the skulls of a pair of twins after their separation. The biggest risk to the Ibrahim twins during surgery would be the separation of the venous sinuses, which drain blood from one child's brain into the other's head, since cutting or tying them off can cause brain swelling and stroke. The venous sinuses can also be easily torn, causing the child to quickly bleed to death. Ahmed has been determined to have better circulation than Mohamed. Prior to separation, surgeons may perform a series of operations to slowly block off the vessels and redirect the blood flow gradually.

Assessment for surgical separation has included CT scans and MRIs, from which life-sized three-dimensional models have been created at no charge by Medical Modeling L.L.C. of Golden, Colorado. Ethicist Alice Dreger points out that the immobility of the Ibrahim twins is an important issue when deciding whether to separate them. "How would you even set up a house around that kind of body?" she asks (Grady 2002). The boys' caregivers have noticed that hints of frustration are beginning to break through their usual good cheer. If surgeons decline to separate them, they will re-

turn to Egypt to live with their parents. They could be reassessed at a later time.

## Identity.

*If it is uncertain where one body ends and another begins, the subject's identity too must remain undecidably singular and plural, individual and collective.* — Elizabeth Grosz (1996)

It has been important to conjoined twins in general to make it clear that a single set of twins is made up of two distinct individuals with differing personalities and tastes. "Yet it also seems evident that the usual hard and fast distinction between the boundaries of one subject and another are continually blurred: speech patterns and even sentences are shared; all their experiences are shared; they do not need to consult over decisions but make them in unison automatically" (Grosz 1996). Stephen Jay Gould (1997) uses conjoined twins as an example in allaying fears about human cloning by pointing out that they and all identical twins are clones, but still maintain a unique individuality. Leslie Fiedler (1978) points out that unjoined identical twins pose the same challenge to distinguish between the individual body and consciousness that conjoined twins do. But Nancy Segal (1999) writes that "while most identical twins get along well, many conjoined twins are masters at negotiation, cooperation and compromise. At the same time, their separate brains allow psychological separateness and selfhood, feelings crucial to all humans. I was intrigued, but not surprised, that families highlighted conjoined twins' personality differences. I suspect physical connection intensifies identical twins' needs to distinguish between themselves, as well as their parents' needs to distinguish between them."

Claudia Wallis (1996) says of Abby and Brittany Hensel, "...their tale of lives unpunctuated by solitude has much to teach all of us about the real meaning of individuality and the limitless power of human cooperation." Since they shared a body, some twins, like Millie-Christine, spoke of themselves as "I" rather than "we." Others defied their chroniclers to choose between the singular and the plural: "…we have sometimes spoken of this extraordinary being as one, and sometimes as two; but this is because it is nearly impossible to use precise language in the description of that which even science fails to tell us whether it be one child only, or two in one," records the Philadelphia *Public Ledger* about the Finley twins (Besse 1874). Most conjoined twins favor speaking in the first person singular, each speaking for him- or herself (Dreger 1998).

Alice Dreger clarifies that because conjoined twins typically exhibit two consciousnesses in one body, singletons assume this means that they are autonomous in terms of mind but imprisoned in terms of body (Dreger 1998). This poses legal and spiritual quandaries. The legal status of conjoined twins varies, whether they are applying for a passport or a marriage license. Their spiritual status is also often in question and has been for centuries. According to Aristotle, a set of conjoined twins constitutes two individuals if they have two hearts and a single individual if they have only one. Differences in temperament were often used as arguments that conjoined twins constitute two persons or souls rather than one (Wilson 1993). Rosamond Purcell (1997) writes, "The question of whether conjoined twins constitute one or two people has kept philosophers and pundits busy for centuries," and the statement still holds true.

*See also* **Hensel, Abigail Lauren and Brittany Lee; McKoy, Millie-Christine**

## Infante, Patricia and Madeleine.
*Twentieth Century.*

Unjoined sisters who capitalized on the fame of the Hiltons by attaching themselves to each other with wire and entering show business as "Violet and Daisy Milton." The ruse was a success until they had a fight with their manager. In their anger, they destroyed a sign billing them as "the only original American Siamese twins" and were brought up on charges of vandalism, ending their career.

*See also* **Hilton, Daisy and Violet**

## Institutionalization *see* Hospitalization

## Ira and Galya *see* Irina-Galina

## Irina-Galina. *Twentieth Century.*

Born in November 1937 in Moscow, these female dicephalous twins were studied at the All-Union Institute of Experimental Medicine by Pyotr Anokhin, who later studied Masha and Dasha Krivoshlyapova. They had separate spines and nervous systems and their heart rates differed, but their circulatory system was interconnected and they shared many internal organs. The girls each had a head and two arms, but they shared a single pair of legs. Photographs of the twins were published in *Life* magazine on September 26, 1938. Several photos have also been published in Luigi Gedda's *Twins in History and Science*. The twins died in December 1938.

*See also* **Krivoshlyapova, Masha and Dasha**

## Ischiopagus.

Twins united ventrally from the umbilicus to a large conjoined pelvis with two sacrums and two pubic symphyses. Ischiopagus twins often share intestines, bladders, and kidneys. The external genitalia are always involved and they have four arms and four legs. Their appearance is usually of a head at each end of the body: "They often appear to be joined end-to-end with the vertebral columns in a straight line, but

**Diagram illustrating typical ischiopagus twins. Courtesy of Rowena Spencer and the W.B. Saunders Co.**

occasionally they are face-to-face with union of the entire abdomen" (Spencer 1996). Occurs in about six percent of conjoined twins (Segal 1999).

## Jamal, Nida and Hira. *Twentieth Century.*

> *Although you can only be awed by the medical technology and mastery involved, the result is bittersweet. Only one of the sisters survived.* — Claire Bickley, *The Toronto Sun*

Conjoined twin girls born in Karachi, Pakistan, to Anwar and Fatima Jamal on October 8, 1992, with a triplet sister named Faryal. The twins were attached at the top of their heads in a slightly rotated position. The physicians at Karachi's National Institute of Child Health encouraged the parents to seek separation in North America, after aborted attempts at separation in Pakistan. The cause was taken up by Prime Minister Benazir Bhutto and became the subject of an award-winning television documentary called "Separate Lives" that aired on the Discovery Channel and the BBC. The twins arrived in Toronto on November 5, 1994. It was learned that their cerebral circulation

was shared and that kidney and heart problems were giving Hira an enlarged heart. Separation was performed at Toronto's Hospital for Sick Children and was "most difficult" relates James T. Rutka, one of the participating surgeons (personal correspondence, June 12, 2001). Preparations included the implant of tissue expanders under the scalps to allow doctors to close the wound after separation; embolization of a major artery and part of the superior saggital sinus in the girls' heads to block part of their shared blood flow; and the transplant of one of Hira's kidneys into Nida to eliminate the need for dialysis after the surgery. The surgery had been pushed back several times because of preoperative complications, but was moved up to January 23, 1995, when Hira began to experience heart failure (Murray 1995).

The surgery, expected to take between six and twenty-four hours, took seventeen hours. The surgical team of twenty-three neurosurgeons, neuroradiologists, plastic surgeons, anesthetists, urologists, nephrologists, and cardiologists was led by chief neurosurgeon Dr. Harold Hoffman. The girls were anesthetized at 8 AM, followed by catheterization. Their scalps were shaved and the incisions mapped out. Guided in dividing the blood vessels by a computerized navigation system employing both CT and MRI images, the surgeons separated the bony union of the skulls and then opened the dura. Nida's vascular system had responded to the earlier embolization and it was hoped that her brain would not hemorrhage when the saggital sinus was moved entirely to Hira's brain. The dura would be closed on both twins using freeze-dried donor dura. Skull defects, which would not be noticeable, were to be repaired in a later operation. The scalp would then be closed, using grafted skin from the girls if the tissue expanders did not provide enough skin. Both twins remained stable throughout

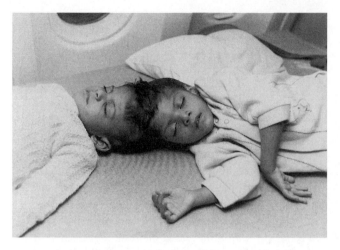

Two-year-old Hira (on the left) and Nida Jamal at the Hospital for Sick Children in Toronto. Courtesy of Rob Terteruck.

their separation, although blood loss was greater than expected and may have affected the blood supply to Nida's brain (Murray 1995).

The girls were expected to remain in the intensive care unit for two or three days, possibly requiring ventilators and, in Nida's case, dialysis. While it was possible that they could be released from the hospital within two weeks, Hira's heart problems and Nida's kidney problems could prolong their stay. Their need for rehabilitation was thought to be minimal, since they were developmentally normal and had walked while joined. The cost of their care was in part raised from private donations by Pakistani-trained Hospital for Sick Children pediatrician Dr. Shahida Khan and from a $100,000 contribution by the Pakistani government (Murray 1995). After the separation surgery, however, Nida failed to improve and remained in a comatose state. Although she had opened her eyes, she was not interacting with her environment and could not swallow properly. Nida died of what was assumed to be cardiac arrest, but may have been a pulmonary embolism or infection. Her parents did not consent to an autopsy on religious and cultural grounds. Had she survived, doctors say that she would have suffered functional deficits, including possible paralysis on her left side.

Hira, on the other hand, made steady progress and was awake, alert, and smiling. She began to feed herself and was expected to develop normally, although her motor functions are delayed since she had been previously unable to sit up, stand, or walk normally. The incision in her scalp may require additional reconstructive surgery. Her heart, weakened from supporting herself and her sister, was improving but not fully recovered. Hira was also malnourished because of the physical demands that had been placed on her body.

## Janus.

An ancient Roman god depicted with two faces. He is thought to have been inspired by conjoined twins, specifically cephalopagus. A form of dipygus twins, united face to face down the middle with each half turned outward, are referred to as *Janiceps* twins (Segal 1999), and such formations were believed to be good omens (Fiedler 1978).

*See also* **Cephalopagus**

## Jodie and Mary.

Pseudonyms used to protect the anonymity of female conjoined twins Gracie and Rosie Attard. Their names were revealed by the British Court after their parents accepted money from the media for telling their story.

*See also* **Attard, Gracie and Rosie; Media attention**

## Johanna and Melchiora. *Sixteenth Century.*

*Each of them would have been a beautiful girl, had they lived and not been thus joined.* — Don Gonalo Fernandez de Oviedo, who saw the twins alive

Female omphalopagus twins born on July 10, 1533, and dying eight days later. They were autopsied in Santo Domingo on July 18, 1533, at the request of the friar who had given them the Last Rites. They were found to have a common epigastrium and umbilicus. Because the livers were the only organs joined, the surgeon Johan Comancho declared that each baby had spiritual independence (Guttmacher 1967).

## "Joined: The Secret Life of Conjoined Twins."

A documentary that aired on the Learning Channel on January 29, 2002, in two one-hour segments as part of the "Mysterious World" series. "Birth" covers the story of the Lawlers and the Lewises and the birth of their conjoined twins and includes an interview with pediatric surgeon Dr. James O'Neill. "Separation" follows Stella and Esther Alphonce through surgery and after, explains why twins like the Schappells cannot be separated, and interviews separated twins Iesha and Tiesha Turner and Hussein and Hassan Abdulrehman.

*See also* Abdulrehman, Hassan and Hussein; Alphonce, Stella and Esther; Lawler Twins; Turner, Ja'Nishia and La'Lishia

## "Joined: The World of Siamese Twins."

A documentary that aired on BBC in October 2001. The show follows Allison and David Lawler through the pregnancy and birth of conjoined twin daughters. "Those girls taught me that imperfections just don't exist," said their father. Although they were carried to term, the twins both died within a half hour of birth. Reviewer Andrew Moscrop criticizes the producers for focusing on the problems facing this individual pair of twins rather than the ethical, medical, and moral issues raised by the case of Jodie and Mary that will affect us all.

*See also* Lawler Twins

## "Joined at Birth."

A one-hour television documentary aired by the Discovery Channel on March 29, 1998. "The documentary addresses conjoined twins who survive the first few months after birth, whether one twin's condition affects the other, surgical problems, and how two conjoined people can live relatively normal lives" (Loft 1998). The program focuses on six sets of twins (Janelle and Shawna Roderick, Abby and Brittany Hensel, Lori and Reba Schappell, Doris and Bessie Gonzalez, Ronnie and Donnie Galyon, and Claire and Emily Taylor) and features an interview with pediatric surgeon Rowena Spencer.

*See also* Galyon, Ronnie and Donnie; Gonzalez, Doris and Bessie; Hensel, Abby and Brittany; Roderick, Janelle and Shawna; Schappell, Lori and Reba; Spencer, Rowena; Taylor, Claire and Emily

## Jones, Charlotte Marie and Paulette Marie. *Twentieth Century.*

Conjoined girls born in July 1976 attached at the chest and abdomen. They were successfully separated at the University of Texas Medical Branch at five weeks of age.

## Jones Twins. *Nineteenth Century.*

Ischiopagus twins born in Russianville (Tipton County), Indiana, on June 24, 1889, to Mr. and Mrs. James Henry Jones. The labor lasted only two hours and was complete before the physician arrived. The twins had a combined birth weight of twelve pounds and were twenty-two inches long (Gould and Pyle 1956). Their mother was convinced that their condition was a result of her having seen two female aerialists fall, twisted together, while she was pregnant. By wrapping the babies around her back, she was able to nurse them at the same time. Curiously, the eye color, hair color, and complexion of the twins was said to differ (Gould and Pyle 1956). Hoping to make a good living from them, the parents exhibited the babies, but they died on February 19 and 20, 1891, at St. John's Hotel in Buffalo, New York (Gould and Pyle 1956). Their body was returned to Indiana and buried in the front yard of the family home. A vigil was kept over the grave night and day for months to discourage grave robbers (Kobel 1959, Bogdan 1988).

*See also* **Maternal impressions**

**Jones, Yvonne and Yvette** *see* **MacArther, Yvonne and Yvette Jones**

**Juarez, Milagro and Marta.** *End of Twentieth Century.*

Female conjoined twins born near Lima, Peru, to twenty-two-year-old Marta Milagros Pascual Juarez in February 2000, sharing a heart, liver, and part of the intestinal tract. With funds donated by the public, the costs of the operation donated by the participants, and their upkeep borne by the Sicilian authorities, the girls and their family (including their father and four-year-old brother) were flown to Italy, where a team of fourteen surgeons led by Dr. Carlo Marcelletti separated them in May at Civico Hospital in Palermo. The operation took place earlier than planned, since the twins' condition was deteriorating. They were dependent on a respirator, had developed a bacterial infection, and were beginning to suffer from bronchial spasms. Preference was given to Marta, the stronger twin, a decision their mother called "a painful choice" (Siamese Twins from Peru 2000). One of the doctors refused to take part in the surgery on ethical grounds, once it was decided that it would not be possible to save both twins, but senior church officials did not condemn the operation (Siamese Twins from Peru 2000). Milagro, the weaker twin, died during surgery as expected — their mother and the hospital's ethics committee deciding that it was better to save the life of one twin than to allow them both to die. The liver was successfully divided and Marta's intestine reconstructed, but she too died on May 27, 2000, when her heart stopped functioning. A funeral was held in Palermo, after which the parents returned to Peru.

**Kelvoyna and Kelvondra.** *End of Twentieth Century.*

Conjoined girls born on July 12, 2000, in Greenville, Mississippi, to Shennikia Malone and Kelvin Howard. They were joined at the hip and stomach and shared a liver, a bladder, and part of the pelvis. They were successfully separated at Children's Hospital of Philadelphia and were released in time to celebrate their first birthday at home.

**Kennedy, Ian and Nathan.** *Twentieth Century.*

Pseudonyms for ischiopagus boys born in New England by Cesarean section in 1991 or 1992. The parents asked the hospital for complete confidentiality to avoid their story being sensationalized. The twins were released at ten weeks and were sent home on oxygen and given sixteen-hour-a-day nursing care. When the weaker and smaller twin became ill, it prompted the parents to research surgical separation. The boys were separated at Children's Hospital in Philadelphia five months after birth. Surgeon-in-Chief James A. O'Neill, Jr., led a twenty-member team that included four general surgeons, two urologists, two orthopedic surgeons, two plastic surgeons, five specialty nurses, and five anesthesiologists. They planned the operation after viewing ultrasound studies, MRIs, CT-scans, and conventional x-rays. The successful surgery took twelve hours. Dr. O'Neill felt that both boys would be finished with other corrective surgery by the time they reached school age.

## Koop, C. Everett.

Former U.S. Surgeon General, Dr. Koop was a pioneer of separation surgery. During his career, he headed three teams and participated in more than eighteen separations of conjoined twins, including that of Clara and Altagracia Rodriguez.

*See also* **Children's Hospital of Philadelphia; Rodriguez, Clara and Altagracia; Separation surgery**

## Korean Twins. *Nineteenth-Twentieth Century.*

Twin boys joined at the breastbone, they were photographed on tour with the Barnum & Bailey Circus in 1903 (Rusid 1975).

## Krivoshlyapova, Masha and Dasha. *Twentieth Century.*

*But after they had written their dissertations the scientists threw us away and forgot about us.—* Dasha Krivoshlyapova

Female conjoined twins born in Russia on January 3, 1950, to a factory worker named Katya. They have fused pelvises and vertebrae, but separate hearts and spinal cords. They have two heads, four arms, and three legs. They have separate genitalia, but share a uterus. They share a circulatory system, a lower intestine, a bladder, and a rectum. Some accounts claim that they were not shown to their mother, but others indicate that she had a nervous breakdown upon seeing her joined babies and was taken to a psychiatric hospital. After birth, Masha and Dasha were "taken away for observation" by the doctors, who did not have the knowledge at that time to attempt separation. Katya was told she should forget about them

**Barnum and Bailey Circus sideshow group, 1903. Among the forty-seven attractions are the Korean Siamese twins. Courtesy of the Circus World Museum, Baraboo, Wisconsin.**

and should try for a normal baby. When she persisted, the doctors — eager to research the twins without interference — told her they had died of pneumonia. In fact, they were alive and well at Moscow's Pediatric Institute.

The girls were raised in Moscow medical clinics under the care of physiologist Pyotr Anokhin and learned to walk at age five while living at the Soviet Scientific Institute for Prosthetics in north Moscow. There they did special exercises to help them coordinate. It was there that physiotherapist "Auntie Nadya" took them under her wing. Coordination was difficult as each controlled the opposite leg (and shared control of the third), but they eventually learned to climb stairs, dance, and ride a bicycle. At age twelve, they were moved to an orphanage school for handicapped children in the small town of Novocherkassk. The school had no plumbing, only a single toilet, unheated dormitories, and no hot water. Masha and Dasha remember it fondly because they met children their own age and the staff tried to make the students' lives as normal as possible, although they were rarely allowed outside the gates. Dasha liked to study more than Masha. The twins were said to have had violent disagreements over their differing tastes in music, television, and exercise (Wright 1997). At the age of sixteen, the twins were issued a single passport. At the same age, they had the vestigial leg that they shared amputated. Both were said to regret the surgery, since they required crutches afterward.

Although their circulatory system is interconnected, the twins react to illnesses differently. Only one of them had the measles, for instance. Dasha is short-sighted and prone to colds. Masha is healthier, even though she is an occasional smoker and has higher blood pressure. Nor do they share feeling. They have four kidneys, but share a single bladder, so they often disagree about when to urinate. They have two livers, two intestines, and one bowel. Encouraged to think of themselves as collaborators rather than specimens since they were children, they were the subject of a medical film produced by the Academy of Medicine in 1957 and have been studied from both a medical and psychiatric perspective. In the film, the twins appear as naked babies sleeping on a sheet. A lab assistant draws a razor across the sole of Dasha's foot, causing her to wake up screaming in pain while Masha continues to sleep. Masha is then stabbed in the stomach with a pin, causing the same reaction. One of the girls is packed in ice to lower her temperature and compare that of her sister. The other is burned and her sister's heartbeat monitored to see how it reacted. Blood was drawn every day and the content of their gastric juices was measured by feeding tubes into their stomachs. Because they had common circulatory, digestive, excretory, lymphatic, endocrine, and skeletal systems, the twins represented the perfect "living laboratory" for the study of resistance to disease, since they rarely shared each other's illnesses (Davis n.d.).

Biographer and friend of ten years Juliet Butler described their lives on BBC2's "Conjoined Twins":

> The USSR was one of the worst possible countries for conjoined twins to be born in. Nobody was allowed to see them. When they were very small the doctors had to get passes to go into the laboratory where they were being kept to see them and they all had to wear masks so the girls were saying they never even saw the doctors' faces. Pain was inflicted on them every day. There were no babies, they used to prick one with a needle to see if the other one would cry, they'd pack one in ice to see how quickly the other one's temperature dropped, they'd starve one and keep feeding the other one regularly, gave them injections of substances to see how quickly it got from one body to the other.

The Krivoshlyapova twins have been quoted as saying that being born in Russia was their real handicap. To this day, they are sometimes told that they should have been killed at birth, according to Butler. They admit feeling that they are not needed, even by medical science. They offered in *Life* magazine to work with doctors who want to study them in exchange for a trip to England, with which they are fascinated.

Juliet Butler wrote a book about the pair entitled *Masha & Dasha: Autobiography of a Siamese Twin Pair*, which was translated into German by Christine Struch and published by Joke Publishing House in Munich in 2000. Butler points out that Dasha is friendly, thoughtful, and flexible, while Masha is hard and unyielding. "If we were both as soft as Dasha," says Masha, "we could only howl the whole time." In the book, their very different voices alternate. The twins sought out the English journalist, Butler, in the Moscow office of *Newsweek*. They wanted to tell their story and to help their readers reach out with genuine understanding to those less fortunate. Butler describes that meeting Masha and Dasha is not at all distressing because of their engaging personalities and sense of optimism. "The past forty years haven't been so good," says Dasha, "but things are looking up for the next forty." Butler notes that they are so physically in accord as to know what the other intends. They do aerobics to keep in shape and keep their hair short.

Masha and Dasha were under the care of Dr. Lydia Mikhailovna until the doctor's death in the early 1990s. They were institutionalized at Home Number Six for Veterans of War and Labour ("the Sixth) just southwest of Moscow. Their room measured twelve by eight feet and Masha complained of having to hide her cigarettes like a schoolgirl and of not being trusted to boil a kettle. They were not allowed to lock their room and so were sometimes the object of uninvited stares from superstitious residents. On one of the rare occasions where they were taken beyond the institution's walls, they went to Red Square but were not allowed off the bus.

With the coming of Mikhail Gorbechev and glasnost, the twins were able to speak out, which they did for two reasons. It allowed them to lobby for better living conditions, resulting in their installment in a modern, more spacious apartment with their own shower, double-bed, and wheelchair. It also allowed them to present themselves to the public and dispel notions of them as embarrassments and rumors that they were mentally challenged. Russians were divided upon seeing them on television, with some disgusted by their appearance, but many sympathetic and ashamed of the way the government had treated the girls. Once westerners learned their story, they sent letters, money, and gifts ranging from food to clothes to dental work. Their meager weekly grant of eight rubles each was increased to twelve rubles. They were invited to visit Germany and marveled at not being stared at, probably remembering when they were taken to a traveling zoo and the zookeeper — who was supposed to have made the visit private — sold tickets to the public to see the "two-headed girl." Masha and Dasha brush each other's hair and straighten each other's clothes. They do their own laundry, since the chlorine in the Sixth's laundry irritates their skin. Dasha is obsessed with cleanliness and dreams of owning her own set of sheets.

Masha and Dasha dislike being treated as one person, particularly the fact that doctors have only a single medical record for them despite different illnesses. (They have had appendicitis and twisted intestines, for which they have undergone surgery.) Their personalities differ, with Masha more energetic and Dasha more serious, temperamental, and submissive. Masha will pull Dasha out of bed to get a midnight snack. Dasha is the more talkative, with Masha quieter and more emotional. Both, though, are meticulously tidy. Dasha often felt like an appendage to Masha, who usually refers to herself in the first person singular and often answers for her and her sister. She tells interviewers, however, that she wouldn't want to be separated from her twin and that she couldn't conceive of life without her. In fact, Masha turned down the offer of a British surgeon to attempt to separate them eleven years ago. Dasha concurs, "We'd never agree to such an operation. We just don't need it." One of the girls is left-handed and the other right-handed. Dasha confesses to being an alcoholic, which makes Masha one too and angers the director of the Sixth when they are open with the press about it. Masha describes herself as the masculine half of the two of them and sometimes wishes being born Dasha's brother. She was not very tolerant of Dasha's brief romance with a boy in her class named Slava, who died after developing pneumonia, and neither has been romantically involved since. Although they menstruated normally, they would have been unable to carry a child because there was no room for their double womb to expand. Dasha explains that they are resigned to being unusual and having unusual fates.

Masha and Dasha were interviewed for BBC2's "Conjoined Twins," which aired in October 2000. They were also reunited with their mother when they appeared on a popular national television program in Russia. The twins learned from her that they had two brothers, but that their father had died in 1980. Masha and Dasha blame the doctors for depriving them of a family life. They complained of finding their mother too late and of having nothing in common with her. If still alive, Masha and Dasha are the oldest living conjoined twins in the world, having been born a year earlier than the Galyon brothers.

*See also* **Galyon, Lonnie and Donnie**

## Lakeberg, Amy and Angela. *Twentieth Century.*

*You have to ask yourself if chain-smoking parents in a trailer park is the most conducive envi-ronment for a sick child.* — Dr. Jonathan Muraskas, Loyola-Chicago neonatologist who advised against separation surgery in the Lakeberg case

*That's a mistake—a big moral mistake. You don't want to allocate medical resources to children based on whether their parents are saints or sinners.* — Art Caplan, director of the Center for Bioethics, University of Pennsylvania

Conjoined twin girls born at Loyola University Medical Center in Chicago on June 29, 1993, to unemployed and uninsured Kenneth and Reitha "Joey" Lakeberg of Wheatfield, Indiana. The nine-pound twins were joined face-to-face at the chest and shared a six-chambered heart and fused livers. Their condition had been revealed at sixteen weeks of pregnancy by an ultrasound and they were told the following week that their was a significant likelihood that both twins would die if the pregnancy were brought to term. The Lakebergs continued the pregnancy and the twins were delivered by Cesarean section. The $375,000 cost of their hospital care was partially reimbursed by Indiana Public Aid. Tests confirmed that the babies had separate lungs, kidneys, and GI tracts and each had a normal brain (Thomasma et al. 1996). Within six hours of birth, the twins became ventilator-dependent due to the way their chest was joined, and remained stable for three weeks. The hospital ethics committee outlined three courses of action: allow the babies to die while keeping them comfortable, attempt separation, or send them to a more experienced facility for separation. Surgery would mean the death of one child, since they shared a heart and transplant was not an option, and possibly both. Doctors at Loyola recommended against separating the twins, since there was little chance the surviving twin would leave the hospital alive, the slim chance of one twin's survival did not merit causing the other twin's death, and the resources could be better spent on cases with better outcomes (Thomasma et al. 1996). The hospital did perform exploratory catheterization that confirmed the complexity of the cardiac anomalies and indicated that Angela would be favored for survival.

"Meanwhile, the parents remained committed to doing everything possible to save the life of at least one of the twins," wrote Thomasma et al. (1996). The Lakebergs searched for a hospital willing to perform the surgery gratis. A decision was demanded after the twins began to show signs of congestive heart failure. Although they agreed that chances of survival of one twin were remote, doctors at Children's Hospital of Philadelphia agreed to consider surgery after an additional test. Amy and Angela were flown to Philadelphia on August 17, 1993. The surgeons at Children's Hospital estimated Angela's chances to be no more than 25 percent and encouraged the Lakebergs to reconsider. The parents pressed forward and the surgery was planned for August 20. "The fact of the babies' continued survival suggested a strength upon which surgery might be built. As the cardiac surgeon in Philadelphia said, the best argument in favor of the separation was the fact that the twins were still alive" (Thomasma et al. 1996). At the age of seven weeks, the red-haired, blue-eyed Lakeberg twins became the thirteenth pair to be separated at Children's Hospital. The doctors at the hospital explained, "You try it because the parents can't accept doing nothing and want to try something, even if it's not likely to work" (Separating Conjoined Twins 1993). Kenny Lakeberg remarked to reporters after saying goodbye to the twins that they were looking for a million-dollar, made-for–TV movie contract from all of this (Thomasma et al. 1996). Chief surgeon James A. O'Neill, Jr., explained to the press that the surgery was risky, but not hopeless, and that the cost should not be a consideration. "We take long odds every day," he said, "but not crazy odds" (Toufexis 1994). "I don't have a positive outlook on this," father Kenny Lakeberg is quoted as saying by BBC2. "I don't

know what to think. Hopefully, everything works out right."

The surgery included separating the organs below the diaphragm and rebuilding the heart, but doctors declined to say which child they would attempt to save. In fact, nurses had painted Angela's fingernails pink, but left Amy's unpainted (Dougherty 1993). Thomasma et al. (1996) describe the operation: "The initial component of the surgery consisted of separating the body wall and liver; then cardiac separation and reconstruction were performed. Angela came off cardiopulmonary bypass uneventfully." During the five and a half hour surgery on August 20, 1993, Amy Lakeberg died, with her family already having made funeral arrangements. The medical team observed a moment of silence, but did not pause long to acknowledge the event. "We were aware at that phase what was happening," commented one of the surgeons, "But minutes really count, and you have to press ahead as fast as you can" (Dougherty 1993). Amy Lakeberg was buried in Indiana four days later. During the funeral, Kenny Lakeberg was involved in a fist-fight over whether the casket would be open or closed (Thomasma et al. 1996).

Angela, who was given a minimal chance of survival, remained in critical condition in the cardio thoracic intensive care unit. Shortly after the surgery, the twins' father was accused of spending some of the charitable donations they had received on fancy restaurants, a car, and cocaine binges (Toufexis 1994). Another report records his purchases as a truck and over $1,300 worth of cocaine, marijuana, and alcohol (Thomasma et al. 1996). In addition, he was said to have purchased drugs with the compensation he received for bringing a video camera into the neonatal unit (Segal 1999, Thomasma et al. 1996). His probation for an earlier assault charge was revoked and he was sent to jail for six months. A week after the separation surgery, doctors removed the breathing tube that connected Angela to a respirator, but she remained on a negative-pressure ventilator because of abnormalities in her chest wall and muscles. The cost of care at Children's Hospital now exceeded $1 million, part of which was reimbursed by Indiana Public Aid ($997 per day) and the rest of which was absorbed by the hospital. Angela was fed through a thin nasogastric tube so that it didn't interfere with her breathing. By late fall, she was able to breathe on her own for brief periods (Toufexis 1994). Kenneth was released from jail in April. He saw Angela only twice during her hospital stay. "Other problems included eviction from the trailer park where they lived and lack of sufficient support that would have been required to raise Angela at home on a respirator," wrote Thomasma et al. (1996), who pointed out that the combination of medical facts and social problems should have weighed against surgery: "The likely poor physiological outcome coupled with the chances of poor physical support in the home environment, with little or no funding for complex home care, negates the possible benefit of prolonging a baby's physiological life."

Angela seemed to be recovering well and her mother, who had made half a dozen trips to Philadelphia, hoped to bring her home to Indiana in the summer. Doctors fully expected to release a healthy child. The baby's emotional needs were met by the nurses, who gave her the attention she lacked from her parents, showing her affection, reading to her, making her laugh (Toufexis 1994). She especially loved to splash in the bath. Therapists were teaching the baby the motions of sucking and eating, and were playing games that helped her learn to sit up. Toufexis (1994) writes, "Far from the tortured existence that many predicted, Angela's brief life was largely free of suffering. Repairs to Angela's heart had rendered it fully functional. Her chest was somewhat misshapen but healing well. Angela did not spend her days entangled in tubes and wires. She needed no sedatives or painkillers or emergency trips to the operating room." In January, however, doctors discovered an obstruction in a pulmonary artery and inserted a small tube to widen the passage. Angela had been progressively weaned from the respirator so that she could be off of it for as long as five hours and learned that if she pulled the cardiac sensors off her chest, the nurses would come running. Joey Lakeberg visited her daughter in April, with the trip paid for by the *National Enquirer* in exchange for exclusive rights to her story and pictures of her with Angela (Burling and Mayer 1994). She said that the operation would help doctors better understand the medical mysteries of conjoined twins, causing critics to label the procedure experimental (Separating Conjoined Twins 1993).

Though her progress had been steady and her weight had reached twenty-one pounds, Angela caught a simple cold in May. Her temperature soared and she developed trouble breathing. When she began to deteriorate, she was ventilated twenty-four hours a day. Doctors suspected she was developing pneumonia, but actually a blocked vessel was keeping blood from flowing to the lungs and it was backing up into her heart (Toufexis 1994). On June 9, 1994, Angela Lakeberg lost consciousness and died after three resuscitation attempts without her parents present. She was twenty days shy of her first birthday. The cause of death, which was to be confirmed at autopsy, was a "cardio-respiratory disorder," a combination of lung and heart problems that led the oxygen levels in her blood to drop precipitously (Burling and Mayer 1994). At the time, her father was in a drug-rehabilitation center. Hours after her death, he was being arraigned on auto-theft charges (Toufexis 1994). Indiana Medicaid refused to reimburse either hospital for the dramatic treatments pursued because they were judged retrospectively to be futile and because the proper pre-authorization forms had not been completed (Thomasma et al. 1996).

Angela was buried next to her sister in Roselawn, Indiana, in a pink dress inside a white casket. She had outlived Amy by only ten months. The Philadelphia team has no doubts that their efforts and the cost were worth it. The lessons learned will help other babies survive. Their mother agrees: "I'd do it all over again," she says. "There is no price on life" (Toufexis 1994). The Lakeberg case did raise many ethical questions about whether so much money should be allocated for such a small chance of success, about the quality of the informed consent, and about the operation whose direct result was the death of one of the twins (Dougherty 1993). Ethicist Dr. Charles Dougherty states that the issue is not that the Lakebergs are uninsured or Kenneth's use of drugs and diversion of funds, but rather that the great expense — which could be used to fund many unmet basic healthcare needs — is not justified by the estimated one percent chance of success. Thomasma et al. (1996) point out that many of those involved in the Lakeberg case may have been influenced or at least distracted by the media attention that surrounded it: "While no explicit decisions about the twins occurred as a result of media attention, there is little question that both institutions received some benefit from the publicity."

Regarding informed consent, Dougherty (1993) points out that allowing the parents an option with such a slim chance of succeeding represents an impossible standard for surrogate decision-making. In addition, he asks, how can parents give morally valid consent for an operation that directly causes the death of one of their children? Alice Dreger (1998) asks about the emotional trauma Angela would have had to face if she survived, knowing that Amy was killed on her behalf. Dougherty discounts the notion that the end justifies the means or that Amy was not really a person. In con-

clusion, Dougherty (1993) writes, "The twins should have remained together. They should have been kept as comfortable as possible. Their deaths should have been accepted. This would have meant choosing to lose a very small, exorbitantly expensive chance of giving Angela more time. But this choice would have reflected an informed consent sensitive to the interests of both patients. And it would have been far more respectful of Amy." David Thomasma et al. (1996) state that the Lakeberg twins can become a paradigm case, like that of Karen Ann Quinlan, for public discussion.

*See also* **Legalities**

**Laloo.** *Nineteenth Century.*

Male child born in Oovonin, Oudh, India, in 1874 with the body of an imperfectly formed twin protruding from his abdomen:

> The upper portion of a parasite was firmly attached to the lower right side of the sternum of the individual by a bony pedicle, and lower by a fleshy pedicle, and apparently contained intestines. The anus of the parasite was imperforate; a well-developed penis was found, but no testicles; there was a luxuriant growth of hair on the pubes. The penis of the parasite was said to show signs of erection at times, and urine passed through it without the knowledge of the boy. Perspiration and elevation of temperature seemed to occur simultaneously in both [Gould and Pyle 1956].

Laloo toured the U.S. and Europe from the age of eighteen, some of that time with P.T. Barnum. The twin was dressed and billed as his "sister" to add to the sensation. In 1899, Laloo participated in the protest meeting in which Barnum's human oddities asked to be called "prodigies" rather than "freaks" (Fiedler 1978). He was displayed before the Pathological Society of London (Dreger 1998). Laloo was killed in a train accident in 1905 while traveling in Mexico.

*See also* **Parasitic twins**

## Lateral union.

Descriptive of twins united side-by-side, with shared umbilicus, abdomen, and pelvis.

***See also* Parapagus**

## Lawler, Mary Grace and Elizabeth Rix. *Twenty-first Century.*

Conjoined twin girls born February 12, 2001, to David and Allison Lawler of South Carolina. Their condition was detected at twenty weeks' gestation when a scan revealed two backbones and possibly a single heart. They were put under the care of Dr. James O'Neill at Vanderbilt University, a pediatric surgeon who has participated in the separation of seventeen pairs of conjoined twins. At 31 weeks of pregnancy, it was determined that the twins shared an abnormal heart that could not be repaired, so neither would survive surgery. The Lawlers were featured on The Learning Channel's "Joined: The Secret Life of Conjoined Twins."

***See also* "Joined: The Secret Life of Conjoined Twins"**

## Lee, Trudi and Sophia. *Twentieth Century.*

Conjoined girls born joined at the head to Kathy and Samy Lee of Zambia. One was reported to have dark skin and the other light skin, so they were referred to in the media as the "Chess Set Kids." In a 1992 interview, doctor Leon Abecele claimed it would be easy to separate the twins.

## Legalities.

Conjoined twins raise several legal questions, especially at the beginning and ending of their lives. Surgeons may consult with legal advisors before performing an operation that will result in the death of a parasitic twin, for instance. And there may be some question whether to issue one birth certificate or two. Legal responsibility may come into question with regard to health insurance coverage and other financial issues. During their lives, conjoined twins confound the legal system. The legal incarceration of one conjoined twin would result in the illegal detainment of the other, so charges brought against them have traditionally been dropped. In a case in Paris in the seventeeth century of a conjoined twin stabbing a man to death, the sentence of death was commuted rather than executing the innocent twin (Thompson 1968). Marriage has also posed a problem for the civil authorities, uncertain in the past whether to issue a marriage certificate at all.

***See also* Attard, Rosie and Gracie**

## Legans, Dominique and Diamond. *Twentieth Century.*

Conjoined twin girls born in California in 1997.

## Lentini, Frank. *Nineteenth-Twentieth Century.*

Francesco Lentini was born in Rosolini, Sicily, in 1889 with three legs and two sets of genital organs. He had two legs thirty-eight and thirty-nine inches long and a third leg, which he could use as a stool, measuring thirty-six inches. To separate the third leg, which had a partial pelvis and was joined at the spine, would have caused paralysis or death. From the day he was taken to visit an institution for the severely handicapped, Lentini never complained about his condition. He toured for years with Buffalo Bill's Wild West Show, Ringling Brothers and Barnum & Bailey, and other shows. Lentini married and became the father of three sons and a daughter. He lived in Connecticut, but retired to Florida.

***See also* Parasitic twins**

## Lewis, Ja'Nishia and Ja'Lishia.

Conjoined twin girls born to Josie Lewis. They breathed on their own, but had an abnormal heart and other ailments. Surgeons hoped to repair their hearts, but were unable. At five years old, the twins remained conjoined and their hearts were giving out.

## Lewis, Tiffany Lynn Brenea and Brittany Lynn Renee. *Twentieth Century.*

Female conjoined twins born on May 12, 1993. Tiffany did not survive separation surgery.

## Libbera, Jean. *Nineteenth Century.*

A male child born in Rome in 1884 with a miniature twin growing out of his body. The twin was named — by Libbera or his manager — "Jacques." Jacques had hips, thighs, legs, arms, and hands and feet complete to the nails on the fingers and toes. An X-ray taken in Germany showed a rudimentary head embedded in Jean's abdomen. Billed as "The Man with Two Bodies," Libbera traveled with Barnum & Bailey and other shows. He married and was said to have fathered four children (Drimmer 1973). Libbera was said to be proud of Jacque's perfectly formed fingernails and toenails and believed he qualified as a person, since he had a rudimentary hidden head (Fiedler 1978).

*See also* **Parasitic twins**

## Lincoln, Charity Mae and Kathleen Faith. *End of Twentieth Century.*

*We'll tell them that they just came in a different packaging.* — Vaneice Lincoln about her daughters

Conjoined twin girls born by Cesarean section at the University of Washington Medical Center on February 21, 2000, to Greg and Vaneice Lincoln. The Lincolns were from just outside Lacey, Washington. They were joined from the bottom of the breastbone to the pelvis, sharing parts of the large and small intestine, the anus, and having fused livers, urinary bladders, pelvises, and reproductive organs. Together they weighed thirteen pounds. Their father remembers, "It was shocking to look at them.... I never got used to looking at the girls" (Casey 2002). The night of their birth, Vaneice examined them closely in the nursery and wondered how they would care for the babies. The twins' website (www.lincolntwins.com) explains, "While it was devastating to see their children misshapen, God did not leave them without hope for separation."

The Lincolns had learned of their girls' condition during ultrasounds in the eighth and eleventh weeks of pregnancy. "I think your twins are conjoined," said their doctor, and referred them to a specialist in high-risk pregnancies (Casey 2002). In December 1999, they met with Dr. John Waldhausen, who diagnosed the twins as ischiopagus tripus and explained to their parents that such twins were among the most difficult to separate, since they often share vital organs (Casey 2002). When Dr. Waldhausen showed them a drawing of ischiopagus twins, Greg remembers, "That was the first time we really came to grips with the situation" (Casey 2002). They explained the situation to their other children later that day. Despite the support of their families, close friends, and co-workers, Greg and Vaneice felt alone and rarely confided in anyone but each other (Casey 2002). Their neighbors did not know of the twins' condition and the Lincolns rarely took them out except to church and doctor appointments. They later decided not to act like they were in hiding, since they weren't ashamed of their girls (Casey 2002).

The twins were released from the hospital ten days after birth. Doctors advised the Lincolns to allow the girls' fused third leg to grow and be tested. They were instructed by physical therapists on how to build up the girls' muscle strength so that they wouldn't favor the outer arm and hand

(Casey 2002). As the weeks went by, Kathleen was thriving, but Charity was getting thinner, even while eating twice as much. The doctors wondered whether the surgery should be weighted toward the twin with the better chance of survival. They also warned that postponing the surgery much past their first birthday might have lasting psychological effects, since the babies would by then have a shared identity. The girls had already begun to develop distinct personalities, with Kathleen more laid back and Charity — a.k.a. the "Pacifier Bandit — more aggressive and curious (Casey 2002). The parents were in favor of separation, but only if both children would survive. "We wouldn't sacrifice one girl for the other," said Greg (Casey 2002). "It'll be like a new birth for them," he added. Their oldest sister Mikayla looked forward to being able to lift each girl from the crib, since she was unable to pick them both up. They also have a brother Troy and sister Annelise.

The girls were separated on September 30, 2000, at Seattle's Children's Hospital and Regional Medical Center. The operation was expected to take up to thirty-six hours and the girls had been given an 85 percent chance of survival through the first month after the surgery. Of the eighteen sets of ischipagus tripus twins that have been separated, six died. There was a 15 percent chance that one or both Lincoln babies could die, but the chance was equal for each. Doctors were encouraged by their normal mental development and their sufficient organ mass. The surgical team directed by pediatric surgeon John Waldhausen included nine other pediatric specialists (representing surgery, urology, orthopedics, plastic surgery, anesthesiology, and radiology) and up to twenty other staff members. "I think everyone was amazed at the level of expertise in this one room at one time," said hospital medical director Dr. Richard Molteni.

Three months prior to the surgery plastic tissue expanders were implanted in the babies' shoulders and hips and fluid was added twice a week to stretch the skin in order to close the surgical incisions. Many blood tests and other procedures were performed. Magnetic resonance imaging allowed the doctors to chart in advance how they would separate internal organs and arteries. They did not know in advance whether some of the organs would be large enough to divide, for instance whether the liver would have enough bile ducts, so the surgery was performed in an order that could be reversed if necessary. "We'd prepared ourselves," explained Vaneice. "We knew we might take them home the way we brought them" (Casey 2002). The twins were admitted to the hospital two days prior to surgery to allow their digestive systems to empty and to run anesthesia lines. As he operated, Dr. Waldhausen discovered that Charity's internal organs were a mirror image of Kathleen's. After the initial incision and exploration, the livers, bladder, and small intestine were successfully divided. The girls were each given one ovary and one fallopian tube and the single uterus and vagina were separated. During the surgery, Kathleen's lungs partially collapsed. Tissue from the removal of the shared, nonfunctional third leg was used to close the abdominal wall; a dimple from the knee was used to create a navel; and bone from the leg was used to reconstruct the pelvises. Separate anuses and urethras were constructed for each twin. Twenty-four hours of separation surgery were followed by several hours of reconstructive surgery during which the surgical teams divided and the girls were worked on in separate operating rooms. Charity was wheeled into the neonatal intensive care unit after a total of twenty-nine hours of surgery. Kathleen, weaker due to lung complications, followed two hours later (Casey 2002).

After surgery was completed on October 1, 2000, the Lincoln twins were listed in critical condition as they were weaned from ventilators and pain medication. They were taken off respirators on October 4, but were still being fed intravenously. The feeding tubes remained in place on October 23 when they returned home to their brother and two sisters. They faced the dangers of lung collapse, infection, and their extensive wounds reopening. Each girl has a colostomy, though doctors hope to be able to give them normal bowel function in the future. It is expected that the girls will be able to bear children, despite their incomplete pelvises, but it was unclear whether they will ever be able to walk with prostheses, since they each have only a single hip and leg. They will require additional reconstructive surgery and will face a lot of physical challenges, according to Waldhausen. The surgeon noted that Charity was thriving and gaining weight, but Kathleen remained on a feeding tube. The girls were undergoing physical therapy to learn to push themselves up, roll over, and crawl.

The Lincolns decided to allow the surgical procedure to be discussed so that the public would know what Kathleen and Charity faced (Holt 2000a) and that they are proud rather than ashamed. They were interviewed by Keith Morrison on NBC's *Dateline* on February 9, 2001, and a transcript of the story made available on the show's website. The Lincolns said that many couples abort, but that was not an option for them as Fundamental Christians. When asked later what their reaction was to the news that their babies were conjoined, Greg Lincoln said, "cry," and Vaneice Lincoln said, "pray." They told their children what to expect — including the statistical possibility that the babies might not live — and then welcomed Charity and Kathleen into their family. The babies' unusual physique posed a number of problems, including getting diapers, clothes, strollers, and car seats to fit. Their surgeon Dr. Waldhausen says, "It always is remarkable to me how well these children adapt and how well these families are able to cope with what initially seem like incredibly daunting challenges."

The twins would have survived without the separation surgery and their parents wouldn't have gone through with it unless both were expected to survive. "It's been a tremendous trial," said father Greg Lincoln. "We feel very good and excited about the future, which will be harder perhaps than for average people. But we do face a bright future" (Holt 2000b). The Lincoln twins' website proclaims, "Their scars are healing and so are ours." A special fund for the twins, the "Kathleen and Charity Special Needs Trust," is maintained by Key Bank. In April 2001, it was reported that the twins were medically stable, but facing additional surgery. Surgeons at Children's Hospital planned to connect the girls' large intestines to give them normal bowel functions. They were expected to be in the hospital about a week. The surgery would eliminate the ileostomies that were put in place during the separation surgery to avoid the infection that may have been caused by stool passing through the suture lines. Surgeons had also planned to operate on the twins to close their hip bones, but physical therapy may make that unnecessary (Thompson 2001).

Vaneice is happy with the outcome of the surgery: "If we could have drawn the perfect scenario, we would have given birth to two separate, perfectly formed little girls. We didn't get the miracle we prayed for, but we got a miracle just the same" (Casey 2002). They make special accommodations for Kathleen and Charity at their family's home in Olympia, Washington, including special cushions in their booster chairs. Both girls are using walkers and will eventually graduate to crutches. NBC's *Dateline* followed up with the twins as they approached their first birthday, as did *Ladies' Home Journal*. They are rolling, crawling army-style, and playing. Socially and cognitively, the Lincoln twins are right on target, calling each other by name, playing peek-a-boo, and suffering no noticeable separation anxiety (Casey 2002). On the *Dateline* website, Vaneice writes, "They are so active, so mobile, so resilient, so happy. It is inspiring…. Their scars are healing and so are ours." Kathleen and Charity have weekly therapy sessions. They have returned to Children's Hospital twice for a virus that caused dehydration and seizures. Because she has difficulty eating enough to gain weight, Kathleen still needs a feeding tube to supplement her oral intake. Charity has had plastic surgery at the incision site and uses a brace. She will likely require an operation to fuse her vertebrae to prevent further curvature of her spine; she is missing a rib and has scoliosis due to the way she pressed against her sister's side in the womb (Casey 2002).

### Lloyd and Floyd.

*I am not saying that a mother cannot love such a double thing — and forget in this love the dark dews of its unhallowed origin; I only think that the mixture of revulsion, pity, and a mother's love was too much for her. Both components of the double series before her staring eyes were healthy, handsome little components, with a silky fair fuzz on their violet-pink skulls, and well-formed rubbery arms and legs that moved like the many limbs of some wonderful sea animal. Each was eminently normal, but together they formed a monster.*— Vladimir Nabokov (1958)

Lloyd and Floyd are the names of the conjoined twins born near the Black Sea in the fictional short story "Scenes from the Life of a Double Monster," written by Vladimir Nabokov in 1950. Floyd explains in the first person that their conception was the result of the rape of their mother, who died shortly after their birth. The twins were raised by aunts and became a regional curiosity. The twins were joined by a cartilaginous band, as were Chang and Eng Bunker. The band was referred to as a "bridge of gold" by their grandfather, who began to charge strangers to see the twins and hear them speak to each other. "By the age of nine, I knew quite clearly that Lloyd and I presented the rarest

of freaks," explains Floyd. "This knowledge provoked in me neither any special elation nor any special shame…" (Nabokov 1958).

From Floyd's point of view, Nabokov (1958) describes the unspoken series of decisions made between conjoined twins: "All of our movements became a judicious compromise between the common and the particular. The pattern of acts prompted by this or that mutual urge formed a kind of gray, evenly woven, generalized background against which the discrete impulse, his or mine, followed a brighter and sharper course; but (guided as it were by the warp of the background patter) it never went athwart the common weave or the other twin's whim." He also explains that it is too late for separation: "In later years I have had occasion to regret that we did not perish or had not been surgically separated, before we left that initial stage at which an ever-present rhythm, like some kind of remote tom-tom beating in the jungle of our nervous system, was alone responsible for the regulation of our movements" (Nabokov 1958).

At the age of twelve, Lloyd and Floyd escape their grandfather's clutches only to be kidnapped by their uncle, who had been negotiating unsuccessfully to take them on a six-month tour. The story is written after twenty years have passed, but their present situation is not revealed.

### Louis and Louise. *Sixteenth Century.*

A pair of pygopagus conjoined twins described and illustrated by Ambroise Paré in his book *On Monsters and Marvels*. They were said to have been born in Paris on July 20, 1570, to Pierre Germain and Matthée Pernelle. Paré described them (impossibly) as a male and a female.

### Makwaeba, Mahlatse and Nthabieseng. *Twentieth Century.*

Conjoined twins born in South Africa in 1994. Separation surgery was performed at Ga-Rankwa Hospital north of Pretoria on June 14, 1994. The surgical team of two dozen was led by Johns Hopkins neurosurgeon Dr. Ben Carson, but resulted in the death of both twins.

## Maria Jose and Maria Fernanda. *End of Twentieth Century.*

Conjoined twin girls born joined at the head on September 22, 2000, to Esmeralda Rodelo of Cartagena, Colombia. Because they had separate brains, it was believed that they could survive independently. But both girls died during an operation to separate them. Maria Jose died on September 23 as the surgery was beginning and Maria Fernanda died of respiratory failure early on September 24.

## Marie-Adèle. *Nineteenth Century.*

Conjoined twin girls born on June 26, 1881, in Switzerland. In feeble health, they were separated on October 29, 1881, by surgeons Biaudet and Buginon. Adèle died six hours after the operation and Marie died of peritonitis the next day (Gould and Pyle 1956).

## Marie-Rose. *Nineteenth Century.*

Conjoined twin girls born in St. Benoit, Canada, in 1878, united at an angle of about 120 degrees. Marie died of cholera infantum at home in July 1879, followed by Rose (Harris 1892).

## Marriage.

*…the observation that marrying female Siamese Twins is at least a way of getting two wives and only a single mother-in-law can still extract a sexist grin.* — Leslie A. Fiedler (1978)

Marriage of conjoined twins has been few and far between, the most publicized brides being Daisy and Violet Hilton. Certainly the most notable married couples are Chang and Eng Bunker and their brides, whose unions produced a combined total of twenty-one children. Leslie Fiedler (1978) raises the irony of conjoined twins being unable to divorce themselves from each other, despite a bad relationship.

*See also* **Blazek, Rosa and Josefa; Hilton, Daisy and Violet**

## Martha and Marie. *Nineteenth Century.*

Ischiopagus female twins born in Copenhagen, Denmark, on April 2, 1848, to a poor and small-statured cobbler and an average and healthy mother. The pregnancy had been normal, until the mother experienced swellings and pains at the end of her term. Delivery was normal, until there was resistance upon pulling the baby past the shoulders and thorax. The conjoined baby was delivered successfully, weighing almost ten pounds, and was transferred the next day to the Delivery Hospital. There, the babies were described as lying in a straight line with the heads at each end, fused in the middle with a single navel, and their limbs protruding from their sides. They had a cloacal opening between each pair of legs, but no external genitalia. Their central nervous systems were determined to be separate, and one child could sleep while the other was awake. Their pulse, respiration, and temperature varied. The babies were baptized as twins. After four uneventful days, Marie became cyanotic and her abdomen became distended. Martha began having cramps a few days later and also became cyanotic. Ten days after their birth, Marie died. Martha followed two or three minutes afterward.

At autopsy, Marie was found to have situs inversus. The fusion of their pelvises was examined. The internal lower body cavities were found to be separated by a transversal, solid membranous separation formed from a doubling of the peritoneal membranes. The girls each had a uterus, but shared a wide common urinary bladder and cloaca. The remains of Martha and Marie are preserved as tissue and skeletal preparations in the Saxtorph Collection of the Medical Historical Museum of the University of Copenhagen. The preparations were described in 1857 by Professor C.E. Levy in an essay entitled "Description of a pair of live born twin girls joined at the lower part of the body."

## Mary and Anna. *Twentieth Century.*

Conjoined twin girls born in Mexico (or Honduras) in 1910 joined by a band of flesh. They toured extensively in the 1920s as the "Honduranian Joined Together Twins." They were said to have very different personalities. Mary and Anna died in 1929 (Rusid 1975).

## Maternal impressions.

> *This Wondrous phenomenon thus had its origin. As the mother of these two children was gossiping with another woman on the street, an unexpected thing happened and struck the two foreheads of the women together; thereupon, the pregnant woman became ill with fright, so that the fruit within her womb had to suffer for it.* — Sebastian Munster, after having seen two six-year-old girls joined at the forehead in Mainz in the mid–sixteenth century

In earlier times, the sight of a conjoined twin (in human or animal form) was believed to put pregnant women at risk of giving birth to such a child. Maternal impression was a legitimate medical theory until the late eighteenth century, but continued as a form of popular wisdom long after it was refuted by medical science (Adams 1996). In the seventeenth century, a Madame Souville was said to have obsessively examined a picture in a French almanac of a monstrous child with two heads that had an excrescence of flesh between them. James Paris du Plessis writes that he examined the stillborn male child that had subsequently been born to Madame Souville and buried in the yard, and its features were identical

(Purcell 1997). More recently, pregnant women were warned against entering the sideshow tent for fear that the very sight of a freak might be enough to deform the gestating fetus; conversely, the freaks on display were described as resulting from maternal impressions themselves (Adams 1996). Robert Bogdan (1988) points out that the theory was less harmful than others, since it blamed neither mother nor child.
***See also* Jones Twins**

## Mathibela, Mpho and Mponyana. *Twentieth Century.*

Conjoined twins born in South Africa in 1987. Mponyana died during separation surgery in 1988.

## Mathse, Pot-en-Pan. *Twentieth Century.*

Ischiopagus female Bantu twins born in August 1946. They lived only seven days, dying on September 4, 1946. Their bodies are preserved as wet specimens at the University of Pretoria Department of Anatomy, but are said to have been "overfixed."
***See also* Specimens**

## McCall, Brenda and Linda. *Twentieth Century.*

Conjoined twin girls born on March 8, 1977, to Arthur and Glenda McCall of Roosevelt, New York. The twins were joined at the chest and weighed a total of three pounds thirteen ounces. Their livers were attached. They were successfully separated in October 1977 by pediatric surgeon Dr. Kenneth Kenigsberg at North Shore University Hospital, where they had remained since birth. The operation involved a team of twenty doctors and took four and a half hours. To ease their transition, the girls were placed in the same bed after surgery. Linda, described as very friendly and more active, weighed nine pounds three ounces. Her sister Brenda, the quiet one, weighed nine pounds seven ounces.

## McCarther, Yvonne and Yvette Jones.
### Twentieth Century.

*God gave them to me, so I guess he'll show me the way to raise them.* — Willa Jones McCarther

Female craniopagus twins born in Los Angeles, California, on May 14, 1949, to a divorced mother of four other daughters. Joined at the head, separation was impossible because they shared a circulatory system. They remained in L.A. County Hospital for two years, after which institutionalization was recommended, since the girls would need full-time nursing and special exercise equipment. The machinery would prevent the muscles from atrophying, but doctors did not expect the twins to achieve more than an awkward crawl (Stumbo 1981). To pay hospital bills exceeding $14,000, their mother accompanied them on a two-year tour with the Clyde Beatty circus, with 30 percent of all earnings applied to the bill, after which they returned to their Los Angeles home to be raised with their siblings.

Their mother remarried and the girls, then almost four, began to walk. Yvonne and Yvette were provided with volunteer tutors from a local school, earning their high school equivalency certificates in 1967. They lived from 1972 to 1977 in Atlanta (or by another account Augusta). Yvette was the quieter of the two, but both were good-natured and liked to laugh, patiently answering questions posed by curious strangers when they were in public. The *Philadelphia Inquirer* reported, "They are unrelentingly friendly, always smiling, joking and reaching out. They know that it is up to them to try to set people at ease. Given the opportunity, they generally succeed" (Stumbo 1981). They explained that they do not get headaches, have no sensation where their heads are joined, and do not suffer from the angle they must maintain when they walk. They told an interviewer how their love of food caused

Yvette to jump from a size 7 to a size 22 and Yvonne from a size 5 to a size 20 (Stumbo 1981).

They corrected comparisons to Chang and Eng Bunker, who were known for their quarrels, by pointing out that they never disagreed. Neither did they dote on the drawbacks of their condition and they were fatalistic about their eventual death, which would of course be mutual. They claimed that they wouldn't want to be separated as adults. They dressed identically, slept and ate at the same time, and both smoked cigarettes, but referred to themselves in the singular tense. "They always eat and drink exactly the same things, in precisely the same amounts, and always at the same time," reports Bella Stumbo (1981). They did not share a wristwatch, a lighter, or a purse, but their purses contained matching sets of everything from vitamin jars to wallets containing the same family photos (Grosz 1996). "I speak for myself, she speaks for herself," said Yvonne (Smith 1988). Their nicknames for each other were "Bonnie" and "Betty." They hoped to marry and have children. Their menstrual cycles differed, but they were in excellent health.

In the 1970s, Yvonne and Yvette performed gospel songs around the country. Yvonne explained (Begley 1987) that they had to achieve perfect harmony or "it kind of sets up a vibration." The twins were featured in the March 30, 1978, issue of *Jet* magazine, became the subject of a pastel drawing and photograph by Joel-Peter Witkin in 1988, and appeared once on the *Geraldo Rivera Show*. In 1987, at age thirty-eight, they enrolled as nursing students at Compton Community College in Long Beach, California, believing that they could do good work with handicapped children (Smith 1988). The following year, they moved from their mother's house into their own apartment. The McCarthers died on January 2, 1993, a few months short of their college graduation. They were found dead of apparently natural causes in their home by a visitor. Nancy Segal (1999) reports that the cause of death was heart failure and that Yvonne, who had an enlarged heart, died first. According to college spokesperson Paula Wilde, "They were wonderful to be around…. They had an excellent sense of humor and spoke their minds freely" (Landau 1997).

### McDonnell, Niamh and Aoife.
*Twentieth Century.*

> *I'd been terrified of what they might look like. You can't really tell from the scans. But when I saw them they were just perfect baby girls who looked as if they have been stuck together.* — Joan Varley

Female conjoined twins born at St. Mary's Hospital in Manchester, England, by Cesarean section on April 8, 1997, to Joan Varley and Paul McDonnell of Levenshulme. The babies weighed a total of ten pounds two ounces and were joined at the chest. They had a single umbilical cord. Their Gaelic names mean "Saint" and "Eve," respectively. Their mother told the *National Enquirer* how the babies were locked together in an embrace when the nurse first brought them to her and described them as "the most incredible sight. They were gorgeous."

The parents had learned that their girls were joined at the chest during a routine scan at twenty weeks of pregnancy. They each had two arms and two legs. Their livers were fused. Their hearts were believed to be contained in a single sac. Termination of the pregnancy was offered, but the McDonnells declined unless the babies also had Down syndrome or spina bifida. After birth, the twins were fed through nasogastric tubes, then began bottle feeding at about two weeks. They were turned every two hours to take the weight off the other, since they couldn't lie on their backs.

The twins were separated at eleven weeks of age in late June 1997 at Great Ormond Street Hospital (Siamese Twins Undergo Surgery 1998). The sixteen-member surgical team was led by Dr. Lewis Spitz and Dr. Edward Kieley. Before the operation, larger and larger pieces of foam were wedged between the twins to stretch their skin. During surgery, one twin was given the existing pericardial sac and an artificial one was constructed for the other twin. A special technique was used to divide the livers: they were drained of blood, cut ultrasonically, the blood vessels sealed with natural-based glue. Very little blood was lost. Post-operatively, the twins were expected to see their doctor every three months or so. They took their first steps in November 2001.

### McKoy, Millie-Christine. *Nineteenth Century.*

> *One from long habit yielded instinctively to the other's movements, thus preserving the necessary harmony.* — George M. Gould and Walter L. Pyle (1956)

Pygopagus female twins born into slavery ten miles from Whiteville, Columbus County, North Carolina, on July 11, 1851, the eighth and ninth of sixteen children of African parents Jacob and Monemia. The parents — and thus their offspring — were owned by Jabez McKoy, a blacksmith in eastern North Carolina. The twins, who weighed a total of seventeen pounds at birth, were known as Millie-Christine. Millie — the twin on the right — was the smaller of the two, accounting for only about five pounds of the total. They were found to have two hearts, two sets of lungs and intestines, two bladders, and a united spinal cord, but one vagina, one uterus, and one rectum. They had shared sensation below their union. Their personalities, though distinct, were in harmony. They learned to walk at twelve months (and could later walk on two or four legs) and to talk at fifteen months. Dr. William Pancoast (1871) later described:

Millie-Christine photographed by Dr. William Pancoast. Courtesy of the Mütter Museum, College of Physicians of Philadelphia.

Pervis waived his remaining interest in the twins for $200. They were acquired by a Mr. Brower for somewhere between $10,000 and $40,000, with the note backed by Joseph Pearson Smith, a merchant from Wadesboro, North Carolina. Brower was quick to exhibit the twins, arranging their display at the first North Carolina state fair in Raleigh in October 1853, with separate viewings for "Ladies only" and "Gentlemen alone" (Martell 2000). Brower then took the twins on the road, billing them as "The North Carolina Twins" and the "Double-Headed Girl." He allowed medical men at each stop of their Gulf Coast tour to examine them and certify them as genuine, a successful publicity tactic. But then Brower accepted an offer of $45,000 worth of land for the twins from a Texan who disappeared with them before providing the deeds. Brower searched for the Texan and the twins for weeks, but then broke the news to Smith,

Though joined at the inferior posterior parts of their bodies by the contiguous sacra, and originally formed so as to be placed back to back, yet they have from their birth instinctively twisted themselves, as if the bond of union had yielded, and their spines have assumed a gibbous form under the exertion, permitting them to assume almost a lateral position, like an expanded V, thus facilitating their movements. They walk each partly sideways, the apex of the V advancing, their main support being from the outer limbs, steadied and guided by the weaker inside legs.

A bill of sale dated May 18, 1852, about ten months after their birth, records that the babies were purchased by John C. Pervis of Chesterfield District, South Carolina, from Jabez McKoy for $1,000 and 25 percent of the proceeds from their exhibition. The document stipulated that they were to be accompanied by their mother. A little more than a year later, on September 30, 1853,

Millie-Christine on a twig-and-branch settee. Courtesy of Milner Library Special Collections, Illinois State University.

who owned the missing twins now that Brower was bankrupt, and to Jabez McKoy's farm to tell Millie and Christine's horrified parents.

Smith paid off his note to McKoy, meaning that he would own the twins outright if he could find them. Smith promptly hired private detective T.A. Vestal of Selma, Alabama, to locate Millie-Christine. The twins were being shown privately to groups of medical men by the swindler, who then sold them to a man who exhibited them in a museum in Philadelphia (Martell 2000). They apparently changed hands several times, finally turning up at age three in August, 1854, as the "Celebrated African United Twins" at P.T. Barnum's American Museum in New York. Meanwhile, Detective Vestal had traveled to Philadelphia, New York, Boston, and finally to Newark, where he learned that the twins had been spirited away to Liverpool by showmen William Thompson and William (Prof. W.J.L.) Millar, who claimed to have found Millie-Christine in Boston. The girls celebrated their fourth birthday aboard the *Arab*, which had sailed from Quebec in July 1855. They were examined in Liverpool by seven physicians, including Dr. Thomas Inman, who signed a medical endorsement:

> We have examined carefully to-day the African twins. They are completely united below the body.... They are interesting, lively, and intelligent little people, and have nothing of monstrosity in their appearance. It is impossible to see them without being pleased with their manners and lively chattering [Martell 2000].

Shortly afterward, on August 14, Professor Millar stole the twins and their Cuban nanny and took them to London and to Dundee, where he allowed eleven doctors to examine them. Millar exhibited the twins to the public for a shilling, offering half price to children.

Thompson caught up with Millar and the twins in Dundee and brought them to the presiding magistrate at Bow Street Police Court for a custody hearing. The judge stated that English Law does not recognize a state's power to confer property right in human beings, so neither claimant could establish title to the twins. Thompson assumed guardianship and continued the exhibit of the twins and their examination by medical men, this time at Drury Lane Theatre. One of the physicians, F.H. Ramsbotham, described them in September 1855 as unable to walk side by side, but active and amiable (Martell 2000). Thompson supported his guardianship claim on his show bills, which claimed that the proceeds went toward freeing the twins' enslaved parents (Martell 2000). After receiving word of their whereabouts from Millar, Joseph Pearson Smith purchased Millie-Christine's entire family (Jacob, Monemia, and seven children) from Jabez McKoy and wrote to Millar in September 1855 offering to pay for the twins. Negotiations dragged on for more than a year.

Millie-Christine continued to tour Great Britain with William Thompson, who promoted them as being from "Tamboo, Africa." Smith — accompanied by the pregnant mother of the twins and joined in New York by William Millar's brother Kennedy — caught up with Thompson in Birmingham, England, in January 1857. The party attended a performance and, after an overwhelming reunion during which Monemia fainted, took the girls away. Thompson swore out a complaint and officers served a writ of habeas corpus to the mother and twins demanding their appearance before the Court of Admiralty. The judge was more convinced by the resemblance of the twins to their mother than the proof offered into evidence. Thompson offered Monemia £10,000 and a house in England if she would allow him custodianship of the girls until they were eighteen, but she preferred to bring them home. Instead, the persistent William Millar convinced them to exhibit with their mother in Edinburgh. Millie-Christine later wrote that they had an audience with Queen Victoria at this time at Osborne House on the Isle of Wight. They were again observed and probed by a number of medical men, including James Syme, James Young Simpson, and John Lizars (Martell 2000). Posters announced their appearance on January 19, 1857, and promoted them as "Christina and Milley Makoi," age five and a half. When Millar was out of town, however, Smith left with Monemia and the twins for Liverpool and sailed for New York aboard the *Atlantic*. They returned to Smith's home in Wadesboro. Shortly thereafter, William Thompson surfaced, but was run out of town when he began agitating local slaves.

The twins lived in Smith's house in Spartanburg, where his wife (who they referred to as their "white ma") educated them and taught them not only to read and write, but to sing and dance. Christine was a soprano and Millie was a contralto, and they were able to accompany themselves on guitar and to play two pianos placed in the form of a "V." The Smiths finally decided to tour with the girls, bringing a slave woman, to attend the girls, and Detective Vestal to the Gulf of Mexico, where they would proceed by steamboat up the Mississippi River. Smith, too, allowed doctors to examine the twins, including Josiah Nott in New Orleans on February 10, 1858. By the end of May, they reached St. Louis, where they were examined by four more physicians on May 28. Millie-Christine had remained healthy throughout the trip except for one bout of malaria. They followed the Missouri River to St. Joseph, where they were examined by another group of five doctors on July 13 (Martell 2000). In the summer of 1859 they were in Tennessee and in February 1860 they were touring Mississippi. February and March 1861 found them the most prominent attraction at the New Orleans Museum.

Millie-Christine photographed at the Gibson & Thompson studio in Philadelphia. Courtesy of Milner Library Special Collections, Illinois State University.

On November 5, 1862, Joseph Pearson Smith died and was mourned by the eleven-year-old twins whom he had made a part of his family and whom he had reunited with their own. Two appraisers charged with settling Smith's estate estimated Millie-Christine's value at $25,000, but they were not among the twenty slaves sold to cover Smith's debts. Legally freed after the Civil War, Millie-Christine remained with Smith's widow, bringing in an income of as much as $600 a week. The twins headed north with their parents and brother in tow. Jacob and Monemia stopped off at Welches Creek, North Carolina, to resettle the family on the land they once worked. The twins exhibited in Raleigh, North Carolina, in March 1866. A month in Baltimore was followed by a stop in Washington, D.C., where they were observed in May 1866 by Professor Charles A. Lee. Now on their own, Millie-Christine objected to intimate examinations, but Professor Lee was able to describe in a letter to a friend that they had begun menstruating some seven months earlier, that their outer legs were better developed than the inner ones, and that their heights were four feet five and a half and four feet six inches (Martell 2000). In fact, it is reported that they menstruated regularly from the age of thirteen (Gould and Pyle 1956). Their weight at the time of Dr. Lee's examination was a combined 159½ pounds. Christine was the stronger of the two, and could lift Millie off the ground. Both girls had suffered fever and ague at the same time, but only Millie had caught diphtheria (Martell 2000). Although they were said to eat separately, they experienced hunger and thirst at the same time. The need to urinate and defecate occurred simultaneously (Gould and Pyle 1956).

In July 1866, Millie-Christine returned to Barnum's American Museum for a month-long engagement. There they attracted Dr. George J. Fisher, the man to whom Professor Lee had written. Dr. Fisher, president of the New York State Medical Society, was writing about "Compound Human Monsters" and was pleased to have the opportunity to see one in person. By 1869, business was bad and the Smiths hired a new agent. At the same time, Millie-Christine wrote their memoirs. *History and Medical Description of the Two-Headed Girl* was the first show business autobiography and the thirty-two-page booklet was sold to patrons for a quarter. The booklet explains, "Although we speak of ourselves in the plural, we feel as but one person." The second half of the booklet included Dr. George Fisher's case study (Martell 2000). In 1869, Millie-Christine toured New England with stops in Massachusetts, Rhode Island, and Maine. In Boston, doctors from the Harvard Med-

Millie-Christine in striped dresses. Courtesy of the Circus World Museum, Baraboo, Wisconsin.

ical School faculty tried in vain to convince the twins to undergo a complete physical exam, but the girls defended their right to personal privacy. In Portland, a Dr. Gardner caused a disturbance because he had been denied an examination and was removed from a performance by the town constable (Martell 2000).

For a time, the "Carolina Twins" toured with Chang and Eng Bunker. In 1870, the twins exhibited in New York, Pennsylvania, Ohio, Indiana, and Kansas. New Year's Day 1871 saw the twins in Baltimore, followed by exhibits in Washington, D.C., and Philadelphia. In Philadelphia, Dr. William Pancoast convinced the girls to pose for a revealing yet modest photograph that shows their union. He wrote, "They clung to their raiment closely, as may be seen, and it was only by earnest entreaty that they were willing to compromise by retaining the drapery as photographed. The expression of their countenances shows their displeasure, as their features ordinarily express great amiability of character" (Pancoast 1871). The photograph appeared in the *Photographic Review of Medicine and Surgery*, along with a less modest drawing by Mr. Faber that illustrated the details of the girls' shared vulva. The two urethra, two clitorises, and two labia majora continuous with each other were diagrammed, along with the common anus. The lyrics of one of the songs they performed read:

> Two heads, four arms, four feet,
> All in one perfect body meet;
> I am most wonderfully made,
> All scientific men have said.

Dr. Pancoast had been called on to treat the girls for an abscess, which he diagnosed as a fistula created during the incomplete formation of a second anus and rectum. Whether it closed spontaneously or he treated it surgically is unknown. In his report, Pancoast (1871) notes that although he found no hymen present, he found the vagina naturally small and contracted as to be expected of an ordinary young unmarried woman. Of the possibility of marriage, he said there were no serious physical objections, but insuperable moral ones (Martell 2000).

Millie-Christine were shown by Dr. Pancoast to faculty and students of the Jefferson Medical College, with newspaper reporters invited to observe, interview, and publicize. Pancoast's own examination showed that their band of union seemed to be chiefly cartilaginous, with some osseous involvement. He noted that their frontal development was remarkably good in each case. He recorded that they experienced hunger and thirst simultaneously, that they both had fever and ague at the same time, and that the viscera were not transposed (Pancoast 1871). Pancoast also suggested that Millie-Christine's mother was not the victim of maternal impressions, since she had never seen the Siamese twins. At this time Dr. Pancoast also carried out some experiments with Dr. William Pepper and Dr. R.M. Townsend to test the girls' sensations. Dr. Pancoast described Millie as weaker physically, but having the stronger will, and advised Christine not to lift her up as she was able to do. Millie-Christine stayed in Philadelphia for two months, during which time they visited two studios to pose for "cartes d'visite" photographs to be sold at their shows. After playing several nearby Pennsylvania towns, the twins sailed for England aboard the ship *City of Brussels* on April 22, 1871, to tour with giants Captain Bates and Anna Swan. Together the troupe attracted 150,000 people during its eight weeks in Philadelphia (Martell 2000).

While in England, Millie-Christine were observed and described by naturalist Frank Buckland:

> I must now describe the "Two-Headed Nightingale." The Siamese Twins [Chang and Eng Bunker] were certainly very wonderful people, but in Christine-Millie we have, I think, something more remarkable. The Siamese Twins are two old gentlemen somewhat advanced in years. The "Two-Headed Nightingale" is composed of two charming young negress girls, who are united back to back by an indissoluble band. I do not recollect to have seen a more intelligent, ever-laughing happy face, than that of Miss Christine. She has dark rolling eyes and jet-black hair, and though her features are those of the daughters of Ham, yet there is a quickness and intelligence about her that shows culture and education [Bompas 1886].

Of Millie-Christine, the *Leader* wrote:

> We can testify that no person of ordinary intelligence can be in her company for half an hour without yielding to the charm of her manner and the fascination of her double smiles. She has you on both sides. If you remove your head from one position, you are immediately the victim of another pair of eyes, which fix you and, in fact, transfix you [Martell 2000].

*Left:* Millie-Christine photographed at the Temple of Art studio in Philadelphia. *Right:* A young Millie-Christine costumed for a show. Courtesy of Milner Library Special Collections, Illinois State University.

The girls again toured Liverpool, wearing a costume cut low in the back to reveal part of their juncture. From there, they returned to London, now selling copies of an updated *Biographical Sketch of Millie Christine, The Two-Headed Nightingale.* After attending the wedding of Anna Swan and Captain Bates on June 17, Millie-Christine performed by command of Queen Victoria on June 24, 1871. Victoria's journal records the event, remarking, "It is one of the most remarkable phenomena possible" (Martell 2000). She presented the twins with a matched pair of diamond-studded hair clips. The twins were invited to Marlborough House by Princess Alexandria, who gave them brooches, and were visited at their shows by the Prince of Wales and other dignitaries. They exhibited in the grand concert hall at the Crystal Palace. They were

said to have appeared before the Queen four times and before the Prince of Wales (later Edward VII) three times (Sullivan 1979).

The crowds back in Liverpool were impressed by the twins' handsome new jewelry and the stories that came with it. The troupe had a one-week engagement in Edinburgh in December, then met up with Tom Thumb's troupe in London in April 1872. After a few more appearances, the Bates and Tom Thumb and company returned to the United States, but Millie-Christine and the Smiths stayed on in England, celebrating their twenty-first birthday during a performance at the Standard Theatre. After Mrs. Smith engaged a manager for the twins and they and the family spent a week's holiday in Brighton, Mrs. Smith and her daughters returned home. Joseph Smith, Jr., continued on with the twins to

Vienna in December 1872; St. Petersburg, Russia (where they probably performed for the czar and his family), in May 1873; and Paris in November 1874 (Martell 2000). The doctors in Paris also regretted the girls' modesty, although Dr. Bertillon was able to report that their light skin and curly (rather than woolly) hair was due to their mother being part Native American, that their hearts accelerated at different rates, and that one didn't usually share the other's migraine headaches unless they were particularly severe. Despite the objections of the twins and Joe Smith, members of l'Académie de médecine — including Pierre Paul Broca — insisted on examining them to make sure the French public wasn't being duped. After negotiations, the twins undressed to the waist with a German woman present. The doctors' observations from head to hips and knees to toes were reported back to the Academy and Millie-Christine was certified as legitimate.

When two women tied themselves together to pass themselves off as conjoined twins, the Cirque des Champs-Elysées, where Millie-Christine was appearing, swore out a complaint to capitalize on the publicity. A more serious event occurred in Tours, France: Millie-Christine's dress caught fire from the kerosene-burning footlights of the stage. Luckily the fire was doused and surprisingly the girls went on with their performance. The twins remained abroad for seven years, during which their original owner Jabez McKoy died. They returned home, arriving in New York on October 1, 1878, and were met aboard ship by a reporter from the *New York Herald*, who reported that they had become fluent in several languages. They welcomed the publicity as they continued to tour. They had a season's run in Boston, another teaching clinic for Dr. Pancoast in Philadelphia, and a month-long show in Philadelphia's Concert Hall in January 1879. They then boarded a train and headed west, where they toured

Millie-Christine photographed by royal photographers W.&D. Downey, Newcastle-on-Tyne and London. Courtesy of Milner Library Special Collections, Illinois State University.

between Denver and Portland for a year and a half. They returned to the South in 1881, spent that winter in Cuba, and appeared back in New York late in the year for a long engagement at Bunnell's Museum.

When George H. Batchellor and John B. Doris tried to convince the twins to tour with the Great Inter-Ocean Railroad Show and asked for their terms, they told him $25,000 for the season with traveling expenses for a maid and man servant, hoping to put Doris and Batchellor off. Instead, the men presented a check and a contract right then and there. The 1882 season lasted thirty-five weeks. They were accompanied by their English companion Blanche Brook. Batchellor and Doris wrote another forty-page booklet about the twins' lives and printed a poster that boasted of their enormous

**Millie-Christine photographed at Bertin studio in Brighton, England, in 1873. Courtesy of Milner Library Special Collections, Illinois State University.**

salary. During the performance, Millie-Christine sang a couple of songs, danced a polka, and bowed in two directions before skipping offstage. The circus toured Pennsylvania, Ohio, Indiana, Illinois, Missouri, Wisconsin, Nebraska, and Kansas, ending up with ten weeks in Texas and two weeks in New Orleans (Martell 2000). The circus competition was vicious and their old rival Adam Forepaugh posted and printed notices that Millie-Christine were disgusting and repulsive to gaze upon. They defended themselves and their livelihood by bringing a libel suit against him for $25,000 that was later settled for an undisclosed amount.

The twins were subject to dangers other than their pride. On October 7, 1882, the Batchellor and Doris circus train on which they were traveling was hit by a freight train, injuring three men, one of them fatally. After wintering at Joe Smith's villa in South Carolina, Millie-Christine signed up for another $25,000 season with Doris (he and Batchellor having parted ways). The season was promoted as her last with Inter-Ocean, and when it closed in Newport, Arkansas, they headed to Whiteville, North Carolina. There they spent the next several months decorating their fourteen-room house, which had been constructed with extra-wide doorways next door to Jacob and Monemia's house. Millie-Christine entertained numerous guests, reserving Sundays for people of color (Martell 2000).

In June 1884, the twins set off on the Wisconsin for another English tour. Their first performance was for royalty at the Marlborough House. In October of that year, their beloved companion Blanche Brook died. In 1885, the twins were seen by C.J.S. Thompson and described in his book *The Mystery and Lore of Monsters.* Before Millie-Christine left England in June 1885, they made an appearance at the Reynolds' Exhibition, a Liverpool wax museum that broke its attendance records that day. Shortly after their arrival back in the U.S., Joe Smith placed an ad asking anyone who wished to engage the twins to contact him. They joined Barnum & London for the 1886 season, where they were described:

> The most truly remarkable human being of which there is any record. A duality of persons in one. Two living mortals combined. Two minds forming beautiful thoughts, two mouths expressing gentle sentiments and two perfect heads receiving impressions and ideas from one common heart. A veritable Female Janus, with two classic faces looking in opposite directions. Undoubtedly the most agreeable, pleasant, and wonderful of living and breathing objects. Two living branches on one stem, talking and singing simultaneously in different languages [Martell 2000].

Instead of traveling with Barnum's outfit to Europe, Millie-Christine stayed in the States and worked the dime museum circuit. They were at the Cleveland Museum and Theatre in November 1887. In February 1888, they appeared at Lit's Museum in Milwaukee.

Millie-Christine signed with F.R. and Lou Blitz for the 1889 season and appeared at the fall state fairs and expositions, beginning with the Buffalo International Fair. When business fell off, Joe Smith would place another ad. The girls were pleased to work at their old Inter-Ocean friend John B. Doris's Harlem Museum in 1890 and appeared in New Haven, Connecticut, at the end of that year.

Their father Jacob McKoy died in spring 1891, at age seventy-nine, having made a will leaving seventy-eight acres divided among nine children and grandchildren. P.T. Barnum died in April of that same year. Millie and Christine turned forty and marked the event with matching gold rings with garnets that they wore the rest of their lives. Mary Smith, their "white ma," died in 1893 at the age of seventy-one. In 1896, Millie-Christine's sister Clarah married Lawrence Yeoman and moved into their house with him. All of them escaped the fire that burned the house down in 1909, but Millie-Christine suffered severe financial losses (Sullivan 1979). They built a modest six-room replacement. During the 1910 census, Millie-Christine were recorded as fifty-nine-year-old unmarried mulatto twins.

Millie-Christine went to the local Methodist churches, organized a school for the local African-American children, and gave money to several local colleges. One of her descendants described, "She was more than just a circus freak. She was a talented, generous black woman who was one of the greatest black women of their time. She said that when God made her, he gave her two heads and two brains because her responsibility was so great" (Martell 2000). Unfortunately, Millie was wasting away with consumption. They took Whiteville doctor William Crowell's recommendation to rest at a sanatorium

Millie-Christine abroad. Courtesy of the North Carolina Division of Archives and History.

in the north, but returned to Welches Creek with Millie uncured. In 1912, the twins converted to Baptists and signed a last will and testament. They were attended by Dr. Crowell on October 8. After consulting with Johns Hopkins Medical College, Dr. Crowell was advised not to try to separate the twins, but to comfort Christine with massive amounts of morphine. He next left a message for Governor William Kitchin asking for official permission to euthanize Christine. It was she who first noticed Millie's passing on October 8, 1912. Christine fought to stay alive, lingering some eight to seventeen hours, praying and singing hymns. Word finally arrived from the governor and Dr. Crowell increased the dosage to ease Christine's death.

After the death of the twins, a neighbor constructed a double-coffin and a wake and funeral were held. They had both been horrified by stories of Chang and Eng's autopsy and rumors of body-snatchers, and therefore wanted their bodies to be cremated. Joe Smith promised to post guards at their grave, which was a four-foot-by-six-foot plot in the family graveyard at the edge of a cornfield. The grave marker had two joined arches:

> Millie-Christine, born July 11th, 1851, Columbus County, N.C. Child or children of Jacob and Monemia McKoy. She lived a life of much comfort owing to her love of God and joy in following His commands. A real friend to the needy of both races and loved by all who knew her.
> Christine-Millie, died October 8th and 9th, 1912. Fully resigned at her home, the place of her birth and residence of her Christian parents. "They that be planted in the house of the Lord shall flourish in the courts of our God." Ps. 92:13.

Their epitaph read, "A soul with two thoughts. Two hearts that beat as one." Their grave was watched by the family for nine months (Martell 2000).

In November 1969, Fred McKoy, members of the Columbus County Historical Society, and two professional preservationists opened the grave of Millie-Christine after receiving permission from her descendants. The collapsed casket was encountered at a depth of fifty-one inches. The skeletal remains consisted of a handful of bone fragments and what appeared to be a vertebra. Also found in the grave were a black dress, a button, two sets of dentures, a hairpin, and two gold rings — one with a garnet and the other with the stone missing. The remains were placed in a one- by three-foot pine box and reburied in the Welches Creek Community Cemetery beneath a flat polished-granite headstone containing the text of their earlier marker. The cemetery is reached via Mille [sic] Christine Road and their grave is mentioned on a state historical marker posted beside U.S. 74-76 Near White Marsh (Martell 2001).

Millie-Christine are the subject of a biography, *Millie-Christine: Fearfully and Wonderfully Made*, by Joanne Martell. The author explains on the publisher's website (*www.blairpub.com*) that she became curious about the twins after reading that their grandnephew often wished he could live the life Millie-Christine did. Martell decided to tell their story, which had been neglected by historians, including those specializing in women's and African-American history. Martell was most impressed by Millie-Christine's faith in God and extreme tolerance for her fellow humans. Before posting a series of provocative questions for reading groups, Martell writes, "That Millie-Christine survived birth and the exploitation of her childhood is remarkable. That she developed her talents to become one of the most renowned performers of her day is amazing. That she overcame what can only be considered a grave physical handicap to flourish into a woman of great character and religious conviction is truly a tale of the triumph of the human spirit."

## Media attention

*That extraordinary bodies continue to be the stuff of spectacle is perhaps no more obvious than in the case of conjoined twins, whose birth and surgical separation consistently excite fierce media interest, including the production of full-length documentaries...* — David L. Clark and Catherine Myser (1996)

News of the birth or separation of conjoined twins often captures popular attention and therefore becomes the focus of stories on television and headlines in the newspapers. Some families try to retain their anonymity. Others embrace the news media for reasons ranging from financial need to management of the public relations angle to a genuine desire to inform the public about children like theirs. Larry Fanning, father of Shannon and Megan Fanning, confronted questions of how open to be with the media upon the birth of his daughters and again upon their separation. He discusses his experiences at length in his book *Separated Angels* (Fanning 1995). "There had been a recent case in the news within our own geographical area involving twin girls. The media had covered this case rather closely, and we had watched with more than just passing interest. In addition, there just happened to have been two television specials concerning two other sets of conjoined twins. We watched these, and wrote down information and questions we thought might be of use to us later on. This included the names of doctors and hospitals we might need to contact" (Fanning 1995). The Fannings also saw a television documentary about Katie and Eilish Holton that they found very moving.

The Lakeberg case was in the headlines during the Fannings' pregnancy. Their doctor discouraged them from allowing the media too much access, but explained that the hospital would be taking photographs during the delivery. Fanning (1995) writes, "We had finally come to realize that there would, at least initially, be a lot of interest in the twins. That is, of course if someone were to let the word out. Knowing how much the Lakebergs were in the news, we could assume the Fannings would be there almost as much. We were trying to protect our privacy and our own personal interests. If there were to be film and/or photos, we wanted control over them." In fact, Fanning provided his nephew Rich, who worked at the hospital, with a video camera to tape the birth. After the birth of his conjoined twin daughters, Fanning's sense of pride overtook his desire for privacy: "I didn't care if everyone in the hospital made some sort of excuse to come see our daughters. I was happy for the safe delivery, and proud of my girls. Besides, everyone who came by was polite and courteous. They all seemed to comment on how beautiful and how per-

fect Shannon and Megan were" (Fanning 1995). At the same time, Fanning was uncomfortable with his celebrity status at the hospital and was embarrassed at being treated differently than other parents (Fanning 1995).

During the separation surgery, Larry Fanning consulted with the hospital's media services representative who had been contacted by the local news station. With his wife, Larry decided to release only basic information about the babies: names, gender, date and place of birth. The Fannings also released basic information about themselves and stated that the twins were undergoing separation surgery. They were dismayed that even so, the resulting news stories were full of errors, for instance substituting the name "Sharon" for "Shannon." They were also disheartened by the negative prognoses offered by doctors who were interviewed as experts, but had never examined or been involved in the Fanning case. Later, they were disturbed by the news media taking their quotes out of context to manipulate what they said and heighten the drama (Fanning 1995).

After the surgery on March 25, 1994, a press conference was held. One of the surgeons spoke first, after which Larry Fanning answered questions. He muses, "Had anyone ever told me that I would one day stand in front of numerous television cameras and microphones, while experiencing absolutely no nervousness or fear, I would have told them they were crazy" (Fanning 1995). Fanning was asked how his daughters looked after the surgery and told the press, "They were gorgeous when they were born and they're gorgeous now, even though they're a little puffed-up and poked full of holes" (Fanning 1995). Though he was still equivocal, Fanning allowed the media to show the girls on television. Fanning was asked if he was insured and was able to answer yes, but revealed that he had not checked to see whether the surgery was covered. A trust fund had been established for the Fannings to receive individual donations. He later dispelled the notion that parents in his and Sandi's position would attempt to benefit financially from the situation, unless cash were needed to pay for medical treatment.

While Sandi was still in the hospital, she received a phone call from the aunt of the Lakeberg twins, offering her encouragement, prayers, and advice. After the separation surgery, they received a letter and photographs from the parents of nine- or ten-year-old conjoined twins who had been successfully separated. Both this family, the Lakebergs, and now the Fannings were aware of media scrutiny of their lives. After the Fanning family returned home, they continued to receive phone calls from local and national television stations and newspapers. "We had already made up our minds to be accommodating, but squeezing in all of these return phone calls was getting difficult to accomplish," explains Larry Fanning (1995). Again he was discouraged when he granted an interview to a local news station broadcast on cable; although they provided him with four questions in advance, none of them were asked during the live interview. He knew the media would move on to the next sensational topic, but explains his frustration: "...it did bother me that some of our comments had been taken out of context. It hadn't been enough to make us look bad or stupid, but had changed our story just a little. Everyone who was watching, listening or reading, was not getting the whole picture" (Fanning 1995).

In an article in *Literature and Medicine*, Catherine Myser and David L. Clark (1998) argue that medical documentaries about conjoined twins reinforce the cultural assumption that there must be a singular self correlated to a single body, using Katie and Eilish Holton as a case study. As they explain, "Medical documentaries are especially vivid instances of the correlation of power and knowledge: although seemingly descriptive, and created in the name of producing a form of lay medical knowledge for a mass audience, they also function in prescriptive ways, reproducing normative assumptions about what it means to be properly embodied" (Myser and Clark 1998). The notion put forth is that embodiment should be a singular condition — one sex, one body, one self — and according to this calculus, conjoined twins are not quite human. Myser and Clark (1998) speak of a medical imperative to separate such twins, despite the risks, to make them conform. Such surgery is assumed and the joined twins are consistently represented in the documentaries with imaginary lines indicating their division into two. Footage of the parents of conjoined twins meeting pairs of successfully separated twins is called by Myser and Clark (1998) the "medical regime's coup de grace." When Eilish Holton died, her surviving twin Katie was described as having in some ways incorporated her characteristics — though they were a part of each other from the start. Myser and Clark (1998) ask, "Even if the twins are physically divided, do the surgeons, do any of us know precisely what 'separation' and 'separateness' mean?"

*See also* **Fanning, Megan and Shannon; Holton, Katie and Eilish; Lakeberg, Amy and Angela; Publicity**

**Millie-Christine** *see* **McKoy, Millie-Christine**

**Milton, Violet and Daisy** *see* **Infante, Patricia and Madeleine**

**Mobility.**

Conjoined twins have more or less mobility depending on their physical anatomy and whether they have been separated. Other undetermined factors may also play a part: the Tocci brothers were unable to walk, but the similarly-formed Hensel twins are able to coordinate their movements to achieve not only walking, but running and riding their bike. When twins sharing two legs are separated, each twin is fitted with a prosthetic leg in addition to one of the natural legs. A vestigial leg may be incorporated or amputated. Conjoined twins each having a pair of legs may be able to lengthen their connection or turn in such a way as to walk forward naturally; if not, they may become accustomed to moving sideways or to one twin moving forward and the other backward. In the most seriously disabled cases, twins may be unable to walk at all, either together or separately, and are provided with walkers, wheelchairs, and other ambulatory aids.

*See also* **Disability; Hensel, Abigail Lauren and Brittany Lee; Tocci, Giovanni-Batisto and Giacomo; Viet and Duc**

## Monstrosity.

Conjoined twins have been referred to as monstrosities or monstrous births over the centuries. The word was first used to mean an abnormality of growth in 1555 (OED 2001). Like the word "prodigy," "monstrosity" also carries with it a sense of being a sign or an omen. The horror that is felt upon seeing a severe anomaly has been interpreted as a warning of external events or a manifestation of our own nightmares. In *Special Cases*, Rosamond Purcell (1997) writes, "The focus in this book remains on the wall of shadow pictures, on the inescapable relationship between a dreamed-up monster and its painfully viable counterpart." The use of the word "monster" to describe conjoined twins was objected to as early as the 1870s, when an editorial about the Finley twins in the *Ohio State Journal* remarked, "No one can look at the two sweet baby faces, see the two pairs of bright eyes, hear the two cooing voices, and say 'monstrosities.' The little prattlers strike too near the heart for that" (Besse 1874).

*See also* **Finley, Mina and Minnie; Freak; Prodigy**

**Moon Creek, Janlee and Janlean.** *End of Twentieth Century.*

Conjoined twin girls born in San Juan, Puerto Rico, on June 9, 2000, to Juanita Creek and James Moon, both described as devout Catholics. An ultrasound first revealed twins, then showed that they were joined at the pelvis. The doctors thought the twins might have extensive anomalies and possibly cerebral palsy. As expected, Juanita went into labor prematurely and an emergency Cesarean section was performed. The babies weighed eleven and a half pounds and had a total of two legs. Although they shared a liver, bladder, large intestine, and much of their reproductive systems, Janlee and Janlean were good candidates for separation. Their father struggled with the decision, knowing that their condition was not fatal. Their mother imagined future repercussions from the girls themselves about why the operation was denied them.

Separation of the Rivera twins, or "Siameses Moon Creek" as they were known in the media, took place at Children's Hospital in New York City. The surgical team was led by Dr. Stephen Stylianos, who explained that Janlean was replacing nutrients for both children because of Janlee's intestinal problem. The separation of the liver was successful, with bleeding controlled and the organ larger than expected. Thirteen hours into the operation, the pelvis was cut and the girls were placed on separate tables. Janlean's surgery took a total of seventeen hours, with Janlee's taking a few minutes longer. Unfortunately, Janlee died after the surgery of cardiac arrest at the age of four months. Her body was transferred to Puerto Rico. Janlean's swelling went down and the sedatives on which she was being maintained were reduced. Their story is chronicled on an NBC *Dateline* program entitled "A Matter of Faith," which aired May 1, 2001.

## Morales, Sarah and Sarahi. *Twentieth Century.*

Twin girls born in Tijuana, Mexico, on January 12, 1996, to Miguel Angel Morales and María Luisa Espinoza, who expected twins but did not know they would be conjoined. The girls were joined at the chest and abdomen, sharing a single set of intestines and a single set of arms and legs. They were transported to Children's Hospital in San Diego a week after birth following a plea from one of the physicians in Tijuana. There they were evaluated for potential separation. Sarahi had a defective heart (due to a malfunctioning ventricle) that was too weak to pump the blood carrying waste products away, a condition that results in acidosis and would have caused the death of the twins within weeks or months if they were not separated. A team of thirty prepared for surgery, using a pair of dolls to anticipate logistical problems. Once surgery began, surgeons found that the girls' livers were joined in a complicated way. Even so, the operation went ahead of schedule and smoothly, with both babies in stable condition toward its completion. Although her heart rate had improved to almost normal and its rhythm was being maintained by an external pacemaker in the operating room, Sarahi did not survive the six and a half hour separation surgery at two weeks of age. Despite her death, doctors considered the operation a success: "We went into the operating room with a pair of doomed twins and came back with one normal baby who will probably live a normal life," said cardiovascular surgeon Dr. John J. Lamberti (Surviving 1996). Sarah remained sedated and on a ventilator after the surgery, but was considered stable. Nitric oxide was administered to improve blood flow through her lungs and antibiotics were given to prevent potentially fatal infections. Some of her sister's skin and bone tissue was used to reconstruct Sarah's chest and a future graft of Teflon material

was anticipated to completely close the chest cavity. She was expected to remain in intensive care for up to three weeks, though doctors were cautiously optimistic about her chances of survival.

Since the parents had no medical insurance, earned very little, and were not eligible for California benefits, doctors in San Diego donated their services, estimated at more than $100,000. The hospital made an international appeal to the public and to the government of Mexico on behalf of the twins. An unidentified San Diego mortuary offered to handle Sarahi's funeral arrangements free of charge. Still, the hospital was faulted by many for providing so much free care to Mexican nationals, particularly for a procedure that may not have succeeded. The twins' parents declined to talk to the media after the surgery, preferring to "keep their thoughts to themselves."

*See also* **Legalities; Media attention**

## Moreno, Hever Arón and Román Alán. *Twentieth Century.*

Conjoined twin boys born by Cesarean section at Scripps Memorial Hospital in Chula Vista, California, on May 16, 1996, joined at the chest and abdomen. They shared a large liver and weighed a total of twelve and a half pounds. Their parents, Román and Andrea Moreno, are from Tijuana, Mexico. They learned that their sons were conjoined during a prenatal test, but doctors there lacked the expertise to separate them. Andrea Moreno crossed the Mexican border six times to see her Chula Vista obstetrician Dr. Jorge Arce. When she arrived for a routine appointment, she went into unexpected and premature labor. The twins are therefore U.S. citizens, but are not eligible for any state or federal government medical funding. After birth, the twins were transferred to the University of California–San Diego for evaluation. The boys were separated in a six-hour operation at the

University of California–San Diego in 1996, two weeks after tissue expanders were inserted to stretch their skin. A special laser was used to prevent bleeding as the liver was divided.

After the operation, the boys were given antibiotics to prevent infection. Nine days after surgery, the twins were discharged and the family took up temporary residence in UCSD's Bannister House, so that doctors could continue to monitor them. A week later, they left for Tijuana. As with the Morales twins, the hospital was criticized for paying the medical bills of Mexican citizens and it was suggested that the separation could have been performed in Tijuana with the assistance of U.S. doctors. UCSD set up a fund to accept donations to defray the cost of caring for the Moreno twins.

## Nabokov, Vladimir *see* Lloyd and Floyd

## Nolan, Bethany and Alyssa. *Twenty-first Century.*

*Being a sceptic, I keep looking for problems, but there have been none so far. She is making the appropriate baby noises and smiling. Everything is stable, and it's a wait-and-see proposition.* — Dr. Scott Campbell

Conjoined twin girls born in Brisbane, Australia, on May 3, 2001, to Shaun and Mary Nolan, the parents of three boys. The girls were joined at the side of the head sharing skull and brain tissue and surgeons planned to wait a year before separating them. Bethany, the weaker twin, had heart trouble and other complications that forced an emergency operation on May 26, 2001, to separate them. Bethany had been born without a gallbladder or kidneys. The surgery, overseen by Dr. Alan Isles and performed at Brisbane's Royal Children's Hospital, resulted in her death. Alyssa suffered two cardiac arrests during the operation, but was revived. Speaking for the parents, a family friend told the press that they had

always known that one of the girls would die. Alyssa was listed in critical condition after the operation. She would require additional surgery to graft bone to her skull (Surgeons Fail 2001) and fix a bone defect at the base of her skull. Alyssa had a cold after the surgery, but the fifteen-week-old baby was meeting all of her developmental guidelines, according to her mother, and returned to the hospital weekly for physiotherapy and other treatment. Doctors were guarded about her long term prognosis, since the cardiac arrests while under anesthesia may have caused permanent neurological damage. Mary Nolan describes that having the twin home was at first nerve-wracking: "We just sat there and watched her. We didn't sleep; we needed to keep checking that she was still breathing" (Roberts 2001).

## Obermaier, Christine and Caroline. *Twentieth Century.*

Female twins born in Chicago in 1980 joined at the head.

## Omphalopagus.

Twins joined face-to-face, primarily in the area of the umbilicus, but with entirely separate hearts. The twins have separate pelvises and four arms and legs (Spencer 1996). The condition often involves shared liver tissue. Occurs in about 34 percent of conjoined twins (Segal 1999).

See illustration opposite and on page 10.
*See also* Xiphopagus

## Onziga, Loice and Christine. *Twenty-first Century.*

*We were able to free them from one another.* — cardiac surgeon Marcello Cardarelli about the surgical separation of the Onziga twins

*At first, this was a bad miracle, but now it's a happy miracle.* — Gordon Onziga

Conjoined girls born on October 28, 2001, to Gordon and Margret Onziga of Leiko in the Democratic Republic of Congo. The babies were joined from the breastbone

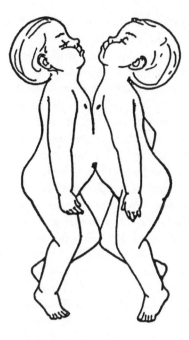

**Diagram illustrating typical omphalopagus twins. Courtesy of Rowena Spencer and the W.B. Saunders Co.**

to the navel and shared a liver, sternum, chest wall, and abdominal wall. They weighed a total of six pounds, with Christine the larger twin. Margret Onziga had intended to have what she thought was a normal child at home, but was taken to the city of Arua, across the border in Uganda, where the twins were delivered by Cesarean section at the regional hospital. "I was not sure if they would survive," said Dr. Richard Amandu, who examined the twins upon arrival. People soon flocked to see the conjoined twins, but the hospital admitted that they could not handle the case (Gibson and Murphy 2002). Two weeks after birth, mother and twins were transported to Mulago Hospital in the Ugandan capital of Kampala, where they were evaluated by pediatric specialist Dr. Margaret Nakakeeto, who said, "Everybody here is so used to death. They believed that the girls would die" (Gibson and Murphy 2002). In Kampala, the girls came to the notice of pediatrics professor Cindy Howard, who was accompanying residents

on an exchange program from the University of Maryland. A CT-scan showed that surgical separation was possible, so Howard called Chief of Pediatrics Jay Perman. Howard explains, "It was a difficult decision for all of us. We didn't want to make any promises that we couldn't keep. But finally, we couldn't just leave them to go back to the village" (Gibson and Murphy 2002). Perman arranged for the University of Maryland Medical Center to accept the twins. Airfare to the United States was donated by British Airways and U.S. visas were granted. The family arrived in Baltimore on February 28, 2002, and have been guests of the Ronald McDonald House and have received assistance from an area church (Goldstein 2002).

Loice and Christine were separated at the University of Maryland Medical Center by a 35-member team of doctors, nurses, and technicians. The team was led by cardiac surgeon Marcelo Cardarelli and pediatric surgeon Eric Strauch. They first underwent a battery of tests, including ultrasound and magnetic resonance imaging. The tests indicated that while each girl's heart had four chambers, they shared an abnormal blood vessel connecting the upper chambers, and Loice's heart was pumping blood into Christine's. Because of the fear of heart failure and the probability of success, the risk of severing the shared artery was found to be worth taking. Separate surgical teams were assigned to each twin and drilled in advance to make sure the plan and all equipment were functioning properly (Bor 2002). The surgery took place on April 19, 2002, and lasted twelve hours. The operation included cutting into the abdomen and chest, separating the liver, diaphragm, and heart, and moving each twin to a separate table where their chests, diaphragms, and abdominal walls were reconstructed with the help of synthetic material. The area of attachment of each girl was about six inches long and four inches wide. After surgery, they were transferred to the intensive care unit, where they were most content when placed in the same crib. The twins remained on ventilators for about ten days, but have experienced no serious medical problems. Each has been left with a slight opening in her heart; Christine's will likely close on its own and Loice's is expected to be repaired nonsurgically with the use of a catheter (Bor 2002).

All fees were waived by the university and its physicians. The decision required careful consideration, as Dr. Perman explains: "We wanted to do the right thing.... We gave to the twins, but they gave to us. Our principal mission is medical education. This was a great learning experience, and it gets us prepared for the next Maryland children who need this kind of care" (Goldstein 2002). The family remained in Baltimore for physical therapy and follow-up care. The twins still arch their backs slightly, but are expected to achieve a normal posture and eventually crawl and walk normally (Bor 2002). Doctors expect their flattened heads to round out with time and their arched backs to straighten with physical therapy. Their personalities are distinct and they are jealous of each other now that they can be held separately by their mother. Their father plans to show them photos of when they were joined together (Pressley 2002).

## Opodidymus.

A condition in which the heads are fused and the sense organs are partially fused. There is a wet preparation of a stillborn infant with opodidymus on display at the Mütter Museum in Philadelphia. The two heads are fused in the back and on the sides, but partially separated in the facial region, where a nodule of skin represents a common ear for each head. There were no visceral deformities other than the division of the esophagus, trachea, and main blood

vessels to supply each head. The specimen was donated by Dr. Benjamin S. Gorder.

## Orissa Sisters *see* Radica and Doodica

## Osorio, Maria de Jesus and Maria Guadalupe Flores. *Twentieth Century.*

Conjoined girls born July 26, 1996, in the Hospital Infantil de Mexico Federico Gomez in Tijuana, Mexico, sharing a single heart. They were flown to Mexico City on August 1, 1996, to be evaluated for surgery to correct a heart condition being controlled with medication. The babies took turns sleeping, since their breathing became labored when they were both awake.

## Padua Twins. *Seventeenth Century.*

Conjoined boys born December 8, 1691, in the village of Ponte de Brenta. They lived only long enough to be baptized and were autopsied three days after their death. The examination revealed two separate hearts, four kidneys, four ureters to two bladders, and one urethra for discharge through the common penis (Harris 1892).

## Palen, Wiktoria and Weronika. *Twentieth Century.*

*The condition of the girls today is testament to the skills and capabilities of the team of nurses and physicians at this institution. It was the combined efforts of general, plastic and reconstructive, and cardiothoracic surgery, along with anesthesiology, radiology, and the dedication of the operating room nurses and care provided by neonatal intensive care nurses before and after surgery that has dramatically improved the chances for Weronika and Wiktoria to have normal lives.* — Dr. Scott Adzick, Children's Hospital of Philadelphia

Conjoined twin girls born at the Medical University in Lublin, Poland, to Krystyna Palen on May 26, 1999, joined at the chest and abdomen. They shared part of the breastbone, ribs, liver, diaphragm, and pericardium. They did not share the pumping chambers of the heart, making surgical separation an option for both of them. They were transferred to Children's Hospital in Philadelphia on August 16, 1999. They were separated on November 3, at Children's Hospital in Philadelphia after two months of preparation during which the skin on their chest and abdomen was expanded. The surgery took five hours and was performed by a team headed by Dr. N. Scott Adzick. It was difficult, since most of Weronika's heart was in Wiktoria's chest. Adzick says, "We thought we could save both, but we knew there was a chance Weronika wouldn't make it, and the mother knew that" (FitzGerald 2000). Krystyna had remained with her daughters since their arrival in Philadelphia. The hospital and the surgeons involved waived their fees, which would have totaled an estimated $1.5 million. Wiktoria was taken off the respirator on November 23. Weronika had to be taken back to the operating room on December 14 to reposition her heart and to fix a malformation in it. She was taken off the respirator on January 10. A week prior to the girls' scheduled discharge from the hospital, Weronika developed a fever. The twins were released three months after separation surgery. A February 18, 2000, news conference was held in conjunction with their discharge on February 11. Dr. Adzick said, "While it was a rocky road at times for them, the surgery performed here has enabled them to lead normal, healthy and separate lives" (Successful Separation 2000). They returned to Poland with nurse Kelli Burns accompanying them to Lublin to help them get adjusted. The family met the twins and their mother in Krakow and took them to their four-room apartment in Stalowa Wola, Podkarpacie. They looked forward to being away from the media attention (Siamese Twins Wiktoria and Weronika 2000). The girls would undergo physical therapy under the supervision of the county hospital and the medical school hospital where they were born. Dr. Adzick said that Wiktoria appeared to be on target and predicted that Weronika would catch up (FitzGerald 2000).

**Palma and Maria.** *Twentieth Century.*

Conjoined twin girls born in Italy on Palm Sunday, 1977, sharing a torso. They were separated in an operation at Children's National Medical Center in Washington, D.C. Maria died about six weeks after separation of complications caused by an infection in the wound.

**Parapagus.**

Descriptive of twins united laterally. Parapagus twins always share a joined pelvis with one symphysis and one or two sacrums. Dithoracic parapagus twins have separate thoraces. Dicephalic parapagus twins have two heads. Diprosopic parapagus twins have one trunk and a single head with two faces on the same side. They may have two, three, or four arms and two or three legs (Spencer 1996). Occurs in about 5 percent of conjoined twins.

See illustration on facing page.

**Parasitic twins.**

*I remember during all the debates how quickly people who wanted to intervene could move into the idea that one twin was like a parasite or an appendage—Language that makes one morally able to divide them.*—Ethicist Alice Dreger about the Lakeberg case

Asymmetrical union in which the smaller twin is dependent on the more fully formed twin. Rowena Spencer (1996) theorizes that the parasite is partially absorbed by its twin: "Considering the high incidence of serious cardiac anomalies and the high pre- and post-natal mortality in conjoined twins, it is not unreasonable to postulate that occasionally one twin with insufficient cardiac function dies during early embryonic life, leaving viable body parts vascularized by the autosite." Such twinning would also include *fetus in fetu*, the presence of an

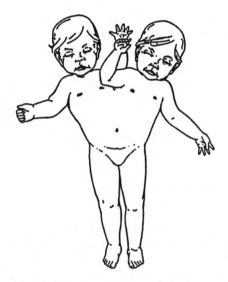

Diagram of typical parapagus twins. Courtesy of Rowena Spencer and W.B. Saunders Co.

abnormal fetus within another individual's body. A very rare form of partial conjoined twinning, in which a parasitic head is joined to the head of a normal cranium, is called cephalodiprosopus.

Examples of parasitic twins include Laloo and Perumal, both of whom were billed as having a sister buried headfirst in their abdomens (though their twin was by necessity the same gender). In his career as a "one-and-a-half," Laloo was unique in refusing to give his upper-body parasitic twin a name. Fiedler (1978) notes that such refusal was more common among those with lower-body parasites, since they could not be fully exhibited without exposing the genitals and their autosites were therefore billed as being multi-limbed. Another sideshow performer, Mexican Pasquel Pinon — shown in photographs with a smaller, fully-featured head projecting from his forehead — is known to have faked his parasitic sibling by fitting a wax replica on top of an anomalous growth on his head.

Gedda (1961) refers to parasitic twinning as "asymmetrical double formation" or "heteroadelphia," with specific terms for the area in which the parasite is attached: the

Figure of a man from whose belly another man issued, from Ambroise Paré's *On Monsters and Marvels*, originally published in 1840.

head ("epignathus"), the trunk ("thoracopagus," "dipygus," "notomelus," "pygomelus"), or a cavity ("fetal inclusion"). Spencer (1996) standardizes the terminology used: "Parasitic twins should not be identified by terms such as epigastrius, dipygus, heteropagus, notomelia and hypermelia; these terms are nonspecific and should be abandoned. The site of attachment of the various and sundry supernumerary anatomic structures will indicate the type of the original conjunction, such as: cranium (not the face), parasitic craniopagus; face and ventral trunk, cephalopagus; chest and upper abdomen, thoracopagus or omphalopagus, depending on whether the heart is involved; ventral pelvis, ischiopagus; dorsal pelvis limited to the sacrum, coccyx, and perineum, pygopagus; dorsal midline union above the sacrum, rachipagus; lateral aspect of the trunk and/ or head, parapagus. The only additional terms needed for identification, other than those listed above, will be those enumerating some of the parts, such as di- (two), tri- (three), and tetra- (four), with –brachius, -pus, -ophthalmia, -otia, and –stomia, referring to arms, feet (legs), eyes, ears, and mouths, respectively (i.e., parapagus tripus tetrabrachius or cephalopagus tetrophthalmia triotia)" (Spencer 1996).

*See also* Atypical twins; Aydin, Bashir; Laloo; Railoun, Aziz; Two-Headed Boy of Bengal

## Paré, Ambroise.

A French surgeon (c. 1510–1590) who studied, dissected, illustrated, and attempted to determine the cause of conjoined twins. He attributed their formation to a demonstration of divine power, punishment of the parents by God, sexual intercourse during menstruation, ejaculation of an overabundance of semen, narrowness of the womb, laziness of the mother, or hereditary disease or accident (Smith 1988). In 1546, he dissected a child with two heads, two arms, and four legs to find that it had a single heart (Thompson 1968). In 1569, Paré was given the dried skeletons of a pair of conjoined twins, which he added to his collection (Wilson 1993). Fiedler (1978) writes that Paré borrowed shamelessly from his predecessors and his contemporaries and that the credit for the first chapter of *On Monsters and Marvels* should have been given to Boiastuau.

See illustrations on pages 131, 133, 168.

## Peter and Paul. *Fourteenth Century.*

Conjoined twins born in Florence in 1316. Their effigy — with two heads, four arms, and three legs — was placed in the stairway of the Florentine hospital along with an inscription by Petrarch (Harris 1892). Gedda (1961) notes that a bas-relief of the twins exists in the courtyard of the San Marco Museum in Florence. He quotes an 1853 source that the babies were born in the old Hospital of Santa Maria della Scala and lived for only twenty days, one dying before the other.

## Pholpinyoh, Naphit and Krisna. *Twentieth Century.*

Conjoined twins born in July 1953 in Khonkaen Province, Thailand, joined at the chest and abdomen. They shared a liver and were said to be in good health by the Thai government, which was caring for them. They were sent to the Albert Merritt Ellings Hospital in Chicago for assessment and possible separation.

## Pregnancy.

*One rash, inconsiderate step will jeopardize the life of three human beings.* — A.B. Cook 1869

Carrying conjoined twins is diagnosed through ultrasound scanning when they are determined to have a single amniotic sac and fixed and tight positions in relation to one another. Before sonography, only 50 to 75 percent of conjoined twinning cases were identified before birth (Segal 1999). The special case that conjoined twins represent was recognized by nineteenth century medical men, one of whom wrote, "Injurious interference will often lead to the death of the children when unassisted nature may be able in time to deliver them alive. The management of the labour will depend very much upon the relative dimensions of the twins and pelvis; the position of the former, and the stage at which assistance is obtained" (Harris 1874). Today, delivery of conjoined twins is most often by Cesarean section to avoid damage to the babies and the mother. But unlike the preferred horizontal cut below the bikini line, their delivery usually

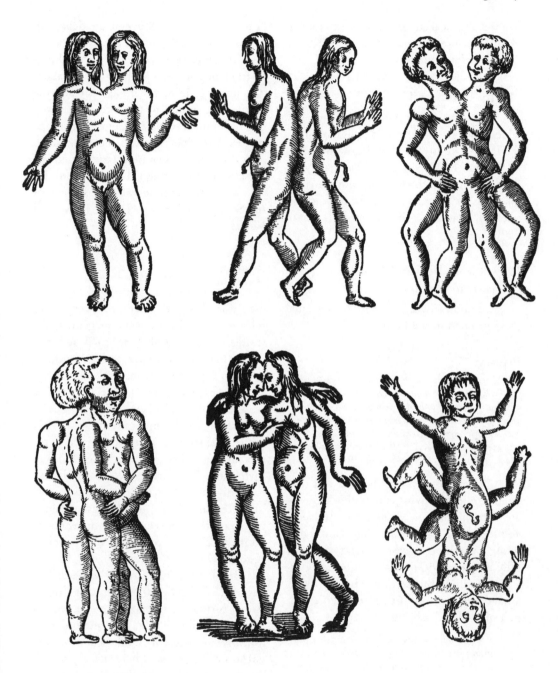

*Top left:* Figure of a girl having two heads. *Top middle:* Figure of two twin girls joined and united by the posterior parts. *Top right:* Figure of a child having two heads, two arms, and four legs. *Bottom left:* Figure of two twins having only one head. *Bottom middle:* Figure of two twin girls joined together by their foreheads. *Bottom right:* Figure of two monstrous children born not long ago in Paris. Photographs from Ambroise Paré's *On Monsters and Marvels*, originally published in 1840.

requires a vertical cut to allow for two joined twins to be brought out (Boseley 2002).

*See also* Abortion

### "Pretty Ladies of Tlatilco."

Pre-Columbian figurines, some of which depict two-headed women once thought to be mythical and now believed by Gordon Bendersky of the University of Pennsylvania to represent diprosopus conjoined twins and therefore to be the earliest scientific medical illustrations (Honan 2000).

### Priestley, Andrew and Grant.
*Twentieth Century.*

Conjoined twin boys born in Australia and separated in the 1970s.

### Privacy.

> *When one imagines a life in which no daily function, no matter how small, can be fulfilled unless it is agreed to by another human being, one can appreciate how extraordinary it was that the twins performed as well as they did and with so little overt conflict.* — Irving Wallace and Amy Wallace (1978) about Chang and Eng Bunker

"What people find difficult to imagine about conjoined twins is how they negotiate such ordinary needs of the body as sex and excretion, and how they can stand doing everything together," points out Natalie Angier (1997). In her biography of Chang and Eng Bunker, Kay Hunter (1964) asks her readers to put themselves in either pair of the brothers' shoes:

> But imagine another You — a mirrored image immediately next to you. This person cannot be removed. He is there permanently, and until the end of your days, joined to you — part of you. Where you go, the other Self goes too, irrevocably. He looks over your shoulder as you read or write, he shares your bath and sleeps at your side. There is no chance of keeping any secrets any more, except in the recesses of your mind. You are watched and accompanied — always.

"Face to Face: The Story of the Schappell Twins" broaches the subject of privacy, pointing out that being forced to do private things in front of another violates a social taboo. The union of joined twins also violates the permissible notion of pleasure. Like many other conjoined twins, Lori and Reba Schappell explain that they can mentally block each other out, when necessary, something the Hilton sisters claimed to be able to do.

*See also* "Face to Face: The Story of the Schappell Twins"; Hilton, Daisy and Violet

### Prodigy.

While the word "prodigy" has been used since the mid–seventeenth century to refer to a child of precocious genius, the word's use to describe abnormal or monstrous beings dates back at least another century. Conjoined twins have been characterized as prodigies and subject to another sense of the word as something extraordinary from which omens are drawn (OED 2001). The study of monstrosities led to fetomancy, teratoscopy, and other methods of divination. The Greeks held birth defects to be divine warnings or symptoms of past indiscretions. Their mythology abounds with representations of double-monsters, as do the history and prehistory of most races (Grosz 1996).

In his work *The City of God*, Saint Augustine (A.D. 352–430) reasons that if monstrous births are human, they descended from Adam like all other humans and were not mistakes made by God: "For God, the Creator of all, knows where and when each thing ought to be, or to have been created, because He sees the similarities and diversities which can contribute to the beauty of the whole. But He who cannot see the whole is offended by the deformity of the part, because he is blind to that which balances it, and to which it belongs" (Augustine 1950). Monsters were thought of as signs of God's wrath through the early years of the Reformation, but by the end of the seventeenth century, only popular literature (ballads and broadsides) treated them in this way (Semonin 1996). From being a manifestation of divine warning, prodigies came to be understood as simply nature's sport or *lusus naturae* (Thompson 1996).

*See also* **Monstrosity**

## Prosecution *see* Legalities

## Publicity

*Greater attention to the medical support and public reaction new families of conjoined twins can expect may help prepare them and their children for the uncertainties lying ahead.* — Nancy Segal

The families of most pairs of conjoined twins choose to stay out of the public eye, particularly when they do not (or cannot) opt for surgery. "Conjoined twins are relatively rare, and first-person (singular or plural) accounts are even rarer, so it is difficult to know what the experience of a permanent coupling is like. There are now ... usually only two possible fates for conjoined twins: separation, with the attendant dangers it poses for the children's physical and emotional well-being; or isolation from society, either through institutionalization or through a kind of self-imposed segregation" (Grosz 1996). Much biographical material exists about Chang and Eng, but little of it is autobiographical. As David L. Clark and Catherine Myser point out, "...the grainy black and white stills of their 'inscrutable' faces so easily become a mute surface upon which almost anything can be projected."

Conjoined twins in show business had a reputation as publicity seekers, objecting loudly to paying double fares, for instance, in order to garner newspaper copy. Examinations by medical men put the seal of approval on their performances and increased their paying customers. Today, publicity may result in the establishment of funds to pay for the care of twins whose appearance in the media has provoked both sympathy and generosity.

*See also* **Media attention**

## Punk.

In show business, "punk" has been used since 1923 to refer to a youth (OED 2001). The word was easily transferred to the teratology specimens — including conjoined twins — featured in "unborn shows" or "life shows." Because the babies on display at carnivals are often preserved in formalin, the adjective "pickled" was added, so such specimens have been familiarly referred to as "pickled punks." Such exhibits were often faked, as showman Howard Bone (2001) admits. He defines a "punk" as an "artificial freak, made of rubber of some pliable substance, intended to be displayed in a formaldehyde-filled jar. Examples would be two-headed babies, foetuses, heads of famous criminals, or other body parts with malformations. The list of punks is long. They look real but are not." Bone explains that they were displayed as an annex attraction (for additional charge) with the sideshow acts or as an exhibit of their own.

*See also* **Dufour, Lou; Freak Show; "World's Strangest Babies"**

## Pygopagus.

*Pygopagus twins, as a rule, are more viable than other types of united twins, such as the craniopagus, thoracopagus, or ischiopagus. Perhaps this is because the union in pygopagi involves no vital organs and, moreover, allows a carriage nearer the normal.* — M.A. Perlstein and E.R. LeCount 1927

Descriptive of twins joined by a shared coccyx and sacrum, sharing the perineal regions and sometimes the spinal cord. There is usually one anus with two rectums. The union typically results in back-to-back positioning and the twins have four arms and four legs (Spencer 1996). Occurs in about 18 percent of conjoined twins (Segal 1999).

See illustration on following page.

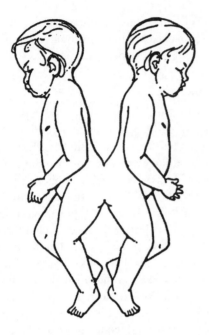

Diagram of typical pygopagus twins. Courtesy of Rowena Spencer and W.B. Saunders Co.

## Quiej-Alvarez, Maria Teresa and Maria de Jesus. *Twenty-first Century.*

*Everyone had goosebumps at the end of the procedure. People were cheering, people were clapping, people were crying.* — Dr. Houman Hemmati, U.C.L.A. Medical Center

Craniopagus twin girls born to Wenceslao Quiej Lopez and Leticia Alba Alvarez in Belen, on the southern coast of Guatemala, in 2001. They were joined at the top of the skull facing opposite directions. Their brains were not meshed, but they shared bone and blood vessels. The twins were brought to the United States by Healing the Children, a nonprofit group. They were separated in an operation that began on August 5, 2002, at the University of California, Los Angeles Medical Center and lasted twenty-two hours. The medical team of fifty at Mattel Children's Hospital separated the skulls, sorted out the individual blood vessels, and separated the brains, which allowed them to push the babies apart. The surgery had gone as expected, with no unforeseen complications. One of the twins lost a lot of blood during the surgery and was given transfusions. Four hours after surgery Maria Teresa suffered a subdural hematoma and had to have another five-hour operation to relieve the build-up of blood. Both girls remained in the Intensive Care Unit. Lead neurosurgeon Jorge Lazareff said that despite Maria Teresa's complications, the outlook for both twins was positive. The Guatemalan press followed the story closely and referred to the twins as "Las Maritas," the "Little Marias." Neighbors and friends held prayer sessions and had candlelight vigils in the local churches and were collecting money for the twins' care. Six days after surgery, the girls were more alert as their sedatives were reduced, but were still in critical condition. They were on intravenous nutrition. Ten days post-operatively, Maria Teresa had to have three additional hours of surgery to drain an accumulation of blood that doctors believe may have contributed to a bacterial infection in the lining of her brain. Maria Teresa underwent a third operation on August 22, which lasted ninety minutes, after which she was on a ventilator and again under sedation. Both twins will require follow-up surgeries to reconstruct their skulls (Conjoined Twins Split 2002).

## Rachipagus.

Descriptive of twins with backbone or spinal column fused above the sacrum. The condition is so rare that generalization is impossible, but the union may involve the occiput and segments of the vertebral column and the twins usually have four arms and four legs (Spencer 1996).

See illustration on facing page.

## Radhakrishna. *Twentieth Century.*

Child with two heads born in Nalla Sopara, India, on January 4, 1999. Parents decline to identify gender and consider the baby a reincarnation of Vishnu.

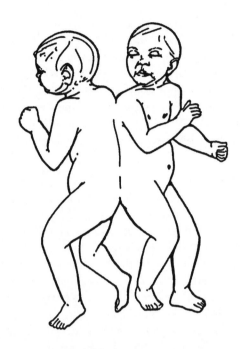

**Diagram illustrating typical rachipagus twins. Courtesy of Rowena Spencer and the W.B. Saunders Co.**

## Radica and Doodica. *Nineteenth Century.*

Female conjoined twins born in Orissa, India, in September 1889, joined at the chest by a cartilaginous band two inches wide and four inches long. The band was flexible enough that the twins could sit on either side of each other (Gould and Pyle 1956). When one child ate, the food appeared to satisfy the hunger of both and medicine given to either twin would affect both. Their portrait was shown at the World's Fair in Chicago. The twins were exhibited in Europe in 1893 under the management of showman Captain Colman. They spent considerable time in a Paris hospital, after they fell ill, but continued on to England after they recovered. Soon Doodica was diagnosed with tuberculosis. The thoracopagus twins were separated in Paris in 1902 as Doodica was dying. Radica survived for two more years, succumbing to the same disease.

## Railoun, Aziz. *Twentieth Century.*

Male child born by Cesarean section to Ebrahim and Ghairu Railoun of Cape Town, South Africa, with two pelvises, two sets of sex organs, two bladders, and four legs. Surgeons removed one pelvis, one set of sex organs, and two of the legs in a ten-hour operation at Cape Town's Red Cross Children's Hospital. Although several plastic surgeries will be required, the doctors expected Aziz to be able to walk normally.

## Rainey, Bethany and Hannah. *Twentieth Century.*

Female conjoined twins born in Texas c. 1995 to Scott and Elaine Rainey, who have two other daughters, Emily and Amanda. They were joined from the chest to the hip and shared a leg. They were separated at Wilford Hall Medical Center, Lackland Air Force Base, Texas, in 1995 at the age of six months. The surgery took twenty-eight hours and was conducted by a twenty-nine member team of Air Force, Army, and civilian specialists. Air Force Major Dr. John Doski commented, "It was a moving experience and brought a hush to the OR when we completed the surgical separation at 2:30 in the morning of March 7th. I will always remember the family's reaction to first Bethany and then Hannah being brought out of the OR as separate little girls" (Mitchell 1997). On March 7, 1997, Bethany and Hannah Rainey met reporters for the first time and were described as happy and lively two-and-a-half-year-olds. They were learning to walk on their prosthetic legs. They both required additional surgery after the separation. Each required reconstruction of her portion of the shared limb and her bowel, and Hannah will required additional urologic surgery.

## Randall, Randi. *Twentieth Century.*

Surviving conjoined twin born c. 1975, she was joined to her sister at the chest. They each had a heart, but shared a pair of kidneys, a liver, a bladder, and the large intestine. The girls shared a rectum and a single set of sexual organs. The twins were separated at Children's Hospital in Philadelphia by a team led by Dr. Harry C. Bishop that included a urologist, an orthopedist, a plastic surgeon, anesthesiologists, and nurses. During the twenty-two-hour surgery, a second bladder was constructed. The smaller child tolerated the surgery well, but developed complications and died several days later. Randi, though able to breathe on her own, was critically ill for several months, after which she was finally able to rejoin her family in New Jersey. Randi will return to Children's Hospital for check-ups and to be fitted with a prosthesis for her leg.

## Red Cross Children's Hospital.

More than thirty separation surgeries have taken place at the Red Cross Children's Hospital in Cape Town, South Africa, including that of the Alphonce twins.

*See also* **Alphonce, Stella and Esther**

## Relationship.

*The one on the left— I mean the one on its left … the one that was west of his brother when they stood in the door.*— Patsy Cooper describing Luigi Cappello in Mark Twain's *Those Extraordinary Twins*

Several methods of labeling the physical relationships between conjoined twins have been devised and used over the years. Dr. Rowena Spencer points out that since twins are rarely united quite symmetrically, the measurements between anatomical landmarks on one side will be broader than on the other. She therefore suggests Schwalbe's method in which the broader ventral aspect, when the twins are placed in a position that exposes more of their abdomen(s), is referred to as "secondary anterior" and the opposite surface as "secondary posterior." Once "anterior" and "posterior" have been determined, the infants can be identified as the

"twin-on-their-right" and the "twin-on-their-left," and shortened to "right twin" and "left twin." For completely symmetrical twins for whom "secondary anterior" and "secondary posterior" are indistinguishable, Dr. Spencer suggests identifying the relationship of the twins arbitrarily as 1 and 2 or A and B (Spencer 1996).

## Religion.

It has been debated for centuries whether conjoined twins should receive one of the Roman Catholic Holy Sacraments of Baptism and Last Rites or two. The first known autopsy in the New World (1533) was performed on conjoined twins at the request of the priest who had baptized each of them and it proved him right, since each twin was complete. The Hartley twins were each baptized in 1953, though they had been issued a single birth certificate.

*See also* **Johanna and Melchiora; Legalities**

## Representation.

*Not only have photographers captured on film the freaks of their time, but after a while they were portrayed in fiction as well. No sooner, in fact, had the novel been invented, than it too began to portray the monstrous and malformed as objects of pity and fear and— however secularized— wonder, always wonder.*— Leslie Fiedler

Today, conjoined twins are usually represented by photographs — in the popular media, in medical textbooks. Before photography was discovered, their appearance was conveyed in print and through sculpture. Purcell (1997) captures the Romanesque bas-relief of dicephalous twins in the capital of a column from the Abbey Church of Mary Madeleine in Vézelay, France, and a second example from a column in the Church of the Trinity, the Holy Cross, and the Virgin Mary at Anzy-le-Duc, both early twelfth century. Purcell also reproduces a frieze of conjoined twins born in 1317 and treated during their brief life at the hospital of San Martino della Scala in Florence, where the stone sculpture hung. The stories of some twins are known only through such sculptures.

Conjoined twins have been the subject of art photography and medical photography. Diane Arbus and Joel-Peter Witkin both used them in their work, taking advantage of the medium that allows its viewers an extended gaze to appease their curiosity — a gaze that results in humanizing the subjects, though the images may be manipulated. Medical photography achieves the same objective, as Rachel Adams (1996) explains: "Sepia-toned photographs of limbs grown massive and misshapen with elephantiasis, the bodies of conjoined twins, the scars of Civil War veterans continue to be moving, for they represent the failure of medical science to alleviate such conditions and the camera's audacity in daring to preserve them on film. Contemporary viewers have grown accustomed to understanding freaks as artistic projections, and it is the impersonality of the camera's eye that now repels." The viewer is allowed to stare at who the camera objectively recorded and who the artist subjectively presents. Medical photography "turns wonder into pathology," to use the words of Rachel Adams (1996), but some artists reverse this. Rosamond Purcell, for instance, does more than merely document the conjoined twins and other specimens in medical museums — she makes what have traditionally been considered grotesque into objects of beauty and contemplation.

*See also* Freaks

## Reproduction.

The idea of conjoined twins engaging in intercourse has been considered repulsive over the years. So — by extension — has the idea of one (or both) of the pair carrying a pregnancy to term. Whether pygopagus twin Rosa Blazek ever did so in the nineteenth century is not undisputed. In twentieth century interviews, however, craniopagus twin Lori Schappell indicates her desire to give birth, though she and her sister have no intention of being separated. Ironically, one of the goals of the separation of conjoined twins is to provide each child with the capacity for natural reproduction. Surviving separated twin Clara Rodriguez is reported to have given birth to a baby in 1994.

*See also* Blazek, Rosa and Josefa

## Ritta-Christina. *Nineteenth Century.*

*Christina-Ritta ceased living, this single heart flew away, this double heart ceased beating, and already Mr. Geoffroy Saint-Hilaire proceeded to the autopsy of the strange phenomenon; this charming creation, these two young children in only one body was subjected to the scalpel of the operator: the scalpel today answers all the questions beyond the usual world, it slices without pity the node which attaches the possible one to impossible, ad infinitum finished, this single heart with this double body.* — Jules Janin, *A Woman with Two Heads,* 1829

Female twins born in Sassari, Sardinia, on March 23, 1829, to thirty-two-year-old Maria Teresa Parodi. The ninth and tenth of her children, the girls had a single pelvis and a single pair of legs, but two heads and four arms. Ritta had a poor appetite, was pale and sickly, and had occasional attacks of cyanosis and difficulty breathing. Ritta was said to have transposed viscera and an abnormal vascular system (Harris 1892). Dr. Robert P. Harris writes (1892):

> The Rita-Christina [*sic*] had four arms and hands, two vertebral columns, and two sacra, with two perfect legs and feet. Within the body were four lungs; two hearts in an undivided pericardium; a double liver, with a central sulcus and two gall bladders; two stomachs, one transposed in position; two spleens; two pancreases; two uteri, one imperforate; and one bladder.

The twins breast-fed at the same time and urinated and defecated simultaneously. They had a common large intestine, so

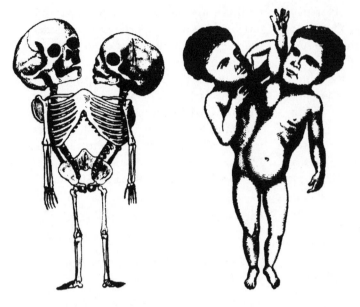

Print of Ritta-Christina and her skeleton. Courtesy of Jan Bondeson, M.D., Ph.D.

were blamed in the popular press but which could have been prevented, ironically, by allowing the parents to legally exhibit the twins. Ritta developed acute bronchitis and three days later, on November 23, 1829, died at the age of eight months, causing the seemingly healthy Christina to cry out and die in the same instant. Even before their deaths, there was much speculation on what the autopsy would show and which museum would get the skeleton of such an anatomical rarity (Bondeson 2000), and the doctors were criticized for not trying hard enough to keep Ritta-Christina alive.

Christina was able to ingest enough nutrients to help support her sister. Impressed by the interest shown in their babies by both doctors and the public, and fearful of Ritta's ill health, the poor parents began a brief tour of some Italian cities. The twins were then smuggled into France despite that country's objections to the exhibition of Siamese twins, and were shown in Paris in October 1829 when a mere six or seven months old. The popular fear was "that a sight of them might cause some of the French women to breed abnormal children of a similar type; an opinion that is by no means confined to France, nor excluded by the medical profession…." (Harris 1874). After the magistrates closed the show down, the parents exhibited the girls surreptitiously to journalists and members of the medical profession (Bondeson 2000).

Ritta is described as "feeble and of a sad and melancholy countenance," in contrast to her vigorous and happy sister (Gould and Pyle 1956). Neither would withstand a cold winter night in an unheated room, however, a fate for which the parents

Jules Janin writes in 1829, "The monster is contained in a bottle of amphitheatre, and you will be able to see it three times per week between craniums of Papavoine and Castaing!" According to contemporary accounts, anatomist Geoffroy Saint-Hilaire arrived in the company of the police to persuade the twins' father to allow them to be dissected and the autopsy was carried out in the Anatomy Theater of the Jardin du Roi (Bondeson 2000). According to Gould and Pyle (1956), the postmortem was secured with some difficulty due to the authorities ordering the bodies to be burned.

The autopsy of Ritta-Christina was performed by Dr. Manel, with Saint-Hilaire, Georges Cuvier (d. 1832), and other famous medical men present. The event had been advertised in the newspapers. The twins were shown to be mirror images of each other. Their hearts shared a pericardium. Ritta's heart was severely deformed, but was compensated by Christina's normal circulatory system. Their upper digestive organs were double, but their common large intestine allowed Ritta to benefit from

Christina's healthy appetite. There was a single fused liver, but each twin had her own stomach, gallbladder, spleen, and pancreas. The two spinal columns fused into a single pelvis. There were two uteri (one of them deformed), but only one set of external genitals. Anatomist Etienne Serres published a 300-page study of Ritta-Christina containing descriptions and illustrations in 1833; he suggested that they would have been able to bear children and concluded that they were two people. Their skeleton (specimen A8599) was exhibited for years alongside other teratological specimens at the Musée d'Histoire Naturelle in Paris, where Stephen Jay Gould saw it as recently as 1982 (Bondeson 2000, Gould 1982).

## Roderick, Shawna Leilani and Janelle Kiana. *Twentieth Century.*

*It was a unique set of circumstances, but we coped.*—Michelle Roderick

Twin girls born by Cesarean section in California to Michelle and Jeff Roderick on May 1, 1996, joined at the abdomen. They shared a liver (with separate bile ducts) and weighed a total of eleven pounds four and half ounces. "I didn't even think to look at where they were joined (after delivery), and I didn't," Michelle says, "I just looked at them as two individuals and my daughters, and just was so happy in the moment. We are very blessed with two beautiful daughters" (Loft 1998). The parents soon considered separation: "We felt that since the chances were so good that they'd come out of it as healthy individuals, we didn't think it would be fair not to try," said their mother (Angier 1997). Shawna and Janelle were separated thirty days after birth in a seven-hour operation on May 30, 1996, at University Medical Center in Loma Linda, California. The surgical team, led by Dr. H. Gibbs Andrews, included perinatologists, neonatologists, surgeons, anesthesiologists, and nurses. The story was covered by *Good Morning America, This Morning, Today,* and other national and regional media.

A dedication ceremony was held for the Roderick twins at their Seventh-Day Adventist church on October 19, 1996. By spring 1997, Shawna weighed fourteen and a half pounds and Janelle weighed sixteen. Shawna was more assertive and slept better, with Janelle more passive. The Rodericks now live in Prescott, Arizona. Their grandfather Will Degeraty directs (and their mother co-directs) the organization Conjoined Twins International.

***See also* Conjoined Twins International**

## Rodriguez, Christopher George and Timothy Elias. *Twentieth Century.*

Male conjoined twins born on February 17, 1978, to Elias and Georgeann Rodriguez. They were delivered at North Side Hospital in Youngstown, Ohio, joined at the chest. The twins shared — in addition to a liver — a three-chambered heart that would make separation extremely risky. They were transferred to Children's Hospital in Pittsburgh in May 1978, but soon contracted pneumonia and died.

## Rodriguez, Clara and Altagracia (Alta). *Twentieth Century.*

*I believe in God, and I believe in heaven, and right under that I believe in Dr. Koop.*—Farida Rodriguez

Ischiopagus twins born by Cesarean section in San José de Ochoa in the Dominican Republic on August 12, 1973, to Farida and Salvador Rodriguez of the village of Las Auyamas, two hours away. "Joined together at the lower trunk and pelvis, they looked as if they were sitting in each other's lap" (Drake 1974). Their gastrointestinal, urinary, and reproductive systems were partially united. They had a total of four vaginas, but shared a liver, a colon, and a rectum, and their ureters crossed to the opposite

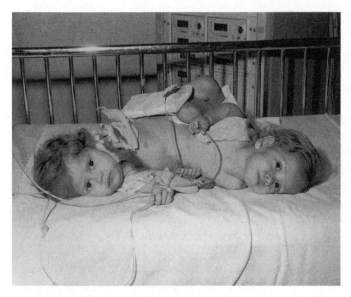

Clara and Alta Rodriguez before separation surgery. Courtesy of the Mütter Museum, College of Physicians of Philadelphia.

bladder. Together they weighed ten pounds at birth. They were believed cursed by many of their superstitious neighbors and doomed by local doctors. Their mother was at first told they were dead. When she learned they were conjoined, she prayed for the strength to care for them, but was certain they would not survive. Clara was the larger and more dominant twin and Alta soon had numerous scars on her upper arms from Clara's bites. Though they shared circulation, Alta had a severe allergic rash to her hospital bracelet, while Clara showed no reaction at all. To assure better medical care for the twins, the Rodriguezes rented a small cinder-block house near the hospital (It's Home Again 1975).

The babies were brought to Philadelphia at one year of age to be separated by Dr. C. Everett Koop. If they remained conjoined, they would never be able to sit up at the same time. Dr. Koop (1975) writes, "I knew then that any risk to separate them was justified. Just the thought of their going through life so grotesquely attached was overwhelmingly tragic." The trip was sponsored by Mrs. Joseph Zimnock of Warrington, Pennsylvania—who heard about the

twins from her sister's maid, a cousin of the Rodriguezes — and her church group. Upon arrival the girls were anemic and undernourished and had a urinary tract infection. They weighed a total of twenty-one pounds. They were separated by Dr. Koop and a team of twenty-three doctors in a ten-and-a-half-hour operation at Children's Hospital on September 18, 1974, after ten days of detailed studies, discussions, and rehearsals. Dr. Koop knew from the photograph he had been provided before meeting the twins that the operation would be extremely difficult and could require a colostomy for one child.

The surgery was recorded by medical photographer Ed Eckstein and described by Dr. Koop (1974). Each twin was anesthetized and intubated. An intravenous arterial line was inserted and a central venous pressure line introduced into the superior vena cava. Clara and Alta were then hooked up to the cardiac monitors and scrubbed down with iodine. The babies were draped and positioned on foam-rubber cushions on the operating table. An incision was made and expanded. The liver was divided with an electrocautery. Their crossed ureters were detached and their pubis was divided with a saw. Before the final separation, Alta was given a blood volume boost of albumin and packed cells as a precaution against hypovolemia and possible cardiac arrest, but she experienced no problems. With modest tension, the surgeons were able to close Clara's skin over her incision. They elected to do posterior osteotomies bilaterally on Alta's pelvis to close her wound with her own skin (Koop 1974). As stated in *People* magazine (It's Home Again 1975), "Dr. C. Everett Koop … succeeded in forming two separate beings

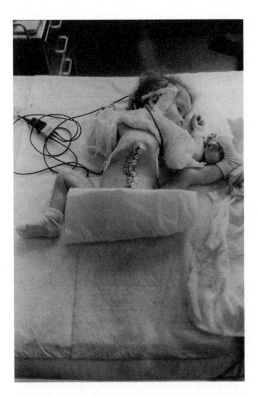

Clara Rodriguez after surgery. Courtesy of the Mütter Museum, College of Physicians of Philadelphia.

out of the twins' own tragically jumbled genetic code." The single rectum was given to Clara and Alta's was constructed with a section of colon and her imperforate anus corrected. Two of the vaginas were sealed off and it was believed the girls would be able to reproduce normally. In a Christian publication, Dr. Koop attributed the surgery's success to God's love: "He had cared enough to give us the skills to change one helpless form into two beautiful people" (Koop 1975).

After the operation, the twins were placed in the same crib and Clara reached out for Alta's hand. Surgeon John Templeton, Jr., said, "To be honest, they seemed almost relieved to be separated" (Angier 1997). They were maintained on curare and on respirators, Clara for forty-eight hours and Alta for seventy-two hours. When their mother couldn't be with them after the separation, the hospital played a recording of her voice to cheer them during their recovery. The girls remained in the intensive care unit for eighty-two days, with their care exceeding $32,000, not including the donated services of Dr. Koop and the other surgeons. In addition to his surgical services, Dr. Koop spent countless hours on the telephone to the Dominican Republic trying to arrange medical care and supplemental food supplies for the family's return home. Clara was taking fluids by mouth on the sixth post-operative day and Alta did the same two days later. Less than a week after surgery, however, Alta required an operation to remove an intestinal blockage. Clara was admitted a few days later with severe diarrhea and vomiting. When they were apart, a photograph of both twins was placed in each child's crib. By the twelfth day after surgery,

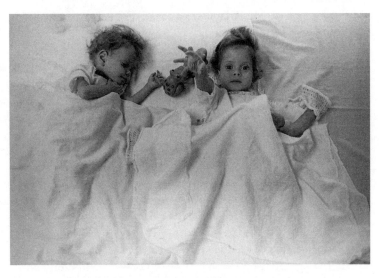

Clara and Alta Rodriguez post-operatively. Courtesy of the Mütter Museum, College of Physicians of Philadelphia.

both twins were eating solid foods and all monitoring and in-dwelling lines were removed. Alta soon caught up with her sister in weight, with each topping thirteen pounds, and her personality began to become more aggressive. A month and a half after separation, Clara had additional surgery to reshape her pelvic bones to enable her to walk, the procedure that had been done on Alta just after the separation. Alta was therefore the first to crawl after the operation, but they were both soon sitting up.

The parents sold the story rights to *Ladies Home Journal* for $10,000 and planned to use the money — supplemented by private donations — to buy a house with electricity and sanitation. The twins returned home in January 1975, after their mother was given lessons in nutrition and sanitation (Innerst 1974). They were gradually reintroduced to the food and water of their native region. The family had help from the local religious group in bathing the girls, which needed to be done twice a day to keep their thin skin protected from the infections to which they are easily susceptible. Clara and Alta were outfitted with orthopedic shoes and Alta wore a corset because she has no abdominal muscles. Dominican President Joaquín Balaguer awarded Dr. Koop a medal for his surgery and honored Mrs. Rodriquez with a presidential decree allowing her to travel to Puerto Rico to obtain baby supplies and medicine not available in her own country and to bring them back duty-free (It's Home Again 1975). They were also to return to the U.S. at the expense of the *Ladies Home Journal* for tests that weren't possible to obtain at home.

The Rodriguezes subsequently moved into a house in Santo Domingo built for them by the government on land that they purchased. Unfortunately, a year after their separation Alta choked to death on a bean. At the age of twelve, Clara Rodriguez — whose mother said she did not remember her twin sister — returned to Children's Hospital to have a bladder stone removed. She was photographed during her reunion with Dr. Koop. Her American sponsor Mrs. Zimnock was trying to raise money to buy Clara a hearing aid, since she is completely deaf in her right ear and has partial hearing in her left ear. In 1997, it was reported that Clara had given birth to a healthy baby boy in 1994 (Angier 1997).

## "Rope."

The name of a project carried out in 1983–1984 in which performance artists Linda Montano and Tehching Hsieh attached themselves to each other with an eight-foot rope tied at the waist for a one-year period. The enforced intimacy mirrored the interdependency of natural Siamese twins, evoked taboo topics (particularly since one artist was a woman and the other a man), provoked the same questions that conjoined twins do about private functions, and brought out the differences in their personalities (Dennett 1996).

*See also* Privacy

## Rozycki, Anna and Barbara. *Twentieth Century.*

*We are definitely two parts of the same whole.* — Anna Rozycki

Conjoined twin girls born in May 1970 in Coventry Hospital, England, joined at the breastbone and sharing a liver. The birth lasted 72 hours and nearly killed their mother. They were taken to the Birmingham Children's Hospital, where they were determined by X-ray to have separate kidneys. The twins were separated within twenty-four hours of their birth by Dr. Keith Roberts. They each have a scar from the separation, but no physical disability. They feel a deep bond. Today they are healthy adults with full life expectancy. Barbara has two children and Anna still lives with her parents, as her father explains: "The fact that Anna lives with us and doesn't have a job has nothing to do with being a Siamese twin. They are both well and happy and they have lived very normal lives. They don't go round telling everyone, 'I'm a Siamese twin,' but normally it comes out. I tend to tell people because I'm so proud of them" (Edge 2000).

## Sacrifice surgery *see* Separation surgery

## Saint-Hilaire, Isidore Geoffroy.

Isidore Geoffroy Saint-Hilaire (1805–1861) is the doctor who coined the term "teratology." He published the first teratology treatise in 1832, in which he arranged terata into fifty genera, 23 natural families, and five orders (Wilson 1993). Saint-Hilaire developed the following classifications for conjoined births: union of several fetuses; union of two distinct fetuses by a connecting band; union of two distinct fetuses by an osseous junction of cranial bones; union of two distinct fetuses in which one or more parts are eliminated by the junction; union of two fetuses by a body union of the ischii; fusion of two fetuses below the umbilicus into a common lower extremity; bicephalic monsters; parasitic monsters; monsters with a single body and double lower extremities.
*See also* Teratology

## Sami, Perumal. *Nineteenth Century.*

Born in India in 1888, this man had the body of a parasitic twin protruding from his chest. He toured widely in America.

## "Scenes from the Life of a Double Monster" *see* Lloyd and Floyd

## Schappell, Lori and Reba. *Twentieth Century.*

*We're just like any other person; just because we're conjoined doesn't mean we have to like or dislike the same things. We're two human beings that happened to have an egg not split, and that is where it begins and ends.* — Lori Schappell (Loft 1998)

Born at Reading Hospital in Reading, Pennsylvania, on September 18, 1961, Lori and Dori (who later changed her name to Reba) are the only living adult conjoined twins in the United States joined at the head. They are densely conjoined through the frontal bone, parietal bones, and one side of their faces. Their appearance is of one person leaning to whisper in another's ear (Anthony 1993). Lori is of average size and pushes her sister — who has spina bifida, has no use of her legs, and is four inches shorter — on a stool. Reba's lower organs were incomplete and she had other congenital anomalies that required surgical procedures as an infant. They were their mother's fourth and fifth children and the pregnancy had been uneventful. After birth, their father was protective and didn't allow photos of the twins, who were expected to die. The twins cannot pinpoint their first awareness of their unusual anatomy (Segal 1999). They knew they were different, but were taught to ignore stares and unkind comments (Jackson 2001). The girls were institutionalized in 1968 at Pennsylvania's Pennhurst State School and Hospital (later renamed Hamburg Center), a state facility for the mentally retarded, and remained residents for twenty-four years. Their parents visited every Sunday, but they considered the staff their family, and from the hospital employees learned about the outside world. They were "adopted" by Herman Sonon, who they called "Papa," and his wife June, who brought them home on visits and took them out shopping. Lori sold Avon products to the hospital staff members.

It was assumed when they were children that they couldn't learn, since the hospital was intended for patients with an I.Q. of 70 or less, but it was Reba's desire for an education that led to their release. With the help of the governor's wife, Ginny Thornbaugh, their intelligence was tested and they were allowed to leave the institution. They live on their own in a fifteenth-floor apartment in a senior citizen high-rise in Reading, Pennsylvania (Anthony 1993). Reba has a pet, a small dog. They point out that there was always someone to depend on at the institution and there was no transition for them when they moved out. They explain that they were unfairly disadvantaged by being institutionalized, but are not bitter about it. They are seen regularly by their doctor at Children's Hospital of Philadelphia. As young adults they were treated by Dr. John Templeton, Jr., now retired, and Reba's care required urgent surgery. Dr. Templeton reports (letter to the author, February 10, 2002) that the twins have both been in good health for the last seven or eight years. He calls the Schappells "remarkable":

> Both of them are amazing examples of what can be accomplished in spite of significant handicaps. Their ability to cope has been a source of significant inspiration to many people who have met them both as patients and as individuals [letter to the author, February 10, 2002].

Rather than "handicapped," Reba and Lori consider themselves "handi-capable," a word that they coined. A recent MRI shows that Lori and Reba share some 30 percent of their brain tissue, mainly the frontal lobe. They don't share each other's pain, but they do share some of their blood supply. Their link gives them no pain at all (Anthony 1993). Templeton describes to BBC2, "We can see the tremendous amount of conjoined brain tissue in here. The fusion is sort of a dense flow of nerve tissue that all comes together. There's not a dotted line in here." The twins rotate their bodies so that the one talking faces the front.

Lori and Reba have declined in-depth interviews over the years, but Reba's singing and guitar-playing sometimes provokes publicity. She won an L.A. Music Award for best new country artist of 1997 and accepted in person; awards founder Alfred Bowman said he was impressed with her talent and ability to perform under difficult circumstances (Jussim 2001). Reba has sung her song "The Fear of Being Alone" in Japan, Germany, and Atlantic City, New Jersey. She has also performed on local television, at the governor's mansion, and with Tom T. Hall (Twin Separable 1992). Although they find the display of conjoined twins to the public "distasteful," the Schappell twins appeared on an episode of "Jerry Springer" in 1996 or 1997, mostly to get Reba's music career started. Lori told BBC2, "Her career is her own doing. I support her in that she's my sister and I love her and whatever she wishes to do I back her 100 percent as a sister and I would not stop her for anything in the world because I have no reason to. I'm happy with just flying on her wings, so to speak." Lori sets up interviews for Reba and fields questions about their physical condition, allowing her sister to concentrate on her career, since Reba has always encouraged Lori to pursue hers (Lori now accepts occasional part-time positions). Reba once aspired to be a physician and to design support equipment for the physically disabled. She now wants to live in a house equipped with a music studio and was in 2000 working on a CD entitled "Momma Taught Me." She was also writing an autobiography. She is career-oriented and does not imagine having a husband or children. She wears western clothing and cowboy boots. She affectionately refers to her sister as "Mom." Reba likes to bowl and has racked up two perfect games at the Special Olympics (Twin Separable 1992).

Lori Schappell attended college. Her work as a linen aide in a hospital delivery room and Reba's income, including a small Social Security disability check, pay their rent and other expenses. Lori has also held jobs as a ward clerk and a nurse-receptionist (Jussim 2001). When Reading Hospital worried about Reba's welfare while Lori was on the job, Reba offered to sign a waiver against any liability (Twin Separable 1992).

She reads while Lori works. Lori hopes to marry and have children. In 1992, she was quoted as saying, "Having a baby is one of my biggest dreams! The doctors tell me I'd probably have a normal, healthy baby" (Twin Separable 1992). In the same article, she admits that she is a virgin ("by choice") and relates that if she never meets that "special guy," she would consider artificial insemination. She points out one of the many differences between her and her sister: "Reba's not really fond of dates and boys, and I am. I like meeting people and stuff like that, going to parties, and she's more of a home girl who likes to read and learn" (Edge 2000). Reba is of course present on Lori's dates, but doesn't interfere, as Lori points out: "The guy gets used to that. If he wants to be involved with me, he's got to get used to having her around" (Jussim 2001). Lori would like to live in a house with a big kitchen, full of antiques. She states that she wants to be incredible for what she does, not what she is.

Their differences are many: "Lori is warm and boisterous and maternal. She wants to get married and have babies, she says, and at the age of 36, she wants to do it soon. Reba is quiet and self-contained, and she squirms whenever her sister hugs her in public or tells her that she loves her" (Angier 1997). Lori keeps her brown hair short; Reba colors her wavy hair copper. Lori loves strawberry daiquiris; Reba doesn't drink. The Schappells point out that not only are they different, but each pair of conjoined twins is unique and do not have a lot in common with each other.

The Schappells object to being pitied or considered heroes. They are tired of being referred to as "you two" or "them," and prefer to be called by their names. They are two very different individuals: Lori likes to watch television, shop, and eat sweets, but Reba doesn't. If you acknowledge their separateness, points out Lori, it is okay to ask about their being conjoined. Even so, Lori

complains in a BBC2 interview, "We're not solely conjoined twins. I get tired of everybody thinking about that that's all we are." In another interview (Jackson 2000) in which she was pressed to name some of their similarities, Lori replied, "We have the same last name and we love each other." She said their relationship — like that of any couple — is a compromise, except that they learned it from the beginning. They have a lot in common with Yvonne and Yvette McCarther (d. 1993), craniopagus twins whom they've met. They followed the story of Amy and Angela Lakeberg with interest and, although reluctant to discuss it, strongly supported the parents' decision (Anthony 1993). They also felt strongly about the case of Jodie and Mary and objected strongly to the judge referring to Mary as a "creature." Edge (2000) quotes Lori, "I met another twin who was separated at birth, and her sister died. This lady, who is the same age as me, just can't live without her sister. She thinks about her constantly. It's not something I can imagine."

The Schappells don't want to be separated. When they were born, the equipment did not exist to do the sensitive artery reconstruction that would be needed. If it had, their parents — described as very religious — would have declined the operation. Even today, Lori and Reba would not take the risk of death or neurological damage. "They probably could separate us now, but it would be a very long ordeal — they'd have to separate our bones," explains Reba. "Besides, if you thought the Lakebergs were expensive, you ain't seen nothing. It'd be as high as the national deficit if they tried to separate us" (Anthony 1993). Reba explains that there is no medical or logical reason to separate them and they absolutely do not want it done except in an emergency. "You'd be ruining two lives in the process," explains Reba, and Lori adds, "And we'd miss the other one horribly if she were to die" (Angiers 1997). Lori told the BBC2, "We never wanted to be separated, we never do want to be separated and our families never ever wanted us separated because we fully believe that God made us this way and He had a purpose for us and you do not ruin what God has made."

*See also* "Conjoined Twins"; "Face to Face: The Story of the Schappell Twins"; McCarther, Yvonne and Yvette Jones

## Scottish Brothers. *Fifteenth Century.*

Conjoined boys born near Glasgow in 1490 (Bondeson 2000) and referred to as the "Northumbrian monster" (Wilson 1993). They were brought before King James IV of Scotland, who had them educated and raised at court (Wallace and Wallace 1978), where they lived the rest of their lives. They were separate individuals above the waist, but the lower half of their bodies was fused (they had one set of genitals and two legs) and they shared sensation below the point of union. They learned to sing, one a tenor and the other a treble bass (Mannix 1999); played various musical instruments; and became fluent in several languages, including Danish, Dutch, English, French, Irish, Italian, Latin, and Spanish (Bondeson 2000). They sometimes argued, as described by George Buchanan: "In their various inclinations the two bodies appeared to disagree between themselves, sometimes disputing, each preferring different objects, and sometimes consulting for the common pleasure of both" (Bondeson 2000). The arguments occasionally turned violent: "Between them they would carry on animated conversations, sometimes merging into curious debates, followed by blows" (Gould and Pyle 1956). They lived to the age of twenty-eight, dying a few days apart in 1518 (Thompson 1968, Bondeson 2000). Gould and Pyle (1956) record that the survivor carried his dead brother about before succumbing to "infection from putrescence." William Pan-

coast (1875) quotes Sir J.Y. Simpson in the *British Medical Journal* that "as the dead became putrescent, the living wasted away by degrees."

## Selvaggio, Emily and Francesca. *Twentieth Century.*

Conjoined twin girls born joined at the chest and abdomen to Carol and Charles Selvaggio of Salisbury, Massachusetts. The babies shared an umbilical cord, skin, muscle, and rib cartilage, and were separated at Johns Hopkins University Medical Center on March 6, 1982.

## Separation surgery.

*My own philosophy and that of our department is that Siamese twins are born to be separated.*— Heinz Röde, pediatric surgeon at Cape Town Children's Hospital

*It is significant that today the lives of conjoined twins are considered tragic if the operation to separate them is not feasible. This does not always accord with the feelings of the conjoined twins themselves*— Elizabeth Grosz (1996)

*Just because we can do something, does that mean we have to do it?*— Gretchen Worden (Miller 2001)

Surgical separation of conjoined twins is encouraged when they are young, when the surgery is simple, and when it will not result in death or long-term disability of one of the twins. "Separation is risky, and often involves the death of one or both babies, the disruption of organs or loss of limbs, and major reconstructive surgery" (Loft 1998). Separation allows conjoined twins to assimilate into the world of the "normal" (Fiedler 1978). Psychologically, it is best to separate conjoined twins during the first six months of life, but surgery is often delayed until then to improve trauma tolerance. Segal (1999), however, reports a trend toward earlier surgeries. The separation itself will spare the twins the ridicule of others that will affect their feelings of self-worth. Carrying out the surgery early will ensure that the personality is not fully developed. Dr. C.K. Pepper (1967) cautions: "In counseling with parents of conjoined twins, these developmental steps should be pointed out and the possible areas of emotional difficulty explained. Shame, guilt, inferiority, identity diffusion, and isolation will be constant emotional hurdles for these twins." Segal (1999) notes that separation of conjoined twins prior to their awareness of their condition is believed to promote their psychological well-being, as is keeping them in close physical proximity after the surgery, and points out, "These recommendations are reasonable, although evaluating the behavioral consequences of time and proximity is difficult."

Immediate separation is typically advised when one twin is stillborn, one twin's health status threatens the other's survival, or abnormalities threaten the progress of one or both twins (Segal 1999). But it is considered by many to be unethical to sacrifice the life of one conjoined twin to separate it from the other. According to Alice Dreger (2000), medical ethicist at Michigan State University, "The sacrifice separation of conjoined twins is the only instance in which physicians are sometimes given permission by legal authorities and ethics committees to intentionally kill a child who is not clinically brain-dead." Dreger points out (Angiers 1997) that such action would never be taken if the twins were singletons. Surgeons may consult with law enforcement officials and parents and caretakers with their religious advisors before participating in sacrifice surgery. Yet not attempting separation may raise formidable life-support problems (Sullivan 1981). Jan Bondeson (2000) claims that "'sacrifice' surgery of extensively conjoined twins, in which one twin is deliberately killed to serve as an organ donor to the one best fit for survival, has been practiced several times in the 1980s and 1990s." Unfortunately, "sacrifice surgery" has a poor record of success; the BBC2

reports that of twelve known cases of sacrifice surgery, only two infants have survived for more than a year. Dreger (1998) plainly states, "No sacrifice surgery has ever resulted in producing a viable child," and goes on to say that twins of similar anatomical conformation who were *not* operated on survived for several years and led rewarding lives. But in fact, separation surgery is defined in the medical literature as "successful" if it results in the mere short-term survival of at least one twin.

The earliest documented attempts at separation occurred in Constantinople in A.D. 945, when Byzantine doctors separated adult conjoined twin boys united at the abdomen after one of them died. The "Armenian Twins" had resided in the city and been admired as curiosities, were exiled for a time as a bad omen, and returned to Constantinople during the reign of Constantine. When one of the twins died, doctors separated them at the line of connection, but the surviving twin followed three days later. Arab doctors refused to separate similarly joined twenty-five-year-old twins in A.D. 963, stating that they were not capable of performing such an operation (Pentogalos and Lascaratos 1988). In Germany in 1505, doctors were unsuccessful in saving a ten-year-old craniopagus twin whose sister had died. The first successful separation was performed by Dr. Fatio in Germany in 1689 on twins joined at the navel by a band of flesh (Harris 1874, Landau 1997, Bondeson 2000). An 1866 operation to separate twins united sternum to sternum resulted in the survival of one of them, but an 1881 operation in Switzerland resulted in the death of both twins, the second of peritonitis (Gould and Pyle 1956). Survival of a single surgically separated craniopagus twin did not occur until 1962 and survival of a separated pair did not occur until 1974. A total of 167 pairs of twins have been documented by Conjoined Twins International to have undergone separation surgery, not all of them successfully. Some 90 percent of the surgeries have been performed since 1950. Of these, 75 percent have resulted in the survival of one or both twins (*www.twin-stuff.com*). Roughly 200 pairs of conjoined twins have now been separated, 90 percent of them since 1950. Survival of one or both twins has occurred in close to 150 cases. A 1988 review found a survival rate of 50 percent in newborns and 90 percent in infants older than four months; a 1998 update found 50 percent survival in infants under four months of age, 90 percent in infants six to fourteen months, and 100 percent survival in twins over two years of age (Segal 1999). Separation surgery costs in excess of one million dollars.

In a paper in the *Journal of Pediatric Surgery* (Spitz et al. 1994), separation of a three-year-old pair of ischiopagus twins is described. The twins, born in 1988 joined from the shoulders to the pelvis, were referred to the Hospital for Sick Children in London in 1992 to be assessed for surgery. Numerous tests, including echocardiography, MRI, cytoscopy, and gastrointestinal contrast studies, were performed. Tissue expanders were inserted subcutaneously and regularly injected to increase abdominal girth from 54 cm. to 80 cm. Those in the chest wall became infected and were removed six weeks before separation. At a meeting held one week before the surgery, it was decided to leave one twin with the bladder and urethra and the other with the anus and rectum. As the operation began, the tissue expanders were deflated and the twins positioned and draped. A mid-line incision was made from shoulder to pubis. After exploratory laparotomy, the chest wall and pericardial sac were divided. The ileum of one of the twins was exteriorized as a terminal stoma. After multiple bridging vessels were ligated, complete separation was achieved.

To close the large wounds of the twins described by Spitz et al. (1994), prolene mesh with a polythene liner was used. One of the twins remained critically ill postoperatively and soon died. The surviving twin required two weeks of intensive therapy and the application of new mesh after four weeks. Wound healing was accelerated by the application of sheets of autologous cultured keratinocytes. She was discharged four months after separation and underwent wound debridement, physiotherapy, and fitting for a lower limb prosthesis. Eight months after separation, the surviving twin was thriving, but possibly facing further treatment to establish full urinary continence. The division of the twins at their late age could result in both psychological and physical problems, the latter because there is an increase in postural deformities and a decrease in thoracic flexibility with age. For the surgeons, however, closing the wound was the most pressing concern: "The body wall and skin defects resulting from separation posed the greatest challenge in the separation of these twins" (Spitz et al. 1994).

Leslie Fiedler (1978) refers to conjoined twins as "supernumeraries in a psychodrama starring the doctors who make normal humans out of monsters." Retired pediatric surgeon John Templeton, Jr., expresses the mission of his colleagues differently: "In regard to the vast majority of pediatric surgeons, pediatric urologists, and other pediatric surgical specialists, I would say that all of them approach any potential surgery involving conjoined twins on a completely individual basis.... By focusing on the anatomy, physiology, neurologic function and other important issues with each set of conjoined twins, I think that everyone involved in their care would feel that any decision for surgical separation should be very carefully considered and in some cases denied" (letter to the author, February 23, 2002). According to the BBC2 documentary "Conjoined Twins," no group of doctors has more experience in separating conjoined twins than the surgeons at Red Cross

Children's Hospital in Cape Town, South Africa. There thirty-three pairs have been separated since the mid–1960s, although not all have survived. Johns Hopkins surgeon Benjamin Carson has led a number of separation surgeries and now simulates cases on a virtual reality device. He states, "I do believe we still have a lot to learn. I believe that technology will continue to improve, but I think ten years from now separating conjoined twins will probably be considerably easier than it is now. If you think surgeons of today are good, surgeons of tomorrow will be unbelievable." Carson and his colleagues operate under what Dr. Mark Hoyle (1990) calls "the inherent challenge to restore individuality."

The confidence of the surgeons, many of whom believe separation is essential, is challenged by medical historian Alice Dreger of Michigan State University. Interviewed by BBC2 for "Conjoined Twins," she argued that the twins themselves might take a different view — if they were ever given a chance to express it: "She argues that decisions about who is in pain and who should be fixed — whatever their purported abnormality — must go beyond mechanical or economic or even philosophical considerations to include the voices of those who know best" (Angier 1997). In her own words, Dreger (1998) states:

> The virtual obsession with separation seems to have been and to be far greater among non-conjoined twins (especially among surgeons) than among conjoined twins themselves. Many conjoined twins mature enough to do so have explicitly voiced acceptance of their unusual conditions, and many have even expressed an inability to envision living any other way. Yet there appears to be a willingness on the part of more and more medical professionals to attempt separation at almost any cost, including risking the mobility, reproductive capabilities, or lives of one or both twins; inducing sex-change in one (and only one) of two separated twins; even intentionally sacrificing one

twin, that is, killing one twin to reduce the body in question to only one thinking, feeling mind.

Dreger likens the surgery to an amputation of one of the twins and notes that "in no other realm of medicine can you take a brain-live person and essentially asphyxiate them, to effectively use them as an organ donor." Edward Kiely of Great Ormond Street Hospital agrees that separation is an extremely difficult problem, particularly when there is no overriding medical indication to operate: "You've got two healthy children. You can't make them better than they are if they're healthy. You can certainly make them an awful lot worse and you may kill one or both in the attempt to separate them."

Elizabeth Grosz (1996) elaborates:

> …in spite of the state of health of conjoined twins, there appears to be a medical imperative for surgical intervention and normalization, even if surgery may actually endanger lives that may otherwise remain healthy. It seems that the permanent conjunction of individuals is socially intolerable, and that it is unimaginable to others that these subjects themselves would not wish to be able to lead "normal" lives. Surgery, it is argued, provides the only hope of such a normality, and surgical intervention clearly functions more successfully the earlier it occurs: the younger the children are, the less formed their body-image is…. While psychologically distinct individuals, conjoined twins are nevertheless far closer than another other two beings ever could be, and while there are two identities, they are not sharply distinguished from each other. In separating conjoined twins, one does not thereby create two autonomous beings, only as close as identical twins; conjoined twins are bonded through the psychical inscription of their historical, even if not current, corporeal links. Those who have shared organs, a common blood circulation, and every minute detail of everyday life can never have this corporeal link effaced.

The BBC2 show also points out that the tragedy for conjoined twins who are *not* separated and spend their lives together is that they inevitably die together, too. When one twin dies, the heart of the other twin keeps pumping until he or she is drained of blood. There have been cases, such as that of Radica and Doodica, where successful emergency separation has prolonged the life of one twin after the other dies.

Like other anomalies, such as ambiguous genitals, conjoined twinning invites aggressive attempts at fixing (Angier 1997). Even the surgeons of the nineteenth century knew how momentous, compelling, and risky separation was:

> If the twins, knowing all the risks, demand a division of the bond, a surgeon might, under protest, execute the mechanical part, they relieving him of all responsibility. The success would be an accident, not skill. If one or both died, he could console himself with the thought that he acted in obedience to their commands and not his judgment [Cook 1869].

Today, operability is evaluated before or shortly after birth, by physical examination, electrocardiogram to determine ventricular independence, and angiography with physiologic study to determine the configuration of their blood vessels, in addition to complying with ethical (and legal) considerations (Bergsma 1979). For twins judged inoperable, the choices are passive euthanasia, support of continuous life in a conjoined state, or surgical separation with a single survivor, difficult decisions that should be made with the involvement of the parents. With diagnosis made in the womb, more parents are opting to terminate pregnancies of conjoined twins (Angier 1997).

***See also*** **Attard, Gracie and Rosie; Binder, Patrick and Benjamin; Children's Hospital of Philadelphia; Elizabeth and Catharine; Hensel, Abigail Lauren and Brittany Lee; Hospitalization; Lincoln,**

**Charity and Kathleen; Radica and Doodica; Red Cross Children's Hospital**

## Sexuality.

*The insignificant flat hanging appendage of flesh that linked us was stronger than the tally of its soft tissue, because it could ward off love, and all thoughts of happiness.* — Darin Strauss, *Chang and Eng* (2000)

Speaking of Violet and Daisy Hilton, Leslie Fiedler (1978) writes, "They have in fact only one pair of rivals for the title of the sexiest of all Siamese Twins, Rosa and Josepha Blazek." Fiedler quotes Edward Malone, who was able in 1971, at the age of eighty-three, to recount their stage act: "These two dames were like two Mae Wests, joined at the tail bone. One would wiggle, while the other would waggle, and brother could they put on a great show." He also remembered Josepha's claims to be both a virgin and pregnant (Fiedler 1978).

Katherine Dunn broaches the subject of a conjoined twin engaging in sex in her novel *Geek Love.* Electra and Iphigenia Binewski decide to make men pay for the privilege of satisfying their curiosity firsthand. As Elly describes, "Most of the guys wonder what it would be like to fuck us. So, I figure, why not capitalize on that curiosity? They don't care that I play bass and Iphy plays treble, or whether we both like the same flavor ice cream or any of the other stupid questions they ask. The thing that boggles them and keeps them staring all the way through a sonata in G is musing about our posture in bed."

Medical historian and ethicist Alice Dreger was quoted on BBC2's "Conjoined Twins" as saying: "The notion was ... that if you had two conjoined twins getting married that meant that you'd essentially be sanctioning group sex. What that fails to understand is that conjoined twins when they have sex they always describe it as having sex one on one, that is the other conjoined twin who's in the bed with them simply zones out and pays attention to something else." The Schappells profess to be able to do just that, and the Hilton sisters were said to have learned the trick from Houdini. The number of children produced by the marriages of Chang and Eng Bunker attest to the success of the sex life of each couple.

*See also* **Blazek, Rosa and Josefa; Bunker, Chang and Eng; Hilton, Daisy and Violet; Schappell, Lori and Reba**

## Shrestha, Ganga and Jamuna. *End of Twentieth Century.*

*Ganga and Jamuna are lucky to be born in an age when the miasma of fear and superstition that surrounded such twins has evaporated. In its place is rational, hard-headed science with its clear, demystifying explanations.*— Chua Mui Hoong (2001)

A pair of conjoined female twins born on May 9, 2000, to Bushan K.C. and Sandhya Shrestha in a remote village in Nepal. Joined at the head and facing opposite directions, they share a single skull cavity and their brains are partially fused. The details about their condition were not revealed to their mother until she was discharged from the hospital three months after their birth. Neurosurgeons at Bir Hospital at Kathmandu intended to separate the twins at the age of three months, but decided that the surgery was beyond their skills.

The twins were brought to Singapore, known for the quality of its medical care, and surgery was planned at Singapore General Hospital, although their parents were unsure how it would be financed. The joined twins were visited by Nepal's honorary consul general M.N. Swami and $360,000 was donated to pay for their hospital stay, post-operative care, and long-term needs. In addition, some $500,000 was raised from individual donations in about two weeks. Airfare for the twins and their family members was provided free by Singapore Airlines and the hospital waived many of its charges. "Singapore helped give Ganga and Jamuna a fighting chance for a normal, healthy life. In return, those two little girls gave Singapore a large slice of soul," writes Chua Mui Hoong (2001).

Doctors rehearsed in virtual reality, using a three-dimensional imaging system developed by researchers in Singapore that integrates digital images from an MRI, a CT-scan, and an angiogram. The system, called VizDExter, was first used in 1998 at Johns Hopkins Medical Center. They consulted with Johns Hopkins surgeon Benjamin Carson, who assured them they would know the success of the surgery within forty-eight hours, but warned that their long-term health depends on their post-operative care. The operation was expected to take forty hours. A first attempt to separate the girls was postponed in December because they had an infection.

The twins were separated at ten months of age during surgery that lasted from the afternoon of April 6 to April 10, 2001, a marathon four days. Ganga required a few more hours — a total of ninety-six — than Jamuna. The surgical team of twenty doctors was led by Dr. Keith Goh and Chumpon Chan, with fourteen to sixteen doctors in the operating room at any one time. Dr. Goh described, "[The brains were] wrapped around each other like a helix, going around in a spiral. The path between the two brains was very, very difficult. It wasn't a straight road. It was one of those tortuous routes up a mountain. There were hundreds of blood vessels between the brains that you had to navigate through (Doctors Divide.... 2001). The surgeons used Gore-Tex to replace parts of the dura covering the girls' brains and bone and polymer to rebuild their skulls. The surgery was characterized as a success, but neurological damage may not be immediately apparent. Post-operative risks include infection and hydrocephalus. The girls remained sedated for several days after surgery to keep brain swelling to a minimum and would require further reconstructive surgery to reshape their heads. Both parents cried at the news of the operation's success. But their mother, who had waited eleven months to hold her daughters separately, was prevented from doing so because she had a fever (Sick Mother 2001).

At the age of one year, Jamuna was well enough to eat solid food, but both girls were still in the intensive care unit. They celebrated their first birthday, despite its being against Nepalese tradition, and were wished well by the Nepal royal family. In particular, Princess Shanti took an interest in them (Ng 2001). The family prays for their continued recovery. At a year and a half, they were said to be progressing well, but at different rates, as Dr. Ho Lai Yun explained (Perry 2001):

> Jamuna has the social skills of a fifteen-month-old. She is cheeky and can identify her body parts when asked. Ganga had a more stormy recovery after the operation and is further behind Jamuna. She has the social skills of a six- to seven-month-old, but we have seen a lot of improvement in the past month and she is catching up fast.

Jamuna was sitting up without support. Ganga was having some vision problems. Dr. Chumpon Chan says, "Jamuna seems to have recovered to a near-normal state. As far as Ganga is concerned, there is still a lot of potential for her to recover but it is difficult to pinpoint to what stage at this point" (Perry 2001). Donations of $660,000 had been received for the surgery and the rest was being held in trust for their medical care until the age of five, when a review of fund use would be made.

In November 2001, the twins were released from the hospital and flew home with their parents. Their care would be overseen by Dr. Basant Pant at Kathmandu Hospital, who would be in contact with the Singapore doctors. The girls affected the lives of

hospital staff who had cared for them. Dr. Ho says, "The full impact will probably be felt only the day after they have left, when I go back to their ward to check on them as I have done every day for the past six or seven months, only to find the room empty" (Perry 2001). Because the family's village is located a twenty-four-hour bus ride away from the hospital, they will move to Kathmandu until Ganga improves (Perry 2001).

## Siamese twins.

> While Phineas T. Barnum has been given the credit for coining the term "The Siamese Twins" in 1853, it is evident here [on a letter signed by them in 1832] that Chang and Eng coined the name themselves twenty-one years earlier.— Irving Wallace and Amy Wallace (1978)

Because of the celebrity of Chang and Eng Bunker, who happened to be from Siam (now Thailand), the expression "Siamese twins" has been popularly used since the first half of the nineteenth century to refer to conjoined twins. According to the *OED* (2001), the expression appeared in the *London Times* in 1829 to refer to the Bunkers; Charles Dickens used it metaphorically in 1835.

***See also*** Conjoined Twins

## "Siamese Twins."

An Emmy award-winning documentary written, produced, and directed by Jonathan Palfreman in 1995 for the PBS television series *Nova*. It follows the story of female Thai twins Dao and Duan from their arrival in the U.S. to stay with caregivers Barbara and David Headley, to their preparation for surgery and the surgery itself, to their post-surgical life and rehabilitation. David L. Clark and Catherine Myser (1996) criticize the film for spending so much time detailing the fourteen-hour surgery without considering whether or not the surgery should actually take place and without first making reference to the profound psychological implications of the separation, particularly since the twins were three and a half years old. They also find that the diagrams by the doctors (including pen lines on the twins' skin itself) and the pictures from the many imaging technologies (CT-scans, MRIs, x-rays) objectify the twins unnecessarily, making their bodies a surgical field in which the components can be rearranged at will. The documentary touches on the fact that twins so profoundly joined cannot be divided equally and that organs that cannot be halved are given to the twin believed to have the best chance of surviving and growing. Thus Dao comes out of surgery with one leg, a partial bladder, and half a pelvis, but a complete reproductive system, and Duan receives the third leg, the common rectum, and the largest part of the bladder. Clark and Myser (1996) find fault with the fact that a reproductive life is equated with a productive life and that the virtues of equality, which had been downplayed during the separation, are raised at the end of the film by comparing them to each other as they recover post-operatively.

## Sibley, Walter K.

Sibley (*d.* 1949) is said to be the first carnival showman to exhibit a wet specimen of a deformed birth, having displayed a preserved two-headed baby called "Taka-Tama" at Coney Island in 1893.
***See also* Punk**

## "Side Show."

*Utterly conventional in their desires and aspirations, the twins in "Side Show" experience their bodies as a prison that impedes their profound wish for normalcy. They want nothing more than individuation, which would free them to pursue their dreams of heterosexual courtship and marriage.*—Rachel Adams

A play loosely based on the lives of Daisy and Violet Hilton that opened at the Richard Rodgers Theatre on October 16, 1997, to glowing reviews, although Rachel Adams (1996) calls it a "banal, moralistic translation of the freak show into a Broadway musical." The production stars Emily Skinner as Daisy and Alice Ripley as Violet (incidentally reversed in position in the play), who rehearsed for weeks — sometimes bound together with a corset — before they learned to move fluidly together (Tomlinson 1997). Book and lyrics are by Bill Russell, music is by Henry Krieger, and the play is directed and choreographed by Robert Longbottom, who had seen *Chained for Life* on television. "Though we can't agree on a single response / We want what everyone wants," plead the twins in the show. "I think we're getting more / Than we bargained for," sing her suitors. "I will never leave you. I will never go away," Daisy and Violet reassure each other. Unfortunately, the play closed in January 1998 after only a three-month run. Nancy Segal (1999) theorizes the early closing was due to the lingering perception of conjoined twins as "freaks" and the directness of the stage: "Interestingly, conjoined twins' lives have fascinated people for years, but medical news and magazine articles allow a comfortable distance between readers and twins that live theater may diminish. The carnival sideshow has not survived, even once removed."
***See also* Hilton, Daisy and Violet**

## Smith, Hayley and Jessica. *Twentieth Century.*

Conjoined twin girls born in Bristol, England, in November 1998 and successfully separated thirty hours after birth.

## Smith, Kathleen and Lexie. *Twentieth Century.*

Craniopagus twin girls born in Wynyard, Tasmania, in 1950.

## Smith, Natasha and Courtney. *Twenty-first Century.*

*Both the lives of these tiny girls are equally precious.*—Pro-Life Alliance

Conjoined twin girls born to Tina May and Dennis Smith on April 29, 2002, joined from the top of the chest to the navel. The parents learned that the babies were conjoined during a routine ultrasound, but ruled out termination on religious grounds. Together, the twins weighed 9 pounds 12 ounces. While the twins' shared liver can be divided, they share a single heart that won't support them both and may not support the surviving baby if they are separated. Natasha would receive the heart during the operation, since it resides mainly in her chest cavity. If she survives, she will be the first conjoined twin born with a shared heart to survive separation in the U.K. (Boseley 2002). Perinatal cardiologist Helena Gardiner commented, "If Natasha survives the operation it depends how successful the surgery goes. The first few days will determine whether she can survive. As far as I know there has never been a case of a baby surviving more than a few months when they were joined such as this" (Crilly and McKillop 2002). The twins were delivered at Queen Charlotte's and Chelsea Maternity Hospital in Hammersmith by Cesarean section. Their mother said after the birth, "When I saw them for the first time they looked so beautiful that I melted with love for them. But my happiness is tinged with the agony of knowing the ordeal that lies ahead for us all" (Crilly and McKillop 2002). Three hours after they were born, the twins were transferred to Great Ormond Street Hospital in London for further care. The Pro-Life Alliance has raised the ethical issue of causing Courtney's death by performing the separation surgery, and suggests providing her with a heart transplant. The shared heart has abnormalities (a hole and transposition of the pulmonary artery and aorta) that will require difficult and risky repair. If the surgery is not performed, Dr. Gardiner expects the babies to be symptomatic within six weeks, since the abnormal heart allows too much blood to go to one of their lungs (Boseley 2002).

The day after the birth of Courtney and Natasha, a press conference was held at the hospital. The parents of the Smith twins were paid a substantial but undisclosed sum of money for exclusive rights to the story by *The Sun*, which ran a full-page photograph of the twins on the front page (Crilly and McKillop 2002) and devoted several pages to the story. The hospital succeeded in obtaining a court injunction prohibiting the press from identifying any of the staff involved with the Smith case except for Dr. Spitz and barring them from seeking any information about the twins from hospital staff (Boseley 2002).

*See also* Media attention

### Soto, Darielis Milagro and Sandra Ivellisse. *Twentieth Century.*

*We decided to fight for our babies.* — Ramon Soto

Female twins born to Ramon and Sandra Soto of Manati, Puerto Rico, at Children's Hospital Boston on May 30, 1999. Their union at the chest and abdomen had been diagnosed by ultrasound during a routine examination in San Juan in 1998. The babies shared a single heart and liver, and were both expected to die within a day if they were not separated soon after birth. Termination of the pregnancy was offered, but the Sotos declined: "Doctors in Puerto Rico and even the Sotos' own families had urged Mrs. Soto to end the pregnancy, but the couple, deeply religious and eager to have children, rejected that advice," writes Denise Grady (2000). Grady also quotes Sandra Soto as saying, "We want other parents with this problem to try to save their kids."

Ramon called Children's Hospital in Boston, which he had seen on television. Dr. Steven Fishman offered to evaluate the twins, which he did during Sandra's fifth month of pregnancy in February 1999. There it was learned that the blood from the single heart entered the other twin through arteries in the umbilical cord and drained back through a vein in their shared liver, a situation undocumented in the medical literature. Fishman had hoped that surgery would save one of the twins, but he now explained that surgery would have to take place immediately after delivery, since the umbilical cord must be clamped and that would cause death, which would release deadly acids and toxins into the bloodstream of the healthier sister. After grappling with the news that they would certainly lose one of the twins and possibly both, the Sotos gave Dr. Fishman permission to separate them.

The operation and follow-up care were expected to cost several hundred thousand dollars. Dr. Fishman waived his surgical fee and the hospital waived its charges, since the Sotos had little money and no health insurance. The operation would be an emergency procedure, since the surgical teams had little time to prepare. Obstetrician Lennox Hoyte and radiologist Clare Tempany prepared MRI scans of the twins' intertwined anatomy and assembled the images into a three-dimensional model. Dr. Fishman choreographed the surgery and handpicked the medical team. A week before her scheduled delivery date, Sandra had insomnia, followed by a stomach ache and a headache. Ramon brought her to the hospital at 5 AM on the morning of May 30, 1999. Her blood pressure was elevated and she had protein in her urine, a classic sign of preeclampsia, a condition that put her at risk for seizure and required that the twins be delivered immediately. Dr. Fishman skipped his sister-in-law's wedding and called his team from their Memorial Day weekend festivities. They were assembled at the hospital by 8:30 AM and waited while Dr. Fishman delivered the babies at Brigham and Women's Hospital across the street.

The delivery by Cesarean section went smoothly and was observed by their father, who admitted he was afraid to touch the twins (Grady 2000). The babies were placed in an incubator on top of a gurney, which was transferred over an enclosed pedestrian bridge. By the time they reached Children's Hospital, Sandra had begun to cool and darken and had neither blood pressure nor pulse. Dr. Fishman performed the separation, during which baby Sandra died. The import was not lost on the surgeons, as Dr. Fishman notes:

> As much as we spent months planning for this, and it seemed ethically and emotionally simple, nevertheless when I saw them both initially pink and both crying and moving their arms and having the same size bodies, it was heart wrenching [Grady 2000].

Studies had confirmed that not even a heart transplant could have saved Sandra, since she was missing major blood vessels. Not only were newborn donor hearts virtually impossible to find, there was "nothing to hook a heart into," said Dr. Fishman (Grady 2000).

Dr. Fishman made his incisions as much to Sandra's side as he could to allow additional skin coverage for Darielis' wound. As he closed the incision shortly before 4 PM, Dr. Fishman thanked his team and called the twins' mother. He reported that the surviving baby Darielis was in critical but stable condition. Darielis spent six months in the hospital and underwent additional surgeries to repair a heart defect and an intestinal obstruction. She also had an operation to improve her chest wall, which bulged with tissue from Sandra that was used to protect Darielis' heart. She will require physical therapy and will wear a back brace (Grady 2000).

Sandra's body was buried in a family plot in Puerto Rico. Darielis' parents intend to tell her about baby Sandra: "'When Darielis is old enough to understand,' Ramon says, 'we will tell her about her sister.' 'Yes,' mother Sandra adds. 'She will learn how they came into this world together, and how, in a final embrace, they said good-bye'" (Pekkanen 2001). At the age of four-teen months, Darielis lived with her parents in Paterson, N.J. At two, she still showed no signs of long-term developmental difficul-ties.

## Specimens.

Specimens of conjoined twins have al-ways been a component of museum collec-tions, their precursors "cabinets of curios-ity," and even earlier holdings. The museum of Pompey the Great in first century Rome was said to have included four pairs of con-joined twins (Purcell 1997).

Many of the world's contemporary medical museums and research institutions curate wet and skeletal specimens of con-joined twins. These include the following, though there are many more:

• **The Briest Museum**, a museum of ana-tomical pathology specimens used as an educational aide in the teaching of human pathology at the University of Minnesota

at Duluth, curates a pair of twins that share a single heart. The specimen was acquired some seventy years ago and has been autopsied, but identity, provenance, and clinical information about the case has been lost.

• **The Medical-Historical Museum of the University of Copenhagen** preserves a number of historical specimens they refer to as "diplopagus," along with papers and books about conjoined twins. Specimens include female ischiopagus twins Martha and Marie, b. 1848; dicephalus thoraco-pagus, b. 1888; dicephalus ischiopagus, b. 1876; and others. The collection is known as the Saxtorph Collection, after founders Matthias Saxtorph (*d.* 1800) and his son Johan Sylvester Saxtorph (*d.* 1840).

• **The Mütter Museum of the College of Physicians of Philadelphia** curates a number of wet and dry specimens of con-joined twins, as well as the joined livers of Chang and Eng Bunker.

• **The National Museum of Health and Medicine** curates and displays several wet

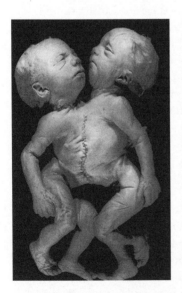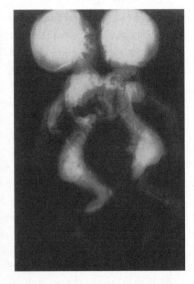

*Left:* Dorsal view of the body of conjoined twins who died approximately seventy years ago and were more recently autopsied. *Middle:* Ventral view of conjoined twins. *Right:* X-ray of specimen of con-joined twins. Courtesy of Arthur Aufderheide, Department of Pathology and Laboratory Medicine, University of Minnesota.

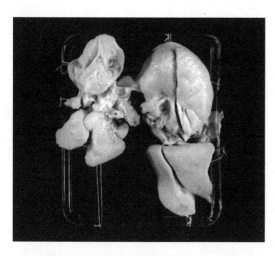

The joined hearts of conjoined twins. Courtesy of Arthur Aufderheide, Department of Pathology and Laboratory Medicine, University of Minnesota.

specimens of stillborn conjoined twins, along with skeletal preparations.

*See also* Exhibition

## Spencer, Rowena.

Dr. Rowena Spencer, a retired pediatric surgeon from Tulane Medical School and Louisiana State University Medical Center in New Orleans, has participated in the separation of a number of pairs of conjoined twins. She has also documented more than 1,200 cases in the medical and historical literature. In 1996, she published an article in the *Journal of Pediatric Surgery* proposing the nomenclature that is used today to describe the eight types of unions exhibited by conjoined twins.

*See also* Cephalopagus, Craniopagus, Ischiopagus, Omphalopagus, Parapagus, Pygopagus, Rachipagus, Thoracopagus

## Spitz, Lewis.

Dr. Lewis Spitz, a pediatric surgeon at Great Ormond Street Hospital in London, has been involved in nineteen cases of conjoined twins, including several cases where separation was not possible.

## Stark, Alexandra Esther Kanikava and Sydney Wilhemina Kanikavi.
*Twenty-first Century.*

> *We could keep them together, and we could keep them forever or we can try to make their lives better with the potential that we may not be bringing them home.* — Emily Stark

Conjoined twin girls born March 9, 2001, in Denver, to Emily and Jim Stark. Their thirty-year-old mother, who was Miss Colorado in 1995, always wanted to have twins and the couple had a feeling she was carrying two babies. During an ultrasound in November 2000, Emily's hunch that the twins she was carrying were joined was confirmed. They were put under the care of Dr. Robert McDuffie, a specialist in high-risk obstetrics. An MRI was performed to decide on the quality of life the girls could be offered and whether abortion should be an option. "We cried all night," said Jim, "and the next morning, we told our families and closest friends. But ultimately, we wanted to be alone. We had to figure out for ourselves whether or not to keep the babies.... Quality of life was always our main focus, so we instantly agreed that if we had them, we'd have them separated" (Cohen 2002). Pediatric neurosurgeon Dr. Michael Handler told the Starks that the babies were joined at the base of the spine, so separating them would come with the risk of paralysis or death. They were pygopagus, joined at the lower back, rump, and hip. They shared parts of the spinal cord and column, some bone and musculature, and the lower portion of their gastrointestinal tract, but did not share any major organs. But Dr. Handler cautioned, "What we don't know is exactly how commingled are the nerves that control the function of the legs." The parents decided to proceed with the pregnancy, but told only their family and close friends that the babies were joined.

Remembering the image of her babies sucking their thumbs on the MRI, Emily says, "There was no way in hell I was going to give them up" (Cohen 2002). Despite the fact that Emily had been confined to her bed to prevent premature delivery, the twins arrived eight weeks early. A large incision was made to deliver the babies by Cesarean section. Emily recalls, "They were even more beautiful than I had dreamed." Jim gushed, "They were purple and gross — and yet so heart-stoppingly beautiful that my fears flew away instantly" (Cohen 2002). They were joined at the spine and shared an imperforate anus. Each baby had her own arms, legs, and reproductive tract (Cohen 2002). After birth, they were breathing on their own but Sydney was having difficulty, so she was given oxygen. They were brought to the neonatal intensive care unit, which is where they were baptized. Just ten hours after birth, they underwent surgery to provide them each with a colostomy.

The Starks moved into a new house. Their father explained that since they necessarily do everything for both twins at the same time, it was almost like having a single baby. They described the girls as sleeping mostly on their backs, often holding hands (Cohen 2002). Their mother was concerned with how she would diaper and feed the girls. Their grandmother Joy Stark, a gifted seamstress, made their clothes. The parents wondered if people thought they took them for walks in a single stroller because they couldn't afford a second one. The Starks decided that they wanted the twins to experience life. They became more accustomed to the curiosity of strangers.

"Lexi" and "Syd" were the subject of an episode of the CBS documentary *48 Hours* entitled "Twin Miracles" and reported by Jane Clayson, which begins before their birth and ends with their successful separation on October 9, 2001, at Denver Children's Hospital. At the parents' request, the image of the twins' physical juncture was blurred. The Starks, who planned to have the twins surgically separated from the start, were prepared for any outcome. They would

care for their babies if they were paralyzed; they would donate their organs if they did not survive the operation (Cohen 2002). The surgery was expected to last eighteen hours. The surgeons claimed that they knew they were doing the right thing, but were frightened by the risk of paralysis. For the next seven months, fifty-seven medical personnel took part in the planning of the operation, which also involved representatives from Kaiser-Permanente. The Starks' insurance company covered much of the cost of the surgery, but the family still had significant out-of-pocket expenses (Cohen 2002). The surgical team, led by pediatric surgeon Joseph Janik, was assembled from staff at Kaiser, Children's Hospital, and Exempla Saint Joseph Hospital. It was hoped that both girls would be able to walk afterward.

To prepare for surgery, doctors used a computer to prepare a replica of Alexandra's and Sydney's spines. They determined that the girls had enough skin to cover a 42-centimeter wound, so they installed tissue expanders in their backs. The parents grieved over the fact that conjoined was how their babies were given to them, but referred to the day of the operation as "independence day." The family prayed with twenty friends, who waited with them in the hospital for the hourly updates. In the operating room, the surgeons first took turns cutting through layers of skin and bone, using tools that cut and cauterize so that there is very little bleeding (Cohen 2002). The twins' reflexes were tested with a nerve stimulator throughout the surgery. The surgeons separated the two sets of intestinal tracts, then cut through muscle to separate the tailbone. Individual buttocks were constructed for each child. When the twins were flipped over, some of their skin had blistered, which left less of it to use in closing the wound. Once the nerves were carefully separated, the girls became "two patients" eleven hours after surgery had begun. The parents found the moment significant, but also felt that a weight had been lifted from their shoulders. Jim Stark described relief and the joy of realizing their dream. Surgery was now in the hands of the plastic surgeons.

The doctors had to wait until the anesthesia wore off to assess whether there was any nerve damage. They had found during the surgery that the girls shared the sac around the spinal cord, but not the cord itself (Cohen 2002). Sydney was the first to awake and began moving all four limbs, followed by Alexandra. Doctors predicted they would both be able to walk. It would be another two or three years before they could assess whether the twins had normal bowel control. "They're just little miracles. I think they have proven so many things," said their mother, who confessed that reality wouldn't hit her until she was holding one baby at a time in her arms. Soon she was able to do just that. Only eight days after surgery, the Stark twins were released from the hospital and spent their first Halloween at home — each in her own costume. An article about the Stark twins in Rosie O'Donnell's magazine describes, "When Lexi sleeps in her own crib, she now loves to spread out, enjoying her newfound freedom. Her scar is shaped like an S, so she'll always carry her sister's initial where they were joined. Syd still finds her twisted-sideways position the most comfortable. Both seem to enjoy the independence they unknowingly longed for" (Cohen 2002).

**Statistics** *see* **Frequency; Survival rates**

**Stillbirth** *see* **Abortion**

**"Strange Medicine."**

The August 13, 2001, episode of this weekly drama on *Lifetime* television featured the story of a couple whose strong opposition to the separation of their conjoined twins — which would save the life of one child, but result in the death of the other — was overruled by the hospital ethics committee.

**Study** *see* **Teratology**

**Superstition** *see* **Prodigy**

**Survival rates.**

Approximately 40 to 60 percent of conjoined twins are delivered stillborn. A mere 35 percent survive longer than a single day. The overall survival rate is between 5 and 25 percent, with some 600 sets of conjoined twins surviving over the past 500 years (*www.twinstuff.com*). The majority of survivors are female, since conjoined males tend to have more health problems.

Separation surgery is considered "successful" if it is survived by at least one twin. Edge (2000) writes, "Worldwide, there have been around 200 attempted separations since 1950, three quarters of which have resulted in the survival of one or more babies."

*See also* **Frequency**

**Symbolism.**

*Freaks are powerful symbols of a common anxiety that underneath the apparent normality of our bodies we are as divided as the conjoined twins, as fragmented as the human torso, as excessive as the fat person.* — Rachel Adams

The physical union of conjoined twins has been used to express different sentiments, based on the times in which they lived. An editorial cartoon in *Harper's Weekly* (February 7, 1874) depicts labor and capital as conjoined twins, with the words "the real union" inscribed on their connecting band. Conjoined twins Chang and Eng Bunker became symbols of the divided country during the American Civil War. Allison Pingree puts this into larger context: "Conjoined twins arrest the attention and imagination of the American public because they embody both a national fantasy and a national nightmare. That is, the prospect of merged selves corporealized in conjoined twins both reflects a democratic imperative — where all selves are in a sense the same, interchangeable self— and imperils the stability of unique selfhood so stressed by American individualism." Pingree (1996) notes that the Bunker twins were used to sell democratic nationalism, but that patriotism was also employed to "sell" the twins to the paying public. The democratic symbolism backfires when one of twins avoids prosecution for assault so that the innocent twin won't be punished, suggesting ominous possibilities of the guilty going free (Pingree 1996). But the fact that doctors declined to separate Chang and Eng reinforced the value of national cohesion and loyalty (Pingree 1996).

Pingree also points out that Violet and Daisy Hilton were intriguing, but somewhat unsuccessful symbols of career women: "The twins' particular form of aberration perfectly embodies what many by then had come to fear: that a woman's body might not be able to be controlled; that heterosexual, companionate marriage might not be the only form of intimate 'bonding' between two people; and that the division between public and private might not be so clear after all. Despite a host of attempts — futile as they were — to master this enigmatic figure, the image of Daisy and Violet remained, like the New Woman, a symbol of 'disorder and rebellion.'" In general, conjoined twins are used to convey themes of cooperation and sharing. Rachel Adams (1996) writes, "Conjoined twins remind us that we are all inextricably bound to other human beings." A recent advertising campaign by Earthlink features an illustration of Chang and Eng Bunker with the slogan, "Get Connected." A 1995 advertisement for Van Halen's compact disk "Balance" depicts young female twins attached at the hips, one in pain and the other expressionless (Segal 1999).

Because the birth of Vietnamese conjoined twins Viet and Duc was blamed on the use of the deforestation chemical Agent Orange, the twins became symbols of the horrors of war and the need for international unity. The use of conjoined twins and other "monstrosities" to further a cause has sometimes obscured their needs, as Dudley Wilson (1993) points out: "What has been the role of the monster in all this? Certainly, he or she has found it more than difficult to achieve individuality and freedom. In general the condition has been exploited, sometimes in the name of a multitude of good causes: used by God to declare his glory and power, used by man to obtain money and provide a spectacle, sponsored by science for the advancement of the same. In many people's eyes all this is ending. They may be right, but the exploitation and the isolation of the monster, consented to or not, are far from finally over."

***See also*** **Bunker, Chang and Eng; Hilton, Daisy and Violet; Viet and Duc**

## Symmetry.

*We may truly wonder at the diversity of nature, yet we always find her true to herself in the anatomical structure of united twins.* — H. Besse (1874)

Wright (1997) notes that mirror imaging — ranging from the location of the eruption of the first tooth to having organs on the wrong side of the body — appears frequently in conjoined twins. In fact, mirror-image reversal of traits such as handedness and hair whorl occur among 25 percent of all identical twins. Gedda (1961) referred to mirror imaging as "specularity" or "reversed asymmetry" and noted that it has both anatomical and functional implications. Although many conjoined twins appear to be mirror images of each other, modern surgeons know that this is not necessarily the case. Internally, their organ systems sometimes differ dramatically. In fact, *situs inversus,* the physical reversal of internal organs such as the heart or liver, does not occur more frequently in twins than in singletons, so its frequency in conjoined twins may be unique to some forms of conjoined twinning (Segal 1999). In the case of craniopagus twins, their bodies may be rotated to a greater or lesser degree so that they are not facing the same direction, but in general conjoined twins exhibit the symmetry that marks their shared origin: "The finding that conjoined twins are typically connected in symmetrical (mirror-image) pose by corresponding body parts is also consistent with their one-egg derivation" (Segal 1999).

### Tahiri, Hasna and Ihsane. *Twentieth Century.*

Conjoined twins born in Morocco on November 19, 1999.

### Tamulevicious, Vilia and Natalia. *Twentieth Century.*

Conjoined girls born in Lithuania on May 27, 1987, joined at the head. Separated in 1989.

### Taveras, Rosa and Carmen. *Twentieth Century.*

Female conjoined twins born in Santiago, Dominican Republic, on November 15, 1992, to Ana Lia Martinez and Wilson Taveras. The delivery was vaginal and the twins weighed ten pounds. They shared organs and parts of their pelvis, but had four legs and did not share a heart. They had a single anus and two urethral openings. The twins' differences soon became apparent. Carmen was more outgoing and demanding. Rosa was more relaxed and accepting.

The family was referred to Dr. Luis Cuello Mainardi, a cardiologist at Corazones Unidos Clinic in Santo Domingo. Dr. Cuello contacted Healing the Children Midatlantic Foundation, a charitable group that brings children from all over the world to the U.S. for treatment. The foundation brought the twins from the Dominican Republic for evaluation and possible separation and arranged for the Taveras twins to stay with hosts Debra and Stephen Scaturro, who agreed without even seeing a photo of the girls. The Scaturros picked up the twins at Newark Airport on December 12, 1992. At their home, they propped the twins up so they could see each other. They were examined by Dr. Pater Altman of Columbia-Presbyterian Medical Center. Without the surgery, they would never be able to sit, stand, or walk. The hospital prepared by assembling a team of fifty-two doctors, nurses, respiratory therapists, and technicians. The use of the high-tech equipment, laboratories, operating room, intensive-care bed, and the services of the staff would be donated. The operation would consist of five separate procedures (Tanne 1993).

To familiarize themselves with the twins' anatomy, the surgeons performed a number of tests. Carmen and Rosa spent three days in the radiology suite. They were examined by endoscopy. A cystogram showed two bladders, but Rosa's urine was backing up into her kidney so she was put on antibiotics to prevent infection. A CT-scan showed that each twin had two kidneys, but Carmen's was unusually low in the body. An ultrasound showed that each twin had a normal liver, spleen, pancreas, gallbladder, and spinal cord. Each of the girls had a urethra, a vagina, a uterus, and two ovaries. A barium enema revealed that they had separate small intestines, but shared the large intestine and a single anus. After the surgery, doctors expected to have two functional little girls. The most difficult part of the surgery would be reconstruction of the pelvis and assuring ample soft tissue for coverage after the bowel reconstruction (Tanne 1993).

Tissue expanders were inserted under the skin of each twin's lower belly on March 8, 1993, by plastic surgeon Mark Sultan.

The Scaturros injected sterile water into tubes leading to the balloons every other day over the next two months to stretch the skin. The surgery began on June 7 in a very warm operating room, with their legs wrapped in sterile gauze for additional warmth. The twins were positioned and attached to heart monitors, each with her own anesthesiologist. They were swabbed with antiseptic solution and hooked up to respirators. Incisions were made and the tissue expanders were removed. Another incision separated the twins between their legs, after which the bowel was divided. They were each given a colostomy with the hope that later surgery could provide them with new anuses. The temperatures of the twins were maintained by covering them with pads soaked in warm saline solution. Next a catheter was threaded up into each twins' bladder. With their ureters detached, the girls were separate and Carmen was moved to a separate table. After separation, the babies remained in the same operating room. One team worked on Carmen's bowel while the other worked on Rosa's urinary tract, then they switched. Their legs were loose and floppy because their pelvises had not yet been reconstructed. Orthopedic surgeons pulled the bones of Rosa's pubic symphysis together with long sutures threaded through wires in the bones. The same was done on Carmen. The tissues in Rosa's genital area were carefully arranged, her colostomy neatened, and her perineum was sewn. The skin of Rosa's abdomen was closed with staples and a belly button was created. Carmen's incisions were opened to find the severed blood vessels were evident from her swollen right leg. Rosa was the first to be transferred to the pediatric intensive care unit, followed three hours later by Carmen (Tanne 1993).

After the surgery, Debra Scaturro spent every day of the next two weeks with the twins. Her husband and son Andrew visited as often as they could. The hospital staff made sure the babies could see and hear each other and delighted in their enjoyment of their new freedom of movement. On June 22, casts were put on Carmen's and Rosa's legs to help turn them to a normal position. The casts came off in July and the twins worked with a physical therapist to learn to crawl and stand. At eight months of age, their development from the waist down was comparable to three-month-old children. Doctors suggested that the twins needed several months to recover, learn to walk, and let their muscles heal before they were returned to their parents in the Dominican Republic. The publicity the twins generated may have been responsible for improving their living conditions at home (Tanne 1993).

The separation of the Taveras twins was recorded by the hospital's television crew for teaching purposes. Also present was a crew from WNBC and a photographer and a reporter from *New York* magazine, who described the room as "jammed" (Tanne 1993). The video of the surgery was transmitted down the hall to the pediatric anesthesia conference room where it was viewed live on a large-screen television by hospital staffers. The entire surgical team is identified in a photograph that accompanies an article in *New York* magazine. Letters, photographs, and videotapes of Carmen and Rosa were sent by the hospital staff to their parents to show their progress following the separation (Tanne 1993).

### Taylor, Emily and Claire. *Twentieth Century.*

Female twins born on February 12, 1984, at St. Mary's Hospital Medical Center in Madison, Wisconsin, to Richard and Mary Taylor of Portage. They were joined at the pelvis and abdomen with most of their organ systems involved. For their parents, there was no question but to separate them. "'They were conjoined much more severely than we had anticipated, and that changed everything,' Mary said. 'There was no choice in our minds that they would be separated, no matter what. We would expect that if they didn't make it through the surgery, it was meant to be'" (Loft 1998). Two days after birth, Emily and Claire were flown to Children's Hospital of Philadelphia for assessment. Each baby had her own heart, lungs, and kidneys. They each had a liver, but they were attached. They shared a urinary tract, a digestive system, and a reproductive system. On June 18, 1984, the twins were separated by a surgical team of eighteen led by James A. O'Neill, Jr., and John M. Templeton, Jr. (Herskowitz 1984).

They are now active teenagers, each with a prosthetic leg, and aspire to have careers as an emergency room doctor and an actress, respectively. They still live in Wisconsin (Loft 1998).

*See also* **Children's Hospital of Philadelphia**

## Tejeda, Nichelle and Michelle.
*Twentieth Century.*

Twin girls born thirteen weeks prematurely in Texas on May 15, 1995, joined at the head. They were separated at the age of thirteen weeks at St. David's Hospital in Austin in August 1995. After the thirteen-and-a-half-hour operation, they were in critical but stable condition in the hospital's neonatal intensive care unit, each weighing six pounds four ounces. Nichelle, however, was terminally ill from a herpes infection inherited in the womb. The disease destroyed part or all of her intestines, stomach, bladder, kidneys, liver, and brain. The hospital kept Nichelle comfortable until her death. Michelle had no signs of infections, but battled other problems and had a "guarded" prognosis.

## Terata Anacatadidyma.

The class of conjoined twins that are joined at the midportion of the body and are separate above and below the shared region. Includes thoracopagus, omphalopagus, and rachipagus.

*See also* **Omphalopagus, Rachipagus, Thoracopagus**

## Terata Anadidyma.

The class of conjoined twins that are single in the lower portion of the body and double above or a pair of twins joined by some lower portion. Includes dipygus and syncephalus (now called cephalopagus), and craniopagus.

*See also* **Cephalopagus, Craniopagus**

## Terata Catadidymus.

The class of conjoined twins that are single in the upper portion of the body and double below. Includes diprosopus and dicephalus (now called parapagus), ischiopagus, and pygopagus.

*See also* **Ischiopagus, Parapagus, Pygopagus**

## Teratology.

*Fascination with monstrous births — especially with the appearance of conjoined twins — is universal.* — Rosamond Purcell

The study of abnormal human births. In its biological sense, the word dates back to 1842, according to the *Oxford English Dictionary* (2001), but was designated by Geoffry Sainte-Hilaire in 1860 to refer to the study or consideration of monsters or anomalies of organization. Anomalous bodies had been considered by Aristotle, who placed monsters along a graded and hierarchical continuum with normal being superior: "Although Aristotle's approach to monsters is partly ethical and philosophical, it is essentially physiological and medical, and in this he is in many ways the founder of the science of teratology" (Wilson 1993). Pliny, on the other hand, was content to record the variety of nature and

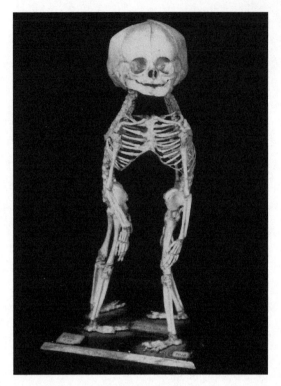

Cephalothoracopagus skeleton. Courtesy of the Mütter Museum, College of Physicians of Philadelphia.

wrote of (but did not guarantee) the existence of monstrous races (Wilson 1993). Augustine saw monsters as being examples of the variety of God's creation and as playing an essential part in a universe which is both harmonious and mysterious. He felt that much of the universe was inexplicable and that it should be wondered at, rather than analyzed and explained: "Augustine points out that, if the baby with two heads is marvellous, the fact that most babies only have one head is equally and possibly even more legitimately, a source of wonderment" (Wilson 1993). His thought was echoed by Montaigne (*d.* 1592), who offered the following reflection after observing a conjoined twin: "Those which we call monsters are not so with God, who in the immensitie of his worke seeth the infinitie of formes therein contained" (Wilson 1993). Monstrous births had been given a special place in the schema

developed by Francis Bacon in 1620 (Semonin 1996). Their religious treatment in the literature of the Middle Ages and Renaissance gave way to an encyclopedic interest that resulted in treatises patterned after Albertus Magnus's *De secretis naturae* and quickly copied into "prodigy books" like Ambroise Paré's *Des Monstres et prodiges* for popular consumption (Semonin 1996).

Anomalous bodies had been studied popularly in cabinets of curiosity, museums, and sideshows. "In a definitive bifurcation from the popular, nineteenth century science officially enunciated teratology as the study, classification, and manipulation of monstrous bodies. As scientific explanations eclipsed religious mystery to become the authoritative cultural narrative of modernity, the exceptional body began increasingly to be represented in clinical terms as pathology, and the monstrous body moved from the freak show stage into the medical theater" (Thompson 1996). Grosz (1996) notes that teratology being driven by medicine rather than superstition rendered what is horrifying and fascinating about such individuals into neutral facts described in scientific terminology that places them within a continuum that has normal as the ideal. Alongside the scientific and philosophical pamphlet, the broadside — which retained elements of superstition to enhance the story — proliferated (Wilson 1993).

Early teratologists included Ulisse Aldrovandi (1524?–1607) and Victor Albrecht von Haller (1708–1777). Other teratologists included Friedrich Ahlfeld (1843–1929), J.W. Ballantyne, Johann Friedrich Blumenbach (1752–1840), George Jackson Fisher, Hans Hübner, Schenkius, and Ernst Schwalbe. Also among them is natural philosopher Fortunio Liceti, who is credited with one of the few realistic posthumous portrayals of conjoined twins, reproduced in his 1616 book *De Monstris*, in which he attempted to catalog all teratological births (Purcell 1997). The nineteenth century was

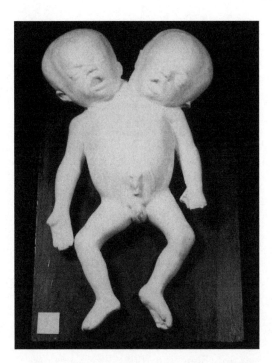

**Plaster cast of bicephalic twins. Courtesy of the Mütter Museum, College of Physicians of Philadelphia.**

the heyday of scientific teratology, particularly in Germany and France, where it had been helped along by the detailed anatomical studies conducted by the learned societies that were formed in the eighteenth century (Wilson 1993). "In addition to dissecting every malformed infant that came into their hands, the pioneer teratologists reviewed the old annals of strange births to discover historical cases of rare malformations" (Bondeson 2000). Isidore Geoffroy Saint-Hilaire (1805–1861) is considered the first modern teratologist because he "was not only committed to advancing a methodological study of human deformities, but also to combatting what he believed were the naïve and superstition myths surrounding them" (Grosz 1996). Saint-Hilaire divides the history of monstrous births into three periods: the first lasted until the end of the seventeenth century and is dominated by superstition and prejudice; the second lasted until the mid–eighteenth century and

is characterized by careful observation driven by curiosity; and the third, and contemporary, period is associated with the search for true scientific knowledge and the effort to advance it (Wilson 1993).

Dudley Wilson (1993) writes, "Halfway through the twentieth century the monster-freak seems quite suddenly to disappear, and the rapid development of caring for those who are handicapped seems set to herald a new era in which the monster comes in from the cold. Indeed, developments in embryological research and genetic engineering threaten his very existence." Teratology has come a long way.

*See also* **Prodigy**

**Teratology Society.**
1767 Business Center Drive
Suite 302
Reston, Virginia 20190-5332
*www.teratology.org*

A multidisciplinary scientific society whose members study the cause, process, and prevention of abnormal development and birth defects. The group conducts annual meetings.

**Teratoscopy.**
Divination based on examination of abnormal births.
*See also* **Prodigy**

**Terminology.**
Types of conjoined twins were grouped and classified by Alan F. Guttmacher and B.L. Nichols in 1967. The nomenclature used to describe the anatomical relationships of conjoined twins was standardized by Dr. Rowena Spencer in a 1996 article in the *Journal of Pediatric Surgery*.

*See also* **Atypical twins; Dorsal union; Lateral union; Relationship; Spencer, Rowena; Terata Anacatadidyma; Terata Anadidyma; Terata Catadidymus; Ventral union**

## Thoracopagus.

Twins united face-to-face from the upper thorax to the umbilicus, sharing the chest wall. The union always includes the heart, even if it is joined by only a single vessel, and often includes a common liver and intestines. The pelvises are not united and the twins have a total of four arms and four legs (Spencer 1996). Occurs in about 40 percent of conjoined twins (Segal 1999).

There is a wet preparation of thoracopagus fetal twins on exhibit at the Mütter Museum in Philadelphia. The specimen, on permanent loan from the Wistar Institute, has autopsy incisions.

**Figure of two girls joined together by their anterior parts, from Ambroise Paré's *On Monsters and Marvels*, originally published in 1840.**

## Tocci Brothers *see* Tocci, Giovanni-Batisto and Giacomo

## Tocci, Giovanni-Batisto and Giacomo.
### *Nineteenth Century.*

*In their general appearance there is nothing repulsive. They have bright, intelligent faces, not of the peculiar case common to cripples. They are educated and write their names as souvenirs for visitors.* — Scientific American 1891

Dicephalous twin boys born in Locana, in Turin, northern Italy, on October 4, 1877, to thirty-two-year-old Giovanni Tocci and nineteen-year-old Maria Luigia Mezzanrosa (Bondeson 2000), although *Scientific American* (Tocci Twins 1891) records their birth date as July 4, 1875, and their mother's name as Antonia Mezzano. Under the care of a midwife, the eight-hour labor and delivery of the eight-pound twins was said to have been easy, but the reaction of the father (who had to be restrained temporarily in a lunatic asylum, according to one source) was not (Bondeson 2000). The heads presented one at a time, followed by the body and legs and a single umbilical cord and placenta (Harris 1892). The Tocci twins had two heads, four arms, two hearts, four lungs, two stomachs, two vertebral columns, one penis (with a rudimentary secondary organ located posteriorly), one anus, three buttocks, and two legs. They were fused, as described in *Scientific American* (Tocci Twins 1891): "The twins are connected from the sixth rib downward, and have but one pair of legs and a single abdomen. The spinal columns are distinct until the lumbar region is reached. There they unite at an angle of 180 degrees. The sacrum seems to be a single bone." Their circulatory systems seemed to be distinct and they were observed to breathe at different times. They were examined by doctors at the Academy of Medicine when they were only a month old. The doctors confirmed that the boys had two hearts and two sets of lungs, but didn't believe they would live long. A month later they had gained an additional three pounds (Tocci Twins 1891).

After his recovery at their appearance,

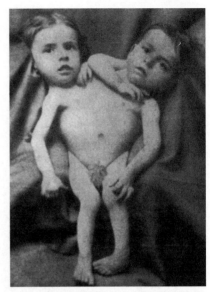

*Above left:* An illustration of the Tocci brothers being fed, from an 1879 article by Dr. Grunwald in *Virchows Archiv.* Courtesy of Jan Bondeson, M.D., Ph.D. *Right:* A photograph of the Tocci brothers in 1881. Courtesy of Jan Bondeson, M.D., Ph.D.

their father decided to exhibit them. Four weeks after their birth, the Tocci brothers were shown in Turin and examined there by Professors Fubini and Mosso, who complained about the restrictions placed on their investigations. Dr. Harris (1892) later explains: "The parents appear to be impressed with an idea that there is danger in a physical examination, whereby the hope of their gains might be destroyed; and the manager even opposes the answering of questions of a simple character put to the boys." At that time, the twins weighed nearly nine pounds and could not yet talk. Exhibits followed in Austria, Germany, Switzerland, England, America, and France (Harris 1892). The twins were shown in Paris in May 1878 and in Lyons in October 1878. In Lyons, they were examined and described by two doctors. They were developing at a normal rate, both physically and intellectually, and were said to be in good health. The medical men determined that they had two sacra and two coccyges.

Both Giacomo and Giovanni were able to write. Giacomo was the more talkative

and quick-tempered. Giovanni was quieter and fond of drawing. They had blond hair and grayish-blue eyes. Each boy controlled half of the body and they could dress themselves, but they were unable to coordinate their movements enough to walk without assistance, although they could stand. Dr. Robert P. Harris writes (1892), "This last is the most inconvenient of all of their structural points, for neither head can will to walk with both legs, and the two wills cannot effect a co-ordination of movement and balance of any practical value in progression." Their control of the legs was proven by the determination that the pulse in either leg was synchronous only with the cardiac beat of the same side (Harris 1892). In photographs, they appear supporting themselves with a chair. Giacomo's foot had a form of clubfoot (talipes equinovarus) that prevented him from resting it flatly on the floor (Bondeson 2000). Giovanni was said to be better formed and stood more erect (Harris 1892). At home, they most often used their inner arms to pull themselves along on the floor. They had large regions of shared

**The Tocci brothers photographed with their inner arms raised and clasped. Courtesy of the Circus World Museum, Baraboo, Wisconsin.**

sensation, but their appetites and sleeping habits did not always correspond. Giovanni, for instance, liked beer (and drank it in considerable quantities, according to the 1891 *Scientific American* article) and Giacomo drank mineral water. They did not necessarily share illnesses. They normally got along well, but had regular disputes, sometimes settled with their fists. The Toccis both liked music, but only Giovanni had a talent for drawing. Curiously, the boy on the left was right-handed (Harris 1892). In addition to their native Italian, the boys spoke French and German. They agreeably entertained questions from the audience.

Giovanni and Giacomo toured Europe with their parents throughout the 1870s and 1880s. They made daily appearances in the larger cities of Austria, France, Germany,

Italy, Poland, and Switzerland. They may also have traveled to England. In 1879, the Tocci twins were demonstrated before the Swiss Society for Natural Science in Bern and described as healthy and likely to live (Bondeson 2000). They are said to have spent their adolescence touring the Sardinian countryside. In 1891 at age sixteen, the Toccis appeared in Vienna billed as the "Greatest Wonder of Nature" and at the Panoptikon in Berlin. Giovanni-Batisto was described as clever and alert, but Giacomo was characterized as "somewhat idiotic" (Bondeson 2000). It was claimed that they, like other male conjoined twins, sometimes settled their differences with their fists (Harris 1892). They were examined and described by pathologist Rudolf Virchow in 1886 and 1891. The year 1891 also found them in the United States, where they were paid a reported $1,000 a week. They were promoted as the "Blended Twins" or the "Two-Headed Boy," signing their names as souvenirs and selling photographs for two dollars.

The Toccis were examined by Dr. Robert P. Harris in Philadelphia in 1892. Dr. Harris wrote (1892) that their vitality "would indicate that their anatomical organization is sufficiently perfect to admit a much longer existence." He classified them as belonging to the order Xiphodidymi and to the class Dicephalus tetrabrachius dipus and was well aware of how unusual their condition was:

> The rarity of type in the Tocci twins, and the fact that no case like them has ever been exhibited in the cities of the United States, make them to be regarded by teratological students with unusual interest. Besides which we are to consider the fact that no analogue has attained their present age since the year 1518, and that only one of the type has grown to mature years in the past six centuries [Harris 1892].

He likened their appearance to the shape of the letter "Y" and describes, "In mind and character they are two individuals, but in body are so intimately blended that their interior anatomy is an interesting study, which is still only partly completed, and their abdominal viscera are either in duplicate or are held in common" (Harris 1892). He described them as "high-chested" and "top-heavy," with their shoulders crowded together (Harris 1892). He confirmed that they each had two lungs and independently functioning hearts and assumed from the medical literature about similar twins that they each had their own spleen, pancreas, and small intestines. He was less sure about whether the twins shared a liver and how many kidneys they had. Of their sexual organs, he reported their appearance as normal and wrote that they would probably develop late. Their testicles were regarded as large in infancy, but grew slowly since. "In manhood there may be some curious discoveries made in their sexual partnership," Harris (1892) writes.

The twins were described by Charles E. Davis, who saw them in Hartford, Connecticut, and had the rare opportunity — through an interpreter — to talk to them. They told him that far from enjoying their travels and success, they were often sad and disturbed by their condition (Bondeson 2000). This is in contrast to the 1891 *Scientific American* article in which they were said to "live on excellent terms with each other, and seem unconscious of any misfortune in their condition." After a three-week stay in New York, the Tocci brothers went on to Boston under the management of Frank Uffner. A three-page biographical booklet, *Tocci, The Wonderful Two-headed Boy (Giovanni and Giacomo)*, was printed and sold.

The twins were described as "probably the most remarkable human twins that have ever approached maturity" in *Scientific American* in 1891. In October 1892, the twins appeared in Chicago, where they may have been seen by Mark Twain. Twain had

Cabinet card of the Tocci brothers with their arms around each other's neck.

published a sketch about them in *Packard's Monthly* in 1869. He then made them characters in his novel *Pudd'nhead Wilson*, but took them out and published their farcical story as *Those Extraordinary Twins*. The boys remained in the U.S. well into 1894, having toured the country successfully for a full five years (Bondeson 2000). In 1897, however, they decided to retire. Now of legal age, they returned to Italy and bought a high-walled villa near Venice, where they lived in seclusion. Their story made headlines in the French and Italian newspapers in 1904, when it was learned that they had married two women despite having only a single set of genitals. In fact, the twins were most likely impotent. Jan Bondeson (2000) remarks that despite much bawdy speculation, "The simple explanation that the twins felt a need for human company in their lonely life, after their long and dismal career as sideshow monsters, does not seem to have entered anyone's mind." The Toccis stayed out of sight, prompting a rumor in 1906 that they had died. German teratologist Hans Hübner confirmed that they were alive in 1911 and French teratologist Maurice Gille claimed that they had been seen alive in 1912. In *Human Oddities*, French writer Martin Monestier writes that they died childless in 1940 at the age of 63 (Bondeson 2000).

### Turner, Iesha Da'Sean and Tiesha Ra'Sean. *Twentieth Century.*

Conjoined girls born in Harris County, Texas, on April 19, 1991, to Lester Wilson and Jacqueline Michelle Turner, joined at the chest and abdomen. They weighed a combined nine and a half pounds and were admitted to the Texas Children's Hospital neonatal intensive care unit. After birth it was determined that they had separate digestive systems and kidneys, but their livers were fused. Echocardiograms showed two separate heart structures. They were released from the hospital on May 13, 1991.

An MRI at ten months led to preparation for surgery at one year of age. Theirs was the first case of conjoined twins in which tissue expanders were inserted and injected periodically with saline solution to expand the skin. Dr. Samuel Stal explained, "The use of tissue expanders to stretch the pre-existing skin allowed for complete protective coverage of the wound which would not have otherwise been possible. In addition, we were able to selectively stretch their chest wall skin so normal breast development can occur" (Conjoined Twins Celebrate 1997). The twins were separated at Texas Children's Hospital on June 9, 1992. The surgical team included a pediatric surgeon, a cardiovascular surgeon, and plastic and reconstructive surgeon, a pediatric anes-

thesiologist, a cardiovascular anesthesiologist, and a pediatric cardiologist. They will require additional surgery (bony remodeling of the sternum and ribs) to improve their chest contour. They had to return to the operating room after their separation to repair chronic intestinal obstructions. Iesha was discharged from the hospital on August 13, 1992. Tiesha had pneumonia and remained in the hospital until October 15.

The twin girls have appeared on *Maury Povich* and are in good health. They see cardiologist Dr. Michael Nihill for annual evaluations. They reunited with their doctors five years after their separation on June 9, 1997. "We are excited to reunite with our team of doctors," said the twins' maternal grandmother Lark Turner. "The twins have been through a lot in the last five years and gone through a lot of changes. They've grown up and developed a love for life, the outdoors and — ice cream" (Conjoined Twins Celebrate 1997). The Turners live in Beaumont, Texas. Most recently, the twins were featured at age nine on "Joined: The Secret Life of Conjoined Twins."

### Twain, Mark.

*Not until he encountered real conjoined twins, first the Siamese Twins, Chang and Eng, and then the Tocci Brothers or the Two-headed Boy, did Twain find the right metaphor for his inseparable other. But having found it, he could not quite make it work, though he tried three times....—* Leslie A. Fiedler (1978)

American author Mark Twain (*d.* 1910) had an interest in conjoined twins. He was fascinated by Chang and Eng Bunker, although he never met them, and included a satire on their lives called "Personal Habits of the Siamese Twins" in his book *Sketches New and Old.* He then wrote what began as a farce and became a comedy about conjoined twins. Eventually, the twins were transformed into separate identical twins and the novel became *Pudd'nhead Wilson.* But the short story about the conjoined twins, called "Those Extraordinary Twins," was also published. It was inspired by the lives of the Tocci brothers: "I had seen a picture of a youthful Italian 'freak'— or 'freaks'— which was — or which were — on exhibition in our cities — a combination consisting of two heads and four arms joined to a single body and a single pair of legs," writes Twain (1980). Twain's story was in turn said to have inspired the screenplay *Chained for Life.*

**See also** **Bunker, Chang and Eng; Cappello, Luigi and Angelo;** *Chained for Life;* **Tocci, Giovanni-Batisto and Giacomo**

### "Twenty Fingers, Twenty Toes."

A play based on the lives of the Hilton sisters that was performed in December and January 1990 at the WPA Theater in New York. Book is by Michael Dansicker and Bob Nigro, music and lyrics are by Michael Dansicker, and the performance was directed by Bob Nigro.

**See also** **Hilton, Daisy and Violet**

### *Twin Falls Idaho.*

A 1999 film written, directed, and starred in by identical twins Mark and Michael Polish portraying twins Blake and Francis Falls, who are joined at the chest and share many vital organs. The plot focuses on their search for their mother, their relationship with a prostitute named "Penny," and the illness that threatens one — and therefore both — of the brothers' lives. The film conveys the brothers' intimacy through private gestures and whispered conversations that the audience is unable to comprehend. When the twins meet Penny, Francis resists the idea of incorporating an outsider into their solitary companionship. Issues of curiosity about their bodies — by the public and by Penny — are confronted, but the sexual relationship between Blake and Penny remains unconsummated. Con-

veniently for the plot, Francis becomes fatally ill and the brothers undergo emergency separation surgery. "The bittersweet conclusion of *Twin Falls* does not celebrate the fact that, absent his other half, Blake is at last free to be an individual. Nonetheless, this film attests to the difficulty of envisioning a long-term arrangement that so dramatically defies social norms," writes Rachel Adams (1996).

### "Twins."

The name of a play about conjoined twins Todd and Ted. It was written by Will Schwalbe and performed in New Haven, Connecticut.

### Two-Headed Boy of Bengal. *Eighteenth Century.*

The "Two-Headed Boy of Bengal" was born in India in 1783, but was lucky to have

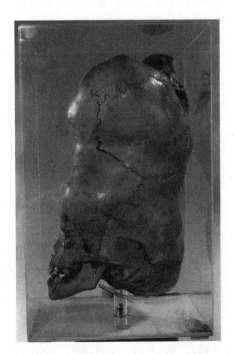

The double-skull of the Two-Headed Boy of Bengal, as it can be seen at the Hunterian Museum (specimen P 1535). Courtesy of the Royal College of Surgeons of England.

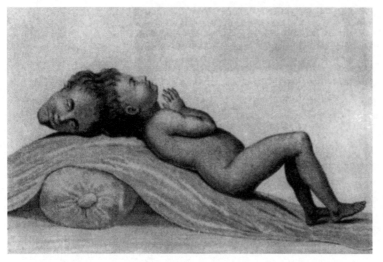

Drawing of the Two-Headed Boy of Bengal that appeared in Sir Everard Home's *Lectures on Comparative Anatomy*, Vol. 4, in 1823. Courtesy of Jan Bondeson, M.D., Ph.D.

ted that no men of science had been able to examine the boy while alive, and while he did see that the two halves of the skull were not separated by a septum of bone, he failed to conclude that the child was an example of conjoined twins of the craniopagus type (Bondeson 1997). The specimen remains in the collections of the Royal College of Surgeons of England.

See also **Parasitic twins**

survived at all. The midwife who delivered him was so frightened by his appearance that she threw him into the fire, leaving him badly burned. The boy had the remnants of a conjoined twin in the form of a second head upside-down on his own. The two heads were of the same size and covered with black hair at their junction. The upper head ended in a necklike stump and showed reflexive movements, absent corneal reflexes, weak reaction to light, malformed ears, and a small tongue. The lower jaw was small, but capable of motion, and the secretion of tears and saliva was plentiful. The two joined heads had independent eye movements. The baby was said to be emaciated. The parents exhibited the child in Calcutta for money, covering him up between shows, until he was fatally bitten by a cobra at age four. His body was buried despite several offers for it, but the grave was predictably plundered. The graverobber, a Mr. Dent of the East India Company, dissected the body (noting that the brains were separate and distinct) and kept the skull, which he presented to Captain Buchanan of the same outfit. The captain presented it to Sir Everard Home upon his return to England. Home regret-

**Two-Headed Nightingale** *see* **McKoy, Millie and Christine**

**Types** *see* **Cephalopagus; Craniopagus; Ischiopagus; Omphalopagus; Pygopagus; Thoracopagus**

**United Swiss Sisters** *see* **Elizabeth and Catharine**

**Ventral union.**

Descriptive of twins united along the ventral aspect, including the umbilicus.

***See also*** **Cephalopagus, Ischiopagus, Omphalopagus, Thoracopagus**

**Viet and Duc.** *Twentieth Century.*

*I firmly say that Viet and Duc ought not to remain merely an object of our sympathy.* — Goro Nakamura

Conjoined twin boys born at Kon Tum Medical University in Gia Lai Kon Tum in the central highlands of Vietnam on March 6, 1980. They were joined at the abdomen and weighed 2.2 kg. They had four hands, but only two legs and a rudimentary "radish-like" leg growing between them in the back

(Nakamura 1986). They have one penis, a single testicle, and a shared anus. They have no "sperm function" (Nakamura 1986). An x-ray revealed that their spines were straight except in the lumbar region. Each boy has his own small intestines and colon and they each have a stomach that is larger than normal. Duc has a heart defect and breathing problems. Their condition, and that of other children born with abnormalities, is blamed on the spraying of the defoliant Agent Orange in their country by the U.S. from 1961 to 1971. The twins were abandoned by their mother after birth at Kon Tum Medical Hospital. "Viet and Duc are not our family members," say their older brother, sister, and parents Nguyen Thang and Ho This Hue (Nakamura 1986). To be assessed for separation, they were transferred at five days (by another account three months) of age to the Vietnam–East German Friendship Hospital in Hanoi, from which their names were derived ("Viet" for Vietnam and "Duc" for Germany). They were legally adopted by a nurse from that hospital. Dr. Ton That Tung recommended against the surgery because it would mean death for one child and considerable risk and plastic surgery for the other, who would remain handicapped for life. Viet and Duc were moved to Tudu Maternity Hospital in Ho Chi Minh City in 1982 (Nakamura 1986). In February of that year, they suffered from pneumonia and measles.

The twins had begun to show signs of intelligence and exhibit dissimilar personalities by the age of one. Viet was generally more cheerful, energetic, and talkative, while Duc was fussy, timid, and quiet. Duc had a healthy appetite, however, and excreted regularly (Nakamura 1986). The staff of the hospital nicknamed them "Ba" and "Bôn," traditionally used to designate the second and third boys of a family before they are formally named. At one year of age, they waved and clapped. Occasionally, one would sleep while the other played. Photo-

journalist Goro Nakamura (1986) describes them at the age of four: "Playing together or quarreling together, their days seemed to be happy in spite of their handicapped bodies." Duc was in a reclining position when Viet sat up, but they were able to ambulate with the help of a cart, even though each controlled one leg. It was difficult for them to stand upright (Nakamura 1986). Their doctor describes, "Viet is playful, and fond of fruit. Duc is industrious and fond of sweets. They both like cars. As many people have taken their pictures, they shy away from them, saying 'we are not ready yet.' Their disobedience show us their egos are developing normally" (Nakamura 1986). However, compared with other children, Viet and Duc's physical and mental development are considerably retarded (Nakamura 1986).

Professor Bunro Fujimoto, of the Department of Education at Shiga University, describes the twins as being in good health, other than Duc's weak heart. He describes their mental growth as normal and says they fight from time to time but are generally on good terms. Although they sometimes say, "I hate my body," their awareness of their handicap is not yet a source of suffering (Nakamura 1986). Professor Fujimoto said to himself, "To make the people aware of everyone's right to live, I'll build a wheelchair for Viet and Duc. The chair will contribute to their growth. Above all, our present from over the sea will encourage handicapped people all over the world. It will bind them with friendship, and strengthen worldwide solidarity" (Nakamura 1986). He enlisted the help of his colleagues and in mid–1985 the Group Hoping for Viet and Duc's Development was founded and began an active fundraising campaign for a new wheelchair for the twins. He hoped that a wheelchair that would help them sit and walk upright would help with their mental as well as physical development because it would free their hands to write, draw, and feed themselves.

He also hoped the device would foster co-operation between them: "Since their bodies contradict each other on a flat bed, life in a wheelchair would help them form more harmonious relations" (Nakamura 1986). With publicity and word of mouth, donations from more than 21,000 people and institutions were received within a year and a half, including contributions from the Japan-Vietnam Friendship Association, Kyoto Teacher's Union, and the Japan Handicapped Association of Kyoto.

Viet and Duc are described in February 1985 by Professor Fujimoto (Nakamura 1986):

> When I gave them a stuffed panda brought from Japan, they scrambled for it. When I took their pictures with my instant camera, they struggled for it. They took a great interest in my camera. After I handed it to them, they curiously wound it up. They had far more capacity than I had expected from their misshapen bodies, and their cooperative steps to walk with the aid of the handcart minimized my awareness of their deformity.

Professor Fujimoto measured the twins in March 1985, collecting data and taking more than fifty photographs from different angles. At that time, Viet was 40 cm. from neck to waist and Duc was 38 cm. Their combined weight was 17 kg. Professor Fujimoto had the twins' medical chart translated into Japanese and interviewed the doctors involved in their care. From them he learned that the twins could live for many years, that they are able to write and speak, and that their counting ability was above average (Nakamura 1986).

After being turned down when he approached the engineering departments of several universities, Professor Fujimoto turned to Mitsuyoshi Yamaguchi, who was paralyzed and had designed his own wheelchair. Fundraising activities — symposia, photo show, charity bazaar, and monthly newsletter — supported the development of the prototype and later a second wheelchair. At the same time, the group received criticism for their narrow focus on a pair of Vietnamese twins when Japan had larger political needs and a needy handicapped population of its own. Some felt the twins' needs should be met by the Vietnamese government and that the United States should accept a larger responsibility (Nakamura 1986). Still, they received a number of concerned letters about the health of the twins — many from schoolchildren — and they responded to each one. Students in a primary school wrote, "We appreciate our good health to be able to play as much as we want. We hope Viet and Duc can do the same in their wheelchair" (Nakamura 1986).

In October 1985, Dr. Nguyen Thi Ngoc Phuong, president of Tudu Hospital, was presented with the adjustable wheelchair created for the twins after a lecture and discussion. Dr. Phuong mentioned attempting to socialize Viet and Duc: "We are gradually allowing them to come into contact with other children, but we are still very careful not to let them become self-conscious about their deformed bodies when placed among normal children. To make Viet and Duc more sociable, we drive them around Ho Chi Minh City. They take an interest in everything, but nowadays they often cry when they see strangers" (Nakamura 1986). She suggested the twins may live another ten or twenty years and jokingly raised the issue of spouses. In a questionnaire completed after the lecture, an audience member wrote, "I was most shocked at the slides shown by Dr. Phuong. But for war, the children would have been born normal. I hope the wheelchair will bring Viet and Duc the health growth that they might have otherwise enjoyed" (Nakamura 1986).

Two months later, Duc and Viet's reaction to the chair was reported: "They play with the wheelchair, clutching and standing on their hands. They push it merrily all over the hospital. The chair is their good play-mate, and the hospital staff has praised the wheelchair highly for its functional construction" (Nakamura 1986). Based on this feedback, Yamaguchi resolved to design a second chair that could be operated with the twins' feet, thereby encouraging them to sit still and free their hands. The Group Hoping for Viet and Duc's Development again emphasizes the larger issues brought to bear by the case of Viet and Duc:

> Some people might think our campaign ended when we handed the wheelchair to Dr. Phuong. The wheelchair has marked a milestone indeed, but it is not the goal of our campaign. Through the campaign, we have learned the importance of peace and international unity, the relation between the handicapped and war, and the love of human lives. What we have learned should be spread to many more people [Nakamura 1986].

The efforts at the time went largely unnoticed by the twins: "Viet and Duc never cry against the menace of herbicide nor do they cry for the necessity of peace. They just innocently smile and continue to exert their powerful hold on us" (Nakamura 1986).

Viet suffered from acute encephalitis that led to a coma in May 1986, threatening both their lives. Dr. Phong arranged for them to be treated by doctors in Japan, which had advanced medical technology and was only three hours away. "Doctors of the Japan Red Cross Hospital promptly responded to her request. Immediately after that, three doctors were sent to Tudu Hospital to administer intensive care to Viet and Duc" (Nakamura 1986). They were flown to Tokyo that same day in the summer of 1986 and were successfully treated. The Group Hoping for Viet and Duc's Development took up additional fundraising efforts and its representative, librarian Masami Kawahara, was deluged with questions from reporters. The twins remained in Japan for four months before returning to Tudu Hospital. They were scheduled to enter primary school in the fall of 1987.

### Villar, Marta and Almudena.
*Twentieth Century.*

Conjoined twin girls born in April 1975, to Saturnino Villar Valin and Lucita, joined at the abdomen. They were separated in less than two hours in La Coruna, Spain.

### Voyoen, Pieternella and Barbara.
*Seventeenth Century.*

Conjoined twin girls born on May 6, 1680, at Claems near Bruges, Belgium, to Roelan Voyoen and Maria Castelmans, joined at the head. Both babies were baptized. They had different eating and sleeping patterns. Their parents were offered smalls sums from visitors to see the children and a large sum for their exhibition (Thompson 1968).

### Wasselinck Sisters. *Seventeenth Century.*

Conjoined twins born November 27, 1657. The left face had a double cyclopean eye in the center and a proboscis above it that was mistaken for a penis, even though the child had a vulva. The baby was said to have four arms and hands, two vertebral columns, and a single sacrum. An autopsy revealed two stomachs, two sets of intestines, and two kidneys (Harris 1892).

### Waterman, Martha and Mary.
*Seventeenth Century.*

A 1664 broadside depicts and describes a pair of female conjoined twins exhibited in London by their father. With the headline "The True Picture of a Female Monster Born Near Salisbury," the broadside records that the babies were born on October 26, 1664, in the parish of Fisherton-Anger, near Salisbury, to John and Mary Waterman. They were joined at the navel, having two

THE
TRUE PICTURE
OF A
FEMALE MONSTER
BORN NEAR
SALISBURY

ON Wednesday the 26. day of *October*, 1664. The Wife of *John Waterman*, a Husbandman, in the Parish of *Fisherton-Anger*, near New *Sarum*, or *Salisbury*, brought forth a wonderful Creature, which cannot be otherwise accounted then a Monster: It having two Heads, four Arms, and two Legs.

The Heads standing contrary each to other, one Head standing where the Feet should be.

There were two perfect Bodies downwards to the Navel, as if there had been two Children, and there they were both joyned together.

The Loyns, Hips and Legs issued out of the sides of the Bodies, just in the middle, where both Bodies were joyned together.

It was dissected, and there were found two Hearts, two Livers, and all the inward parts complete, as the outward to the Navel, except only that it had but two Kidneys.

There was but One Sex to both these Bodies, which was the Female.

This Monster lived two days, and during that time took Sustenance. It would not Suck, but did Eat with both Mouthes; when the one cried, the other did so too, each imitating the other in several actions, and was seen alive by many hundreds of the neighbouring places, which flocked to see so strange a Creature.

The Mother had one Child more at the same time, which was born first, and which also is a Female, and a very comely Child in all proportions, and is yet living.

*This Monster is intended speedily to be brought to* London.
With Allowance, *Roger L'Estrange, Novemb.* 5. 1664.

LONDON,
Printed for *R. P.* at the Sign of the Bible in
*Chancery-lane*, 1664.

"The True Picture of a Female Monster," a broadside printed in London in 1664, reprinted in Rollins, Hyder E., Editor. 1927. *The Pack of Autolycus*. Cambridge: Harvard University Press.

heads, four arms, and two legs. The babies lived for only two days, but during that time took nourishment, cried, and were seen by hundreds of curious neighbors. They became the subject of a ballad by physician Josiah Smith. Other physicians convinced John Waterman to allow them to autopsy the babies, a task made more difficult due to crowds of onlookers.

When the bodies of the twins were dissected, they were each found to have a heart, a liver, and an otherwise complete organ system, but only one kidney. The findings were reported by Robert Boyle to the Royal Society in November 1664 (Pender 1996). The bodies were embalmed ten days after death by Fisherton apothecary Henry Denny, who disemboweled and cleaned them, and placed them in "liquor and gums" to retard putrefaction and discoloration (Pender 1996). They were exhibited in London and brought in twenty pounds on the first day of their exhibition (Pender 1996). The twins were seen by Samuel Pepys and described matter-of-factly in his diary as "two women-children perfectly made, joyned at the lower part of their bellies, an every part perfect as two bodies, and only one payre of legs, coming forth on one side from the middle where they were joined. It was alive 24 hours, and cried and did as all hopeful children do; but by being shown too much to people, was killed" (Wilson 1993).

## Williams, Betty Lou.
### *Twentieth Century.*

An African-American baby born in Albany, Georgia, in 1932, with the body of a parasitic twin protruding from the left side of her abdomen: "For growing out of Betty's left side was part of a little sister in miniature. Her twin consisted of a body from the waist downward, with two legs and a single misplaced arm" (Drimmer 1973). She appeared in the *Believe It or Not* show at the 1934 World's Fair in Chicago and was managed by showman Dick Best. She is said to have been paid $250 a week and earned an additional $500 a week from sales of her photograph. She used her earnings to build her parents a house, buy her family a farm, and send her brothers and sisters to college. She died at age twenty-one after the man she was in love with refused to marry her (Mannix 1999).

*See also* **Parasitic twins**

**Wofford, Jennifer and Lynn.** *Twentieth Century.*

Conjoined twin girls miscarried at twelve weeks on April 29, 1999.

**Wooden, Christine and Betsy.**
*Twentieth Century.*

Conjoined twin girls born in 1973 to Janna Walzeck. Betsy died of a heart defect after separation. Their mother said, "They needed to be separated, and then what would happen, would happen. The stronger would survive, the weaker might not, but that was just—sometimes you have to sacrifice something to … get another life" (Jussim 2001).

**"World's Strangest Babies."**

A traveling carnival show mounted by Ward Hall that toured the U.S. in the 1970s featuring wet specimens, including conjoined twins, exhibited as being the result of immorality and the children of unwed mothers.

**Würtemberg Sisters.** *Fifteenth-Sixteenth Century.*

Conjoined girls born in 1498 with two heads, four arms, one abdomen, and two legs (Harris 1892).

**Xiphopagus** *see* **Omphalopagus**

# ANNOTATED BIBLIOGRAPHY

Able, L.W. 1967. "The Surgical Separation of the Bay City Twins," in *Conjoined Twins*, Bergsma, Daniel, Editor. Birth Defects original article series, Vol. III: 1. New York: National Foundation-March of Dimes. Describes the surgery and post-operative care of thoracopagus twins born in Texas in 1965.

"The Accouchement of Rosa the Pygopaga." 1910. *The British Medical Journal*. May 28: 1313–14. Description of the physique and activities of Rosa and Josefa Blazek.

Adams, Rachel. 1996. "An American Tail: Freaks, Gender, and the Incorporation of History in Katherine Dunn's *Geek Love*." In *Freakery: Cultural Spectacles of the Extraordinary Body*, Thompson, Rosemarie Garland, Editor. New York: New York University Press.

____. 2001. *Sideshow U.S.A.: Freaks and the American Cultural Imagination*. Chicago: University of Chicago Press. A learned look at anomalous bodies in American culture, including carnival sideshows, photography, and fiction. Includes many references to conjoined twins, but no chapter solely devoted to them.

Aikenhead, Sherri. 1985. "The Twins Canada Loves." *MacLean's*. July 15. A news report about the release of Lin Htut from the hospital after his separation from Win.

Allen, H. 1875. "Report of an Autopsy on the Bodies of Chang and Eng Bunker, Commonly Known as the Siamese Twins." *Transactions of the College of Physicians of Philadelphia*. V. 1: 1–46. An exhaustive account of the findings of the autopsy conducted on the bodies of the Bunkers, complete with illustrations, and with particular attention to the physical makeup of the band between them.

Angier, Natalie. 1997. "Joined for Life, and Living Life to the Fullest." *The New York Times*. Dec. 23. A probing look at the lives of Reba and Lori Schappell that includes quotes from ethicist Alice Dreger.

Anthony, Ted. 1993. "Together Forever: Conjoined Reading Twins Lead Separate Lives Together." *The Morning Call*. Sept. 9. A lively account of the lives of the Schappell sisters. Includes many photographs.

Augustine, Saint. 1950. *The City of God*. Translated by Marcus Dods. New York: Modern Library. St. Augustine's fifth-century treatise touches on conjoined twins in a discussion about monstrous births and describes a contemporary pair: "Some years ago, quite, within my own memory, a man was born in the East, double in his upper, but single in his lower half— having two heads, two chests, four hands, but one body and two feet like an ordinary man; and he lived so long that many had an opportunity of seeing him."

"Australian Surgeons Separate Siamese Twins." 2000. www.CNN.com. Oct. 26. A report of the separation surgery of Tay-lah and Monique Armstrong.

Batcha, Becky. 1994. "The Legacy: A Critical Look at Such Surgery." *The Philadelphia Daily News*. June 10: 4+. Touches on the ethical questions posed by the Lakeberg case.

Beecham, Bill. 1979. "Siamese Twins, Joined at Head, are Separated in Utah Surgery." *Philadelphia Inquirer*. May 31: 4-A. A report of the successful separation of Lisa and Elisa Hansen.

Begley, Sharon. 1987. "Siamese Twins: From Ripley's to College." *Newsweek*. Sept. 21. A sidebar about adult twins, including the Bunkers, the Hiltons, and Yvonne and Yvette McCarther.

Bergsma, Daniel. 1979. *Birth Defects Atlas and Compendium, Second Edition.* New York: National Foundation-March of Dimes. Unlike the first edition (1973), this encyclopedic volume includes an entry on conjoined twins that offers diagnostic criteria, terminology, statistics, and photographs.

_____, Editor. 1967. *Conjoined Twins.* Birth Defects original article series, Vol. III: 1. New York: National Foundation-March of Dimes. A well-illustrated volume that includes papers providing facts about the birth, management, and separation surgery of conjoined twins.

Besse, H. 1874. *Diploteratology; or a History of Some of the Most Wonderful Human Beings That Have Ever Lived in Double Form, and a Scrutinizing View Into the Marvelously Strange Freaks of Nature, and Causes of Same.* Delaware, Ohio: Gazette Steam Book and Job Office. An interesting text that includes a detailed account of the lives of Mina and Minnie Finley, including public reaction to their exhibition. Also includes case descriptions by a number of doctors; brief biographies of Millie-Christine, the Blazeks, the Toccis, and other famous twins; and several chapters devoted to the Bunkers.

Bhettay, E., M.M. Nelson, and P. Beighton. 1975. "Epidemic of Conjoined Twins in Southern Africa?" *The Lancet.* Oct. 18. A paper that examines the birth of eleven sets of conjoined twins in Southern Africa in just over a year to determine whether ethnic, geographic, and socioeconomic differences or an environmental agent was a factor.

Bogdan, Robert. 1988. *Freak Show: Presenting Human Oddities for Amusement and Profit.* Chicago: University of Chicago Press. A scholarly treatment of the public display of "freaks," including conjoined twins. Includes a section about Daisy and Violet Hilton.

_____. 1996. "The Social Construction of Freaks," in *Freakery: Cultural Spectacles of the Extraordinary Body,* Thompson, Rosemarie Garland, Editor. New York: New York University Press.

Bolton, George Buckley. 1830. *On the United Siamese Twins.* London: Richard Taylor. A reprint of a paper presented to the Royal College of Surgeons of England that describes Chang and Eng Bunker in great medical detail and includes an illustration of their connecting band.

Bompas, George C. 1886. *Life of Frank Buckland by His Brother-in-Law.* London: Smith, Elder & Co. A biography of the nineteenth century naturalist that includes Buckland's firsthand description of Millie-Christine.

Bondeson, Jan. 1997. *A Cabinet of Medical Curiosities.* New York: W.W. Norton. Includes a detailed account of the life and death of the Two-Headed Boy of Bengal.

_____. 2000. *The Two-Headed Boy and Other Medical Marvels.* Ithaca, New York: Cornell University Press. Medical historian Jan Bondeson offers exhaustively researched and curious cases, including the Biddenden Maids and the Tocci brothers. Lazarus Colloredo is discussed in the preface.

Bone, Howard, with Daniel Waldron. 2001. *Side Show: My Life with Geeks, Freaks & Vagabonds in the Carny Trade.* Northville, Michigan: Sun Dog Press. In this posthumous collection of his anecdotes, carnival midway veteran Howard Bone includes a chapter on "pickled punks," but asserts that they were all fakes.

Bor, Jonathan. 1998. "Parted Twins' Future Bright," in *The Baltimore Sun.* Jan. 11. Story about pediatric surgeon Benjamin Carson's preparation for the separation of Luka and Joseph Banda.

Bor, Jonathan. 2002. "UM Medical Center Team Separates Conjoined Twins," in *The Baltimore Sun.* May 15. Report about the separation of Loice and Christine Onziga.

Boseley, Sarah. 2002. "Outlook Grim for Conjoined Babies," in *The Guardian.* May 1. Detailed account of the birth of Natasha and Courtney Smith and the outlook for their future. Includes comparisons with the Attard twins.

Breakstone, Benjamin H. 1922. "The Last Illness of the Blazek (Grown-Together) Twins," *American Medicine.* V. 17: April, 221–226. A thorough description of Rosa and Josefa Blazek by the doctor who attended them for appendicitis. Includes the results of his manual examination of their vaginas and shared rectum, a brief medical history, and a six-day comparison of their temperature, pulse, and respiration.

Bulwer-Lytton, Edward George Earle. 1831. *The Siamese Twins: A Satirical Tale of the Times.* New York: J.&J. Harper. A tedious, rhyming read in which Chang and Eng Bunker's lives are approximated in the characters of "Ching" and "Chang." Addresses the interest of the medical community in their bodies after death by mentioning a bid by noted dissectionist Sir Astley Cooper to secure them. Expresses the exasperation of the legal system at being unable to punish a single one of them: "...every rascal in shoe-leather/ Would go thus hook-and-eyed together." Touches on their popularity and the commerce it creates: "In every painter's shop one sees/ Neat portraits of 'The Siamese,'/ And every wandering Tuscan carries/ Their statues cast in clay of Paris." And raises the agonizing question of separation: "What hazard in the bold endeavour,/ Those bonds which birth had knit, to sever!/ To break the seal so dreadly set/ Upon their common doom!— to unbind/ The claims which, tho' unnatural, yet/ Nature herself had round them twined!"

Burgess, G.H.O. 1967. *The Eccentric Ark: The Curious World of Frank Buckland.* New York: Horizon Press. A biography of the nineteenth century naturalist that includes brief mention of his meetings with Chang and Eng Bunker and a brief description of Millie-Christine.

Burling, Stacey, and Cynthia Mayer. 1994. "Little Angela, Who Survived Separation from Twin, Dies," *The Oregonian.* June 10. A report of the death of Angela Lakeberg, nearly a year after separation from her sister Amy.

Butler, Juliet. 2000. *Masha and Dasha: Autobiographie eines Siamesischen Zwillingspaars.* Bern: Scherz. The text of this account of the lives of Masha and Dasha Krivoshlyapova through the Summer of 1998 by their longtime companion is in German. The 250-page book includes a section of black-and-white photographs of the twins, mostly as children.

Cady, Marlene L.S. 1987. "My Siamese Twins Have Brought Me Joy," *Redbook.* Feb.: 32–34. A brief memoir of the birth and lives of Ruthie and Verena Cady by their mother.

_____. 1989. "The Pure Joy of Being Alive," *People* 32: 64–71. A lengthy peek into the lives of Ruthie and Verena Cady, written by their mother and heavily illustrated with photographs.

Carson, Ben, with Cecil Murphey. 1990. *Gifted Hands.* Washington, D.C.: Review and Herald Publishing Assoc. An autobiography by the renowned Johns Hopkins University Medical Center surgeon which includes his account of the separation of Patrick and Benjamin Binder.

Casey, Kathryn. 2002. "We Brought Home Two Miracles." *Ladies' Home Journal.* January. A follow-up article on the progress of Kathleen and Charity Lincoln a year after their separation surgery.

"Chang and Eng." 1874. *Philadelphia Medical Times.* Feb. 19: 327–330. An article that explains the circumstances surrounding the autopsy of the bodies of the Bunkers.

Chua Mui Hoong. 2001. "A New Lease of Life, a Large Slice of Soul," *The Straits Times Interactive.* April 15. http://straitstimes.asia1.com.sg. An impassioned account of the birth and separation of Ganga and Jamuna Shrestha.

Clark, Cheryl. 1996. "UCSD Eyes Surgery to Separate Baja Twins," in *The San Diego Tribune.* May 18. About the birth and potential separation of Hever and Román Moreno. Includes photos of newborns.

Clark, David L., and Catherine Myer. "Being Humaned: Medical Documentaries and the Hyperrealization of Conjoined Twins," in *Freakery: Cultural Spectacles of the Extraordinary Body,* Thompson, Rosemarie Garland, Editor. New York: New York University Press.

Clark, Matt, with Mary Hager. 1987. "A Chance to Live Apart: A Team of Surgeons Separates Siamese Twins," *Newsweek.* Sept. 21: 71–72. An article about the separation of the Binder twins.

Clements, Colleen. 2000. "When to Kill to Save a Life: What to Do About the Case of Conjoined Twins Jodie and Mary," *The Medical Post.* Nov. 7. A dissenting opinion that the courts failed to uphold Mary's human rights.

Cohen, Jeffrey Jerome, Editor. 1996. *Monster Theory: Reading Culture.* Minneapolis: University of Minnesota Press. This scholarly volume includes Allison Pingree's essay about Chang and Eng Bunker and Stephen Pender's paper about the display of human anomalies.

Cohen, Sherry Suib. 2002. "Twins Triumphant," *Rosie.* February. A lively article about the birth and separation of Syd and Lexi Stark.

"Conjoined Twins Celebrate Five Years of Separation," 1997. Doctor's Guide to Medical and Other News. June 11. www.docguide.com. Detailed account of the separation and status of Iesha and Tiesha Turner.

"Conjoined Twins Split in 22-Hour Operation: One Has Second Surgery to Halt Brain Bleeding." 2002. *Washington Post.* August 7. Report about the progress of Maria Teresa and Maria de Jesus Quiej Alvarez after their separation.

"Conjoined Twins Successfully Separated." 2000. Columbus Children's Hospital. Press release: Sept. 12. The informative hospital account of the separation surgery of Mary and Decontee Cole.

Cook, A.B. 1869. *Joined Twins: The Obstetrical and Surgical Management, with Remarks.* Louisville, Ky.: Bell & Co. A book that anticipates the modern debate about separation surgery with a number of thoughtful observations.

Also describes the birth, dissection, and separation of specific pairs of conjoined twins.

"Coping." 1984. *People.* Dec. 3: 107+. An interview with the parents of Lin and Win Htut after their separation surgery.

Crilly, Rob, and James McKillop. 2002. "Agony for Parents of Twins Joined at the Heart." *The Herald.* May 1. A news story relating the facts about the birth of Natasha and Courtney Smith and their potential separation.

Dale, Maryclaire. 2002. "At Age 40, Conjoined Twins are Following Their Dreams." *Washington Post.* Aug. 12. Quotes from Lori and Reba Schappell about their lives and their opposition to the separation of the Alvarez twins.

Daniels, Jonathan. 1962. "Never Alone at Last," *American Heritage.* V. XIII, N. 5: August. A fairly thorough account of the lives and postmortem examination of Chang and Eng Bunker.

Daniels, Worth B. 1961. "The Siamese Twins: Some Observations on Their Life, Last Illness and Autopsy," *Transactions of the American Clinical and Climatological Association.* V. 73: lvii–lxv. An account of the life, death, and postmortem examination of Chang and Eng Bunker.

Davis Chiropractic Center. n.d. "The Chiropractic Story of Masha and Dasha." www.davis-chiro.com/masdas.html. A detailed account of the birth and lives of Masha and Dasha Krivoshlyapova on the website of a Michigan chiropractor.

Dennett, Andrea Stulman. 1996. "Dime Museum Freak Show Reconfigured as Talk Show," in *Freakery: Cultural Spectacles of the Extraordinary Body,* Thompson, Rosemarie Garland, Editor. New York: New York University Press.

_____. 1997. *Weird and Wonderful: The Dime Museum in America.* New York: New York University Press. The history of the precursor to the sideshow. Conjoined twins including Millie-Christine and Chang and Eng Bunker are briefly covered in the chapter on "Freaks and Platform Performers."

de Vries, P.A. 1967. "Separation of the San Francisco Twins," in *Conjoined Twins,* Bergsma, Daniel, Editor. Birth Defects original article series, Vol. III: 1. New York: National Foundation-March of Dimes. Describes the surgery of thoracopagus twins born in 1962.

"Doctors Divide Siamese Twins Fused at Head." 2001. *The Arizona Republic.* April 11. An Associated Press report about the separation of Jamuna and Ganga Shrestha.

Donaghy, Kathy. 2000. "Life After Katie." Irish Independent. Sept. 2. www.unison.ie/irish_independent. A sympathetic account of the separation of Katie and Eilish Holton and the life of the surviving twin.

Dougherty, Charles J. 1993. "A Life-and-Death Decision: The Lakeberg Twins." *Health Progress.* Nov. www.chausa.org. An ethical examination of the case of Amy and Angela Lakeberg in a journal published by the Catholic Health Association.

Drake, Donald C. 1974. "Twins Are Separated — and Survive," *The Philadelphia Inquirer.* Sept. 19. A brief report about the successful separation of Clara and Alta Rodriguez, well-illustrated with photographs from the operating room.

Dreger, Alice [Dumurat]. 2000. "Jarring Bodies: Thoughts on the Display of Unusual Anatomies," *Perspectives in Biology and Medicine.* V. 43, n. 2: Winter, 161–172. A thought-provoking paper that describes the mutually beneficial relationship between exhibited "freaks" and the nineteenth century medical community and contrasts it with the contemporary scenario in which those with physical anomalies are obliged to undergo medical study (to prevent more of their kind from being born), but do not benefit career-wise from doctors' testimony and are displayed via "distasteful" venues from which they receive little or no direct profit.

_____. 1998. "The Limits of Individuality: Ritual and Sacrifice in the Lives and Medical Treatment of Conjoined Twins," *Studies in History and Philosophy of Biological and Biomedical Sciences.* V. 29, n. 1: 1–29. A paper pointing out the pressure to separate conjoined babies to make them conform to what is considered a normal body, despite the deficits they will be left with, the possible (or certain) loss of one twin, and the testimony of adult twins who have remained joined. Includes statistical information and uses as examples the McCarthers, the Hensels, and the Cady twins.

_____. 2000. "Why Change the Rules for Twins Like Them?" in *The Washington Post.* Sept. 24: B2. An editorial about the case of Gracie and Rosie Attard by an ethicist at Michigan State University who strongly objects to killing one person in order to save the life of another.

Drimmer, Frederick. 1997. *Incredible People: Five Stories of Extraordinary Lives.* New York: Atheneum Books for Young Readers. This book aimed at young readers includes a chapter on Daisy and Violet Hilton that reviews many other famous pairs of conjoined twins and includes a number of black and white photographs and illustrations.

_____. 1973. *Very Special People: The Struggles, Loves, and Triumphs of Human Oddities*. New York: Amjon. An often-referenced popular book that offers sympathetic and lengthy views of the lives of the Bunkers and the Hiltons, a chapter about parasitic twins, biographies of Millie-Christine and the Tocci brothers, and brief entries about the Biddenden Maids, the Blazeks, the Godinos, Masha and Dasha, and Radica-Doodica.

Dunn, Katherine. 1989. *Geek Love*. New York: Warner. A disturbingly engaging novel that includes a pair of conjoined twins, Electra and Iphigenia Binewski. They and their siblings — including an albino dwarf, an aqua boy, and many others that didn't survive — were conceived by a carnival couple intentionally to have "different" children. The book explores changes to the body, including those that would allow conjoined twins to be separated from each other. Also touches on themes of dominance and personality differences in the twins. Conveys what it feels like to be a "monster," as their brother explains: "We are the things that come to the norms in nightmares." At the same time, the twins are described as having an almost cult-like following in which their fans attached themselves to each other in imitation. Physically, the twins were described as sharing sensations and organs: "They had separate hearts but a meshing bloodstream; separate stomachs but a common intestine. They had one liver and one set of kidneys. They had two brains and a nervous system that was peculiarly connected and unexpectedly separate." In the story, the twins are raped by and kill the man to whom they are betrothed and have his child. After Ellie partially recovers from a lobotomy she was coerced to undergo, she kills the baby and is in turn killed by her sister, an act which necessarily kills them both.

Edge, Simon. 2000. "Siamese Twins," *Daily Express*. Sept. www.lineone.net/express. A brief introduction to and photograph of the adult Rozycki twins, followed by accounts of famous conjoined twins including Chang and Eng Bunker. Includes quotes by Lori and Reba Schappell about their lives and other contemporary cases of conjoined twins.

Edwards, Frank. 1961. *Strange People*. New York: Lyle Stuart. Includes very brief chapters on "Two-Headed Children" and "The Scottish Brothers."

Fanning, Larry A. 1995. *Separated Angels: Shannon and Megan, the Fanning Twins*. Naperville: Storybook Press. A heartfelt journal written by the father of Megan and Shannon Fanning. While the book could have benefited from some professional editing, it offers a biographical and autobiographical account of how the events of the twins' birth and separation unfolded, especially the media attention that both events attracted and resultant privacy issues. The publisher describes, "The accounts of faith shown and support received along with the seemingly miraculous final outcome make *Separated Angels* especially inspirational. The book is written in easy-to-read style ... and should not be offensive to any special interest group.... It is the only true story of conjoined twins written by one of the parents."

Ferraro, Susan. 2001. "Lived and Died as One," in *New York Daily News*. April 17. Account and photograph of Cristal and Paola Colon, conjoined twins who lived only five days.

Fiedler, Leslie. 1978. *Freaks: Myths and Images of the Secret Self*. New York: Doubleday. A frequently quoted book about unusual bodies that examines the many other meanings of the word "freak" and has become a classic because of the author's compassion and ability to put human oddities in cultural context. Includes a chapter on "Siamese Twins."

_____. 1996. *Tyranny of the Normal: Essays on Bioethics, Theology and Myth*. Boston: David R. Godine. In the title essay, Fiedler discusses "freaks" as represented in the media and defends the rights of conjoined twins and others to refuse surgery, despite social pressures to normalize their bodies. He explains, "...the war against 'abnormality' implies a dangerous kind of politics, which beginning with a fear of difference, eventuates in a tyranny of the Normal. That tyranny, moreover, is sustained by creating in those outside the Norm shame and self-hatred — particularly if they happen to suffer from those 'deformities' (which are still the vast majority) that we cannot prevent or cure."

FitzGerald, Susan. 2000. "Once-Conjoined Twins Head Home," *The Philadelphia Inquirer*. Feb. 19: B1. An announcement of the release of Wiktoria and Weronika Palen from the hospital after separation surgery and their plans to return to Poland.

Fowler, O.S., and L.N. Fowler with Samual Kirkham. 1840. *Phrenology Proved, Illustrated, and Applied*. New York: O.S. Fowler. A phrenology text that includes an entry about the examination of the heads of Chang and Eng Bunker.

Gathright, James. 2000. "Spectacular Sisters," *Children's Magazine*. April. A brief account of the pregnancy and birth of Kayla and Kyana Asuncion.

Gedda, Luigi. 1961. *Twins in History and Science*. Transl. Marco Milani-Comparetti. Springfield, Ill.: C.C. Thomas. A now dated, but frequently referenced classic text about twins in mythology, history, science, and medicine. Includes a number of references to conjoining, a diagram of the possible symmetrical double formations, and photographs of conjoined newborns, parasitic twins, skeletal and wet specimens, x-rays, and famous pairs of adult conjoined twins (Bunkers, Gibbs, Godinos, Hiltons).

Gibson, Gail, and John Murphy. 2002. "Trip of Thousands of Miles on the Strength of Hope," in *The Baltimore Sun*. May 15. An informative article about the birth and care of Loice and Christine Onziga.

Gillespie, Charley. 2000. "Twins Recovering: Conjoined Twins from Liberia Surgically Separated," Associated Press. Sept. 12. Report about Mary and Decontee Cole.

Goldstein, Avram. 2002. "Alive, Well and Apart: Conjoined Twins Successfully Separated at U-Md. Hospital," in *The Washington Post*. May 15. Report about the separation of Loice and Christine Onziga.

Goldwyn, Ron, and Dave Bittan. 1994. "The Lakeberg Twins: Infection Kills Surviving," *The Philadelphia Daily News*. June 10: 4+. A report of the death of Angela Lakeberg nearly a year after separation from her sister Amy.

Gonzalez-Crussi, F. 1985. *Notes of an Anatomist*. San Diego: Harcourt Brace Jovanovich. The lively and thought-provoking ruminations of a pathologist that include essays about twins and teratology.

Gould, George M., and Walter L. Pyle. 1956. *Anomalies and Curiosities of Medicine*. Orig. published 1896. New York: Bell Publishing Co. This classic medical text includes an extensive chapter entitled "Major Terata" that covers the scientific history, classification, and famous examples of conjoined twins. Many well-known cases (Biddenden Maids, Scottish Brothers, Ritta-Christina, and others) are included and illustrated with black and white photographs. Also references parasitic twins.

Gould, Stephen Jay. 1997. "Individuality: Cloning and the Discomfiting Cases of Siamese Twins," *The Sciences*. Sept.-Oct.: 14–16. An article that allays fears of human cloning by pointing out that identical twins (including conjoined twins) are clones, but still maintain a unique individuality. Includes photographs of wet and dry specimens of conjoined twins by Rosamond Purcell.

_____. 1982. "Living with Connections: Are Siamese Twins One Person or Two?" *Natural History*. V. 91, N. 11: November. A thoughtful paper that points out that conjoined twins are neither one nor two, using Ritta-Christina as an example. Gould writes, "If we recognize that our world is full of irreducible continua, we will not be troubled by the intermediate status of Ritta and Christina."

Grady, Denise. 2002. "To the U.S., in a Slim Bid for Separate Cribs," *The New York Times*. Aug. 18. A front-page well-illustrated article about craniopagus twins Ahmed and Mohamed Ibrahim and their journey from Egypt to be assessed for separation surgery.

_____. 2001. "Two Babies, One Heart and One Chance at Survival," *The New York Times*. Aug. 10. A lengthy article about Darielis Soto and her separation from her twin Sandra who died.

Grosz, Elizabeth. 1996. "Intolerable Ambiguity: Freaks as/at the Limit," in *Freakery: Cultural Spectacles of the Extraordinary Body,* Thompson, Rosemarie Garland, Editor. New York: New York University Press.

Guttmacher, A.F. 1967. "Biographical Notes on Some Famous Conjoined Twins," in *Conjoined Twins*, Bergsma, Daniel, Editor. Birth Defects original article series, Vol. III: 1. New York: National Foundation-March of Dimes. Covers in some detail the cases of the Biddenden Maids, the Blazeks, and Helena and Judith. Also discusses the first known autopsy of conjoined twins in the New World.

_____, and B.L. Nichols. 1967. "Teratology of Conjoined Twins," in *Conjoined Twins*, Bergsma, Daniel, Editor. Birth Defects original article series, Vol. III: 1. New York: National Foundation-March of Dimes. A paper presenting the early theories about the causes of conjoined twinning, including maternal impressions.

Hall, Ward. 1991. *My Very Unusual Friends*. A self-published, illustrated volume of reminiscences about the people, including Ronnie and Donnie Galyon, with whom the author worked with in the side show business.

Harris, Robert P. 1892. "The Blended Tocci Brothers and Their Historical Analogues." *American Journal of Obstetrics and Diseases of*

*Women and Children.* V. XXV, n. 4. An article that includes more details than most about the Tocci twins, who are then compared to the Scottish Brothers, Ritta-Christina, and other lesser-known twins.

_____. 1874. "Historical and Analogical Record of the Siamese Twins," *The American Journal of the Medical Sciences.* Oct.: 359–377. A paper about Chang and Eng Bunker that concentrates on their medical examination over the years and compares their case to others on record.

Hilton, Daisy, and Violet. 1996a. "Intimate Lives and Loves of the Hilton Sisters, Part 1," in *Shocked and Amazed On and Off the Midway!* Vol. 2. The lurid lives of the Hilton sisters, often in their own words.

_____. 1996b. "Intimate Lives and Loves of the Hilton Sisters, Part 2," in *Shocked and Amazed On and Off the Midway!* Vol. 3. The rest of the lurid lives of the Hilton sisters.

_____. n.d. "Souvenir and Life Story of San Antonio's Siamese Twins." A biographical booklet about Daisy and Violet Hilton prepared for sale to the members of their audiences.

Hluchy, Patricia. 1984. "A New Chance at Life for Siamese Twins," *MacLean's.* Aug. 13. A detailed account of the separation of Lin and Win Htut.

Hollister, Anne. 1984. "Severing the Siamese Twins: From One Life to Two," *Life.* Oct. A report about the separation surgery of Lin and Win Htut accompanied by photographs and diagrams.

Holm, Chris. 2000. "Joined at the Heart — Siamese Twins Are Born Alive," *Scoop Media.* May 3. www.scoop.co.nz. A brief account of the birth of Faith and Hope Emberson.

Holt, Gordy. 2000a. "Olympia Twins Doing 'Just Fine' After Thirty-One-Hour Surgical Separation," in *Seattle Post-Intelligencer.* Oct. 2. Status of the Lincoln twins.

_____. 2000b. "Surgically Separated Twins Go Home," in *Seattle Post-Intelligencer.* Oct. 23. A front-page article and two photographs of Charity and Kathleen Lincoln after their separation.

Honan, William H. 2000. "History of Medical Art Gets Pre-Columbian Chapter," *The New York Times.* Aug. 22. An article about the theory of Gordon Bendersky of the University of Pennsylvania that ancient two-headed figurines were not symbolic, but in fact the first medical illustrations of conjoined twins.

Hoyle, Mark. 1990. "Surgical Separation of Conjoined Twins." *Surgery, Gynecology & Obstetrics.* V. 170: 549–562. A study of the improved survival rates of thoracopagus, omphalopagus, craniopagus, ischiopagus, and pygopagus twins.

Hunter, Kay. 1964. *Duet for a Lifetime.* London: Michael Joseph. A readable biography of Chang and Eng Bunker written by a descendant of Robert Hunter, the merchant who brought them to the United States. Includes some representative illustrations.

"Indigo National Children's Day Bravery Award 1999." 1999. *MONA Newsletter:* November. www.kildare.ie/community/mona/donadea-December-1999.htm. Announcement in a community newsletter that Eilish Holton had received an award for which she was nominated by her sister.

Innerst, Carol. 1974. "Hazards to Twins' Health Abound in Their Country," *The Sunday Bulletin.* Dec. 15. The physical challenges Alta and Clara Rodriguez faced upon returning home after their separation surgery.

"It's Home Again for the 'Miracle' Siamese Twins." 1975. *People.* Jan. 27. A series of captioned photographs describing the return of the Rodriguez twins to the Dominican Republic after separation surgery.

Ivy, Robert H., and Byron E. Boyer. 1970. "Further information on a bicephalic monster, one head with a complete cleft of the lip and palate." *Plastic and Reconstructive Surgery.* V. 45, n. 5: 446–448. An article giving the history of a specimen that had been born in 1929, resurfaced in 1969, and is now in the Mütter Museum.

Jackson, Arthur M. 2001. "Sixth Way of Wisdom." This article about how to develop and adopt a perceptual framework to allow the feeling that life has meaning despite chronic pain is available on the web www.geocities.com/Athens/Oracle/4211/ w2db6.html. It includes an interview with Lori and Reba Schappell.

Janin, Jules. 1829. "A Woman with Two Heads." Electronic collection of the Public Library of Lisieux. http://ourworld.compuserve.com/homepages/bib_lisieux. A very personalized and allusive editorial about the death and postmortem examination of Ritta-Christina. Text in French.

Jaschevatzky, O.E., B. Goldman, D. Kampf, H. Wexler, and S. Grünstein. 1980. "Etiological Aspects of Double Monsters," *European Journal of Obstetrics, Gynecology and Reproductive Biology.* V. 10, no. 5: June. Postulates that there is an exogenous (environmental) factor that influences development and may be related to the way of life of certain populations with a genetic tendency to producing anomalies. The periodic influence of these factors could explain what is regarded as an epidemic phenomenon.

Jussim, Daniel. 2001. *Double Take: The Story of Twins*. New York: Viking. Well-illustrated with black and white photographs, this book intended for readers age 9 and up contains a chapter on conjoined twins that covers both historical and contemporary pairs.

Kaveny, M. Cathleen. 2002. "Conjoined Twins and Catholic Moral Analysis: Extraordinary Means and Casuistical Consistency," *Kennedy Institute of Ethics Journal*. V. 12, no. 2: June. Confronts the case of Jodie and Mary from the Roman Catholic perspective of "ordinary" (morally required) versus "extraordinary" (optional) means, concluding that the surgery should be viewed as an ordinary means of preserving Jodie's life.

Khaikaew, Thaksina. 1999. "Original Siamese Twins are Honored," in *Philadelphia Inquirer*. Aug. 21. About the erection of a statue in memory of Chang and Eng Bunker.

King, Laura. 2001. "Surviving Twin Set to Go Home After Separation," in the *Arizona Republic*. June 16. About the return of Gracie Attard to Malta after separation surgery.

Keese, William Linn. 1902. *The Siamese Twins and Other Poems*. New York: Edwin W. Dayton. Title poem consists of thirteen rhyming stanzas about Chang and Eng Bunker in which they are referred to as "singular dual, original plural" and "two-volumes-in-one."

Kliewer, Mary. 1997. "The Freedome of Love." *CBI Newsletter*: Jan. www.worldinvisible.com/ newsltr/ yr1997/jan/. An article that presents the Hensel twins as religious symbols of sharing and sacrifice: "In the professional business communities of Christian Corps International (CCI) we have quickly discovered the importance of what these twins have grasped — that joy, harmony and peace in living together can only come when we are willing to guard each man's dignity and set aside our own selfish pride."

Kobel, Bernard Lyle. 1959. "Most Siamese Twins Live Normal Lives…" in *The Circus Review*. Fall. Overview of famous pairs of conjoined twins, including the Blazeks, the Bunkers, the Godinos, the Hiltons, Millie-Christine, and the Toccis.

Koop, C. Everett. 1974. "Separating the Siamese Twins." *Medical World News*. Nov. 8. This thorough account by the lead surgeon covers the pre- and postoperative care of Alta and Clara Rodriguez, preparation for their separation, and details and photographs of the surgery itself.

_____. 1975. "A Time of Faith: The Heartwarming, Intensely Personal Story of the Surgeon Who Separated the Rodriguez Siamese Twins," *Guideposts: A Practical Guide to Successful Living*. June. The separation of Clara and Alta Rodriguez from an inspirational perspective by the lead surgeon who credits God with giving him the skills to perform the surgery.

Landau, Elaine. 1997. *Joined at Birth: The Lives of Conjoined Twins*. New York: Franklin Watts. A book aimed at younger children that offers an overview of conjoined twins with the stories of the Bunkers and the Hensels told in greater detail. Includes several color illustrations and photographs, a glossary, and lists of resources.

Langley, Jeff. 1997. "Hurry, Hurry, Hurry … Freaks … Alive on the Inside!" www.texasonline.net/ langley/columns/freaks.htm. Reminiscences of a patron of sideshows over the decades.

Liebling, A.J. 2001. "Masters of the Midway," in *Shocked and Amazed! On and Off the Midway*. Vol. 6. Describes the sideshow careers of Lou Dufour and Joe Rogers, including their exhibit of a two-headed baby in the 1930s.

Loft, Kurt. 1998. "Joined at Birth," in *The Tampa Tribune*. March 29. An article about the documentary "Joined at Birth" that includes a photo of the Galyons as young boys, quotes from the Schappells, and a list of some contemporary cases of conjoined twins covered in the program.

Maloney, E. Burke. 1978. "Hilton Sisters," in *Asbury Park Press*. June 11. A brief reminiscence by a reporter who interviewed Daisy and Violet in 1934.

Mannix, Daniel P. 1999. *Freaks: We Who Are Not as Others*. New York: Juno Books. Somewhat sensationalized accounts of sideshow attractions, including a chapter called "Look Ma, Three Hands" that covers the basic biographies of conjoined twins the Gibbs, the Blazeks, the Hiltons, the Toccis, and many others with parasitic twins or extra limbs. Text is accompanied by many black and white photographs.

Martell, Joanne. 2000. *Millie-Christine: Fearfully and Wonderfully Made*. Winston-Salem, N.C.: John F. Blair. The almost unbelievable lives of Millie-Christine McKoy told through thoroughly researched narrative and the reproduction of photos from a number of archives.

Megargee. 1897. "Seen and Heard in Many Places," *Philadelphia Times*. June 16. A hearsay column focusing on Eng and Chang Bunker.

Millar, Amanda. "Faith Hope." Transcript of 20/20 episode. TV3. www.tv3.co.nz. The transcript of the episode about Faith and Hope Emberson by the reporters they chose to tell their story.

Miller, Kenneth. 1998. "Our Summer Vacation: Conjoined Twins Abby and Britty Hensel Present Their World in Pictures, with Some Help from Mom and Dad," *Life*. A story about the lives and development of Abby and Brittany Hensel, accompanied by photographs the twins took of their family, friends, activities, and favorite things.

_____, and Jen M.R. Doman. 1996. "Together Forever." In *Life*. April. An insightful article about Abby and Brittany Hensel that answers many questions about their lives and is accompanied by a number of moving black and white photographs by Steve Wewerka.

Miller, Robert. 2001. "A Struggle for Survival: Twins Facing Life Joined or Risky Division," *The News-Times* (Danbury, Ct.). July 1: A1, A7, A10. The story of Maria Carmen and Maria Guadalupe DeAndrade and their arrival from Mexico for possible separation.

Mitchell, Dewey. 1997. "Twins Celebrate Successful Surgery," *Air Force News*. Mar. 15. www .af.mil/ news/. A report about Bethany and Hannah Rainey two years after their separation.

Moseley, Ray. 2000. "Britain Awaits Ruling on Fate of Joined Twins," in *The Chicago Tribune*. Sept. 20. Reviews the physical and moral dilemmas faced by the Court of Appeals in the case of Gracie and Rosie Attard (a.k.a. Jodie and Mary).

Mould, Richard F. 1989. *More of Mould's Medical Anecdotes*. Bristol, U.K.: Adam Hilger Ltd. Medical tidbits, including items about Chang and Eng Bunker, Millie-Christine, and the Biddenden Maids.

_____. 1984. *Mould's Medical Anecdotes*. Bristol, U.K.: Adam Hilger Ltd. Includes brief mention of the Tocci Brothers and reproduces a handbill about them.

Murray, Terry. 1995. "Separation Just One Stage for Siamese Twins," in *The Medical Post*. Jan. 31. Discusses at length the case of Hira and Nida Jamal.

Myers, Myer, and William L. Oliver. n.d. *Advance campaign: San Antonio's Siamese Twins Violet and Daisy Hilton*. A booklet of publicity ideas for theaters to tie special events to the coming appearances of the Hiltons, prepared by their manager and press agent.

Myser, Catherine, and David L. Clark. 1998. "'Fixing' Katie and Eilish: Medical Documentaries and the Subjection of Conjoined Twins." *Literature and Medicine*. V. 17, n. 1: Spring, 45–67. A paper that argues that medical documentaries about conjoined twins perpetuate the idea that surgery is necessary to normalize their bodies. The Holton case is used as an example.

Nabokov, Vladimir. 1958. *Nabokov's Dozen: A Collection of Thirteen Stories*. Garden City, New York: Doubleday. Includes "Scenes from the Life of a Double Monster," an amusing story in which Floyd relates the life history of himself and his conjoined twin brother Lloyd, from their conception as a result of rape to their escape from exploitive family members. The twins were described as joined by a band of flesh similar to the Bunkers'. Through the narrator, Nabokov comments on cooperation and the reason the twins don't want to be separated. The story draws on certain perennial themes of conjoined life, including rhyming names and exhibition to the public.

Nakamura, Goro, Bunro Yokoyama, and Masami Kawahara. 1986. *Cheer Up Viet and Duc*. Transl. Mieko Tsuzuki. Kyoto, Japan: Kamogawa Shuppan & Co. A slim and somewhat repetitive volume published in ponderous English by The Group Hoping for Viet and Duc's Development for the stated purpose of spreading the message associated with the lives of these Vietnamese conjoined twins. The group's representative hopes that the book will cause the international community to consider the handicapped and international unity and blames the twins' condition on the spraying of Agent Orange. There is a heavy editorial concentration on the use of the defoliant and the authors blame it for the birth of about thirty pairs of conjoined twins in Vietnam since 1972. Photographically, the book concentrates on the development of a special wheelchair for the twins to use. The photos include some excellent images of Viet and Duc and many of the fundraising and other activities on their behalf.

Ng, Julia. 2000. "Family, Friends Gather to Celebrate Nepalese Twins First Birthday." www. channelnewsasia.com. May 9. Brief update on Ganga and Jamuna Shrestha.

Ostman, Ronald E. 1996. "Photography and Persuasion: Farm Security Administration Photographs of Circus and Carnival Sideshows,

1935–1942," in *Freakery: Cultural Spectacles of the Extraordinary Body*, Thompson, Rosemarie Garland, Editor. New York: New York University Press. An examination of the sideshow that covers the exhibition of live human anomalies and preserved specimens.

Pancoast, William H. 1870–71. "The Carolina Twins," *Photographic Review of Medicine and Surgery.* V. 1: 42–57. A description of Millie-Christine and a photograph of their juncture published by the physician who had recently treated them for an abscess. Pancoast describes their ambulation, their appetites, and their physical point of union.

_____. 1875. Report on the surgical considerations in regard to the propriety of an operation for the separation of Eng and Chang Bunker, commonly known as the Siamese twins. *Transactions of the College of Physicians of Philadelphia.* V. 8: 149–169. A description of the events surrounding the autopsy of the Bunkers by one of the participants, who gives his opinion as to whether separation during their lives would have been a medical possibility.

Paré, Ambroise. 1982. *On Monsters and Marvels.* Orig. published 1840. Translated by Janis L. Pallister. Chicago: Univ. of Chicago Press. A compendium of birth defects by an early surgeon, this book combines what we now know to be fact and fiction. Includes many often-reproduced illustrations of conjoined twins in the chapter entitled "An Example of Too Great a Quantity of Seed."

Pekkanen, John. 2001. "Two Babies, One Heart, One Chance," in *Reader's Digest.* June. A very personal account of the events leading up to the birth and separation of Darielis and Sandra Soto.

Pender, Stephen. 1996. "'No Monsters at the Resurrection': Inside Some Conjoined Twins," in *Monster Theory: Reading Culture*, Jeffrey Jerome Cohen, Editor. Minneapolis: Univ. of Minn. Press. Discusses the public display of conjoined twins, including Lazarus Colloredo, and the common interest in the unusual.

Pentogalos, G.E., and John G. Lascaratos. 1984. A Surgical Operation Performed on Siamese Twins During the Tenth Century in Byzantium," *Bulletin of the History of Medicine.* V. 58: 99–102. An account compiled from historical records of the earliest known attempt at surgical separation of conjoined twins.

Pepper, C.K. 1967. "Ethical and Moral Considerations in the Separation of Conjoined Twins: Summary of Two Dialogues Between Physi-

cians and Clergymen," in *Conjoined Twins*, Bergsma, Daniel, Editor. Birth Defects original article series, Vol. III: 1. New York: National Foundation-March of Dimes. The moral dilemma involved in separating conjoined twins who have only a single heart is approached from the Catholic, Protestant, and Jewish perspective.

Perlstein, M.A., and E.R. LeCount. 1927. "Pygopagus Twins: The History and Necropsy Report of the Bohemian Twins, Rosa-Josepha Blazek," *Archives of Pathology and Laboratory Medicine.* V. 3, n. 1: Jan., 171–192.

Perry, Margaret. 2001. "Ganga, Jamuna Going Home," *The Straits Times.* Nov. 17. http://straitstimes.asia1.com.sg. On-line article about the return home of Ganga and Jamuna Shrestha after surgical separation.

Pingree, Allison. 1996. "America's 'United Siamese Brothers': Chang and Eng and Nineteenth Century Ideologies of Democracy and Domesticity," in *Monster Theory: Reading Culture*, Jeffrey Jerome Cohen, Editor. Minneapolis: Univ. of Minn. Press. Describes how the Bunker twins were used as symbols of national unity, since their unique lives intersected with the American Civil War.

_____. 1996. "The 'Exceptions That Prove the Rule': Daisy and Violet Hilton, the 'New Woman,' and the Bonds of Marriage," in *Freakery: Cultural Spectacles of the Extraordinary Body*, Thompson, Rosemarie Garland, Editor. New York: New York University Press. Describes the Hilton twins as symbols.

Playfair, William S. 1881. "Conjoined Twins," *Transactions of the Obstetrical Society of London.* V. 22: 265–66. A description of Rosa and Josefa Blazek (misspelled Rozalie and Josepha Blazet), who were exhibited to the society on December 1, 1880.

Pressley, Sue Anne. 2002. "Far from Home, Twins' Family Counts Blessings," *Washington Post.* June 24. Update on the status of the Onziga twins, who were separated in 2001.

Purcell, Rosamond. 1997. *Special Cases: Natural Anomalies and Historical Monsters.* San Francisco: Chronicle Books. This beautifully designed "coffee table" book contains historical images chosen by Purcell, in addition to her own color photographs. Illustrations of the Biddenden Maids and Ritta-Christina are offset by photos of anonymous wet and dry museum specimens. A chapter, "Too Much, Not Enough, and in the Wrong Place," addresses conjoined and parasitic twins visually and in the lively text, though they are discussed throughout the book.

"Pygopagus Marriage." 1934. *Time*. July 16. About the refusal of Manhattan authorities to grant a marriage license to Violet Hilton. Includes background on the Hilton twins and a photograph.

"Rare Conjoined Twins Born with Only Two Legs." 1998. CNN Interactive: Feb. 10. www.cnn.com. An account of the birth of Michaela and Gabrielle Garcia.

Reid, T.R. 2000. "Life for One Twin, or Death for Both? British Appeals Court Must Rule on Separation of Conjoined Girls," in *The Washington Post*. Sept. 7: A1 + A22. Explains the issues that faced the Court of Appeals in the case of Gracie and Rosie Attard (a.k.a. Jodie and Mary).

"Rhode Island Siamese Twins, 7; Were Not Expected to Live a Year." 1991. *Providence Journal*. July 22. A report of the death of Ruthie and Verena Cady.

Roberts, Greg. 2001. "As Alyssa Fights on, Her Parents Give Hospital Thanks for Gift of Life." www.smh.com. August 22. The story of Alyssa and Bethany Nolan and Alyssa's current status.

Rossner, Judith. 1977. *Attachments*. New York: Pocket Books. A deliberately lurid novel about an adult pair of conjoined twins and their spouses by the author of *Looking for Mr. Goodbar*. It focuses on the taboo subjects of sex, marriage, and reproduction, while touching on other themes including privacy, identity, public exhibition, media attention, and the psychological implications of separation surgery.

Rusid, Max. 1975. *Side Show: Max Rusid's Photo Album of Human Oddities*. New York: Amjon Publishers. A picture book of black and white illustrations that include the Hilton sisters, the Tocci brothers, and several other lesser-known examples of conjoined and parasitic twins.

Santiago, Roberto, and Emily Gest. 2001. "Joined Girls a Blessing to Siamese Twins' Dad," in *New York Daily News*. April 12. A brief account of the case of Cristal and Paola Colon.

Saudek, Robert. 1941. "The Handwriting of Identical Twins," *Ciba Symposia*. V. 2, n. 10: 717–720. Includes a comparison, with illustrations, of the handwriting of Violet and Daisy Hilton.

Schuknecht, Harold F. 1979. "The Siamese Twins, Eng and Chang: Their Lives and Their Hearing Losses," *Archives of Otolaryngology*. V. 105:

Dec., 737–740. A modern analysis of Chang and Eng Bunker's hearing loss that attributes difference to the placement of their shotguns in relation to one another.

Segal, Nancy. 1999. *Entwined Lives: Twins and What They Tell Us about Human Behavior*. Dutton. A thorough and readable examination of the lives of fraternal and identical twins that includes the chapter "Separate Minds in Shared Bodies: Conjoined Twins." The well-researched chapter includes the development and occurrence of conjoined twins, their physical variations, research on the causes, separation issues, and specific examples (Bunkers, Cadys, Lakebergs, and Schappells).

Semonin, Paul. 1996. "Monsters in the Marketplace: The Exhibition of Human Oddities in Early Modern England," in *Freakery: Cultural Spectacles of the Extraordinary Body*, Thompson, Rosemarie Garland, Editor. New York: New York University Press. Includes examples of the interest the public has shown in conjoined twins.

"Separating Conjoined Twins: The Ethical Dilemmas." 1993. *Issues: A Critical Examination of Contemporary Ethical Issues in Health Care*. V. 8, n. 5: Sept./Oct., 6–8. An article in a publication of the SSM Health Care System that examines the ethical and economic controversy about the separation of the Lakeberg twins.

"Separating the Armstrong Twins — A Team Effort." 2001. *Surgical News Archive*. V. 2, No. 1: February. www.surgeons.org/open/surgical_news. An account of the separation of Tay-lah and Monique Armstrong with a list of participating hospital staff members.

Serres, M. Recherches. 1832. *D'Anatomie transcendante et pathologique: Theorie des formations et des déformations organiques, appliquée a l'anatomie de Ritta-Christina, et de la duplicité monstrueuse*. Paris: Chez J.B. Baillière. An often-referenced 315-page French treatise on "double monsters" that devotes part three to the description of Ritta-Christina. Includes chapters on bone and musculature, circulatory system, nervous system, and abdominal organs.

"The Siamese Twins." 1829. *The Mirror of Literature, Amusement, and Instruction*. No. 401: Nov. 28, 354–356. A contemporary description of Chang and Eng Bunker when they were still on stage in Chinese costume.

"Siamese Twins from Peru Die After Surgery in Italy." 2000. CNN: May 27. www.cnn.com. A brief report of the deaths of Milagro and Marta Juarez after separation surgery.

"The Siamese Twins in Their Own Land." 1874. *Daily Record of the Times* (Wilkes-Barre, Penn.). Feb. 21. An article describing the early life of Chang and Eng Bunker.

"Siamese Twins Saved After 10-Hour Surgery." 1998. Express New Service: May 25. A brief account of the Ahire twins published in the Indian media.

"Siamese Twins Undergo Surgery." 1998. BBC News: Nov. 14. http://news.bbc.co.uk. News of the separation surgery of anonymous conjoined twins that includes details about the separation of Aoife and Niamh McDonnell.

"Siamese Twins Wiktoria and Weronika Palen Are Back in Stalowa Wola After a Six-Month Stay in the United States." 2000. *Central Europe Review*. V. 2, no. 9: March 6. www.ce-review. org. Report of the Palen twins' return home after surgery.

"Sick Mother of Siamese Twins Still Can't Hold Her Babies." 2001. http://news.123india.com. April 11. Brief post-operative report about Ganga and Jamuna Shrestha.

Smith, J. David. 1988. *Psychological Profiles of Conjoined Twins: Heredity, Environment, and Identity*. New York: Praeger. The cases of Simplicio and Lucio Godino, Yvonne and Yvette Jones MacArthur, Millie-Christine McKoy, Giovanni and Giacomo Tocci, and others reviewed from a psychological perspective. Smith uses the fact that most conjoined twins have distinct personalities to examine the influences of heredity and environment, since they necessarily share both. Includes black and white photographs.

Spencer, Rowena. 1996. "Anatomic Description of Conjoined Twins: A Plea for Standardized Terminology," in *Journal of Pediatric Surgery*. Vol. 31, No. 7 (July): 941–944. A milestone paper by a renowned pediatric surgeon that proposes a system of terminology for referencing the physical conditions of conjoined twins, including the types of union, the identification of the individual twins, and their anatomic relationship to one another.

_____. 2003. *Conjoined Twins: Developmental Malformations and Clinical Implications*. Baltimore: The Johns Hopkins University Press. A thorough clinical analysis of conjoined twins by a retired pediatric surgeon who has participated in numerous separation surgeries and standardized the terminology used to discuss conjoinded twins.

_____. 1992. "Conjoined Twins: Theoretical Embryologic Basis," *Teratology*. V. 45: 591–602. A paper by a retired pediatric surgeon in favor of the fusion theory of the development of conjoined twins, in which the embryos do not completely divide. Discusses the process and the terminology.

Spitz, L., M.D. Stringer, E.M. Kiely, P.G. Ransley, and P. Smith. 1994. "Separation of Brachio-Thoraco-Omphalo-Ischiopagus Bipus Conjoined Twins," *Journal of Pediatric Surgery*. V. 29, n. 4: April, 477–481. Report of the separation of conjoined girls that focuses on the interdisciplinary nature of the surgery, the preoperative preparation, and the postoperative results, one of which was the death of one of the twins.

Spitz, Tullan. 1999. "Conjoined No More: Meet the Surgical Pioneer Who Split the Banda Twins Without Neurologic Harm," *Hippocrates*. Feb.: 19–20. A brief interview with Johns Hopkins pediatric surgeon Benjamin Carson.

"Spotlight Falls on UCT Neurosurgeons." 2000. *Monday paper: Weekly newspaper of the University of Cape Town*. V. 19, No. 2: Aug. 7–14. A detailed account of the separation of the Alphonce twins.

Stanton, Jeffrey. 1997. "Coney Island — Freaks." http://naid.sppsr.ucla.edu/coneyisland/articles/freaks.htm. An article about the Coney Island sideshows that mentions the exhibit of Mary and Margaret Gibb and the Godino brothers.

*The Story of Biddenden*. 1989. Biddenden, Kent, U.K.: Biddenden Local History Society. This booklet issued by the village famous for the Biddenden maids includes a chapter providing the details of their legacy, the Chulkhurst Charity.

Strauss, Darin. 2000. *Chang and Eng: A Novel*. New York: Dutton. A fictionalized account incorporating many facts about the Bunker twins, but creating an adulterous relationship between Eng and his brother's wife Adelaide. Strauss explains, "Where I have discarded or finessed or invented the details of Chang and Eng's life, it was only to elbow the facts toward a novel's own idea of truth, which is something else entirely." The book, narrated by Eng, jumps back and forth between childhood and adulthood. Eng criticizes Chang for his love of the stage and his addiction to alcohol.

Stumbo, Bella. 1981. "Siamese Twins: Unique Sisters Full of Laughter." *The Philadelphia Inquirer*. Sept. 6: H-1. An anecdotal introduction to Yvonne and Yvette McCarther accompanied by a photograph of the twins and of their mother.

Successful separation of conjoined twins. 2000. *Cosmiverse*. February 21. www.cosmiverse.com.

A brief report of the separation of Wiktoria and Weronika Palen.

Sullivan, Cheryl C. 1979. "A Strange Kind of Bondage: For the 'Two-Headed Girl' Slavery Was an Inescapable Freak of Fate," *American History Illustrated*. Vol. XIV, N. 7: November. A brief reexamination of the adult lives of Millie-Christine.

Sullivan, Walter. 1981. "Life or Death Choices on Birth Defects," *The New York Times*. June 19: B7. Discusses the ethical issues of sacrifice surgery in the context of terminating the lives of "defective" newborns.

"Surgeons Fail to Save Conjoined Twin." 2001. www.cnn.com. May 27. Describes the case of Bethany and Alyssa Nolan.

"Surviving Twin Stable." 1996. In *The Philadelphia Inquirer*. Jan. 29. Status of Sarah Morales after separation from her sister Sarahi.

Tanne, Janice Hopkins. 1993. "Free at Last," *New York*. Nov. 15: 55–62. A detailed account of the surgical separation of Carmen and Rosa Taveras, complete with before-and-after diagrams and a photographic portrait of the surgical team.

Thomasma, David C., Jonathan Muraskas, Patricia A. Marshall, Thomas Myers, Paul Tomich, and James A. O'Neill, Jr. 1996. "The Ethics of Caring for Conjoined Twins: The Lakeberg Twins," *Hastings Center Report*. July-August: 4–12. Tackles the ethical challenges posed by the case of Amy and Angela Lakeberg, recounting their birth and separation and applying basic ethical principles to their care. These principles include killing one to save another, considering one baby an appendage or an "unjust aggressor," double-effect (in which an act with a good and bad outcome is allowed if it is the good outcome that is intended), and surrogacy (presumed consent from the non-surviving child). The authors also discuss rationing health care.

Thompson, C.J.S. 1968. *The Mystery and Lore of Monsters*. New York: University Books. Reproduces some of the early Paré illustrations and covers the cases of the Blazeks, the Bunkers, the Gibbs, the McKoys, Radica-Doodica, the Toccis, and others. Includes some black and white illustrations. Reprinted by Citadel Press as *Giants, Dwarfs and Other Oddities*.

Thompson, Lorrine. 2001. "More Surgery on the Horizon," *The Olympian*. April 1. An update about the condition of the separated Lincoln twins and the additional surgery they face. A sidebar includes a timeline of their development.

Thompson, Rosemarie Garland, Editor. 1996. *Freakery: Cultural Spectacles of the Extraordinary Body*. New York University Press. This scholarly and somewhat dense collection of essays includes selections by Robert Bogdan and others about the presentation of conjoined twins and other "freaks" to the public. Includes essays about the Hilton sisters, P.T. Barnum, the film "Freaks," and the novel *Geek Love*.

"The Tocci Twins." 1891. In *Scientific American*. Dec. 12. A short article describing Giacomo and Giovanni Tocci, published during their lifetime.

Tomlinson, Tommy. 1997. A Story of two sisters, together, always. In *The Charlotte Observer*. Dec. 7. An informative article about the post-show-business career of Violet and Daisy Hilton prompted by the opening of the musical "Side Show."

Toufexis, Anastasia. 1994. "The Brief Life of Angela Lakeberg: After Ten Months of Great Hope and Healing, the Siamese Twin Rejoins Her Sister in Death," *Time Magazine*. V. 143, No. 26: June 27. www.time.com. A balanced account of the separation surgery and deaths of the Lakeberg twins.

Townsend, Ralph M. 1870-71. "Bicephalic Monstrosity-Ischiopagus Tripus," *Photographic Review of Medicine and Surgery*. V. 1: 58–60. A photograph and physical description of Mina and Minnie Finley.

Twain, Mark. 1980. *Pudd'nhead Wilson and Those Extraordinary Twins*. Ed. Sidney E. Berger. New York: W.W. Norton. When Twain first wrote these two stories in the early 1890s, they were intertwined. He extracted the story about conjoined twins Luigi and Angelo Cappello and published it separately. In his opening remarks, Twain explains, "...it was two stories in one.... I pulled one of the stories out by the roots, and left the other one — a kind of literary Caesarean operation."

"Twin Separable." 1992. *Globe*. March 24. An article in the popular press about Lori and Reba Schappell. Includes several photographs.

"United Unto Death." 1967. *Time*. January 20. An obituary for Mary and Margaret Gibb that is accompanied by a 1949 photograph.

Virchow, Rudolf. 1870. "Die Siamesischen Zwillinge." *Berliner Medicinischen Gesellschaft*. Berlin: Bei August Hirschwald. A nineteen-page paper (in German with no illustrations) by the renowned German physician about his examination of Chang and Eng Bunker.

Wade, Ella N. 1962. "A Tin Coffin for the Siamese

Twins," *Transactions & Studies of the College of Physicians of Philadelphia.* V. 30, n. 1: July. Reprints correspondence from the Bunker family and from the artisan who made Chang and Eng's coffin.

Wallace, Irving, and Amy Wallace. 1978. *The Two: A Biography.* New York: Simon and Schuster. A well-researched and extremely detailed account of the lives of Chang and Eng Bunker.

Wallis, Claudia. 1996. "The Most Intimate Bond: Conjoined for Life, the Hensel Twins Are a Medical Mystery and a Lesson in Cooperation for Us All," *Time,* V. 147, No. 13: March 25. www.time.com. An informative article about Abby and Brittany Hensel and their family life, accompanied by several photographs.

Warrington, Dr. 1850-1851. "Skeleton of a Double-Bodied Monster." *Summary of the Transactions of the College of Physicians of Philadelphia from November 5, 1850, to January 6, 1851,* *inclusive.* Vol. I, n. I: 90–94. A description of the cephalothoracopagus skeletal specimen at the Mütter Museum.

Wilson, Dudley. 1993. *Signs and Portents: Monstrous Births from the Middle Ages to the Enlightenment.* London: Routledge. Traces the interest in anomalous bodies from medieval superstition to the scientific inquiries of the eighteenth and early nineteenth centuries. The text is very scholarly, with numerous well-chosen illustrations, including popular broadsheets and early medical drawings. Includes numerous references to and examples of conjoined twins.

Wright, Lawrence. 1997. *Twins and What They Tell Us About Who We Are.* New York: John Wiley & Sons. This volume about psychological and emotional components of twinhood and how they are applied to human behavior in general includes only a few specific references to conjoined twinning.

# INDEX